Postcolonial Francophone
Autobiographies

Postcolonial Francophone Autobiographies

FROM AFRICA TO THE ANTILLES

Edgard Sankara

UNIVERSITY OF VIRGINIA PRESS · *Charlottesville and London*

THIS BOOK IS MADE POSSIBLE BY A COLLABORATIVE GRANT
FROM THE ANDREW W. MELLON FOUNDATION.

University of Virginia Press

First published 2011

9 8 7 6 5 4 3 2 1

Library of Congress Cataloging-in-Publication Data

Sankara, Edgard, 1970–
    Postcolonial Francophone autobiographies : from
Africa to the Antilles / Edgard Sankara.
        p. cm.
    Includes bibliographical references and index.
    ISBN 978-0-8139-3171-5 (cloth : acid-free paper)
    ISBN 978-0-8139-3172-2 (pbk. : acid-free paper)
    ISBN 978-0-8139-3176-0 (e-book)
    1. French literature—French-speaking countries—
History and criticism.   2. Autobiography.
3. Postcolonialism—French-speaking countries.
4. African literature (French)—History and criticism.
5. West Indian literature (French)—History and
criticism.   I. Title.
PQ3897.S26   2011
848'.920309—dc22

2011015735

CONTENTS

ACKNOWLEDGMENTS

Writing this book has been an intellectual voyage, and I am especially grateful to colleagues and friends who accompanied me and who have read chapters and offered insightful comments: Zan Kocher at the University of Louisiana-Lafayette; Mary Donaldson-Evans, Philip Goldstein, Gary Ferguson, and Cynthia Schmidt-Cruz at the University of Delaware; Lance Donaldson-Evans at the University of Pennsylvania; and Ayo Abietou Coly at Dartmouth College. I am particularly grateful to my colleague and mentor Bruno Thibault who encouraged me throughout the process. I am also indebted to Anne Boylan for introducing me to the Reception Studies Society.

I thank the College of Arts and Sciences at the University of Delaware for a General University Research grant and a one-semester leave, which allowed me to focus on my research and to travel to Northwestern University, the University of Texas-Austin, and Martinique, thus helping me make significant progress.

I would like to express special gratitude to Cathie Brettschneider at the University of Virginia Press for her enthusiastic support and precious collaboration throughout the process from manuscript to book.

I am also grateful to the Modern Language Initiative for supporting my project.

I would like to thank Philip Goldstein and the Reception Studies Society for opening a panel for reception studies of non-Western regions. It was through that channel that I was able to present part of my research and fine-tune my findings. I am grateful to the Melville J. Herskovits Library of African Studies, to the Archives Départementales de la Martinique, and to La Bibliothèque Schoelcher for allowing me to conduct archival research.

A portion and an older version of Chapter 2 first appeared in *The*

Dark Webs: Perspectives on Colonialism in Africa (2005) under the title "Mudimbé: History, Autobiography, and Philosophy." Older versions and portions of Chapters 1 and 3, "Rhétorique de l'exemple et réception chez Kesso Barry et Hampâté Bâ" and "L'appropriation du masculin dans *Kesso* de Kesso Barry" appeared respectively in *Nouvelles Études Francophones* (fall 2010) and *Itinéraires (Littérature, Textes, Cultures)* (no. 2 [December 2008]).

For books available in French only, the translation is mine. I have left the translation in the body of the chapters and moved the original French quotations to the Notes section. For books with an existing English translation (Chamoiseau and Condé), I maintained the translation and moved the French quotations to the Notes. In the chapters on Chamoiseau and Confiant, I intentionally left a few passages untranslated to keep the original meaning in French or in Creole and to make my analysis dependent upon the nuances of those two languages.

Postcolonial Francophone
Autobiographies

Introduction

Postcolonial Francophone Autobiographies: From Africa to the Antilles reflects a broad spectrum of Francophone autobiographies, examining the works of such authors as Valentin Mudimbé from the Democratic Republic of the Congo; Amadou Hampâté Bâ from Mali (formerly French Sudan); Kesso Barry from Guinea; Patrick Chamoiseau and Raphaël Confiant from Martinique; and Maryse Condé from Guadeloupe. To date, there has been a paucity of scholarship in the field of comparative Francophone studies. With its rich geographical and cultural coverage of Africa and the diaspora, this study fills an important gap by juxtaposing works from two colonized entities as they relate to the same colonizer.

This analysis is also original in its use of reception theory as an analytical framework. Many important studies have been made of these writers, but most of them use traditional approaches for exploring their texts, and none takes into consideration the audience these authors address as a shaping factor of their writings. Bringing these writers together and using reception theory in conjunction with postcolonial studies, I argue for an autobiographical tradition that, though geographically dispersed, is equally entangled in the paradox of the target audience and transnational reception. With this book, I hope to generate an interest in the rearticulations of autobiographies in the context of postcolonial and reception studies. In my study, I examine the ways in which Africans endeavor to write in the tradition of classical French autobiography, whereas the Caribbean autobiographers write with the intention to subvert the former colonizer's genre and language. My project examines the relations that, starting in the 1980s, the new generation of Francophone autobiographers has established in dialogue with or in opposition to France and the different ways in which that generation has engaged the question of the colonizing language and their public(s).

Each of the two geographically distinct groups of authors, African and Caribbean, occupies a separate colonial position. Francophone African nations are situated in "postcolonial times," having received their independence from France in 1960, but Caribbean nations such as Martinique and Guadeloupe are still administratively and politically part of France and are considered by some to still be in the colonial stage.[1] Many political parties are actively campaigning for the independence of Martinique: Mouvement pour l'Indépendance de la Martinique (MIM), founded in 1978; Mouvement des Démocrates et des Écologistes pour une Martinique Souveraine (MODEMA), created in 1992; and the Parti pour la Libération de la Martinique (PALIMA), founded in 1999. Guadeloupe, rather than Martinique, has the longer history of movements fighting for independence, dating from the creation of the Groupe d'Organisation Nationale de la Guadeloupe (GONG) in 1963 and followed by the formation of the Mouvement Populaire pour une Guadeloupe Indépendante (MPGI) in 1982. In 1978, Union Populaire pour la Libération de la Guadeloupe (UPLG) and Konvwa pou Libérasyon Nasyonal Gwadloup / Convoi pour la libération nationale de la Guadeloupe (KLING) were established. The existence of these movements, with their emphasis on independence, attests to the sentiment that Martinique and Guadeloupe are still colonies of France. These distinctions between the two geographical groups of authors must be taken into consideration when making any comparative analysis.

THE THEORETICAL FRAMEWORK

Comparative Postcolonial Studies

This study uses a combination of comparative postcolonial studies and reception theory to gain a more complete understanding of Francophone autobiographies. Comparative postcolonial studies provide a framework that analyzes literary and cultural productions by various (formerly) colonized peoples as they relate to their (former) colonizer. Exploring the varied ways in which Francophone authors use autobiography to "write back" to the (former) colonizer against colonialism reveals the complex, and nuanced relationships that exist in a postcolonial world. Through classical paradigms of convergence and divergence, such a comparative framework facilitates the understanding of the different and similar ways in which two, three, or more entities are related to the same or different colonizer(s). Postcolonial studies is dominated by works in English, so a comparative Francophone analysis such as this project aims at creating a dialogue with and collaboration between Anglo-dominated postcolonial studies and Francophone studies. However, unlike other comparative postcolonial analyses, my approach examines two geographically distinct postcolonial groups, each writing in the language of the shared (former) colonizer. This juxtaposition thus proves extremely useful for exploring postcoloniality at work in two groups under the same dominant factors: the French colonizer and the Parisian audience.

The Reader Inside the Text and the Reader Outside the Text

In this study, the reader's characteristics play a crucial role in determining the meaning of a text. However, identifying this reader for purposes of analysis is not a simple matter of recognizing a single entity. It is important to distinguish between the reader addressed in the text (the reader inside the text) from the actual reader (the reader outside the text), as Gerald Prince emphasizes in "Introduction to the Study of the Narratee."[2] Prince establishes that the narratee (inside the text) is the audience addressed by the narrator, the textual teller of the story; that is, the narrator speaks to a narratee. In the structure of narrative communication, following this line of logic, the author addresses actual readers. The author and the narrator are two separate entities in relation to the narrative of fictional texts. In autobiography, however, the author is the narrator, so it is the author who addresses both the narratee (the reader inside the text) and the actual reader (the reader outside the text)—two narrative entities that remain distinct although they may intersect. Both entities are not conceived as fictions, but the narratee has a level of virtuality or generality, and the actual reader is more concrete yet remains a projection in the present and the future. For instance, when the Malian writer Amadou Hampâté Bâ addresses the "lecteur européen," the European reader, in his memoir *Amkoullel, l'enfant peul* (1991), he is thinking of a general, indistinct European reader (the reader inside the text), but Helen Heckmann, his posthumous legatee, is an actual reader. So am I: both of us are actual readers, though I am not a European. Narratologists and reader-response critics have embraced the study of the narratee, but they have focused exclusively on fictional narrative (that is, the Western novel), giving little or no attention to autobiography, let alone postcolonial autobiography. Using a comparative postcolonial perspective, I examine the specific characteristics of the narratee in selected Francophone autobiographies, focusing on the sociopolitical forces that have contributed to its nature.

It is through mapping these two entities, the narratee and the actual reader, noting the sociopolitical forces that have shaped them, that we gain a clearer picture of the complex, even shifting reality of authorial intent. Especially for the postcolonial autobiographer, the relationship between the addressed audience and the actual reader is complicated and either more or less tension filled, occurring at the crossroads of diverse cultures and discourses.

Reception Theory

Having acknowledged a difference between the narratee and the actual reader as well as the importance of mapping the two in relation to each other, we can look at the characteristics of the actual reader, the reader outside the text. For this task, I have found it useful to examine the autobiographies in the context of reception theory, which focuses on the role that the actual reader plays in establishing the meaning of a text. This theory, which found its origins in the writings of Hans-Robert Jauss, makes a clear distinction between the "production" of a work (in this case, the writing by the autobiographer) and the "consumption" of that work (by a public or publics). Jauss stresses the importance of the reader's act of interpretation in creating meaning out of a text. For Jauss, all interpretations exist in history and involve a dialogue between past and present. The temporal condition of interpretation is what allows for multiple and differing interpretations. In addition, each reader brings certain expectations to the text in order to interpret it. Jauss defines the "horizon of expectations" as a set of subjectivities, values, prejudices, and models that the reader uses to interpret the text. The text itself is not the meaning; the meaning lies in the interpretation of the text. Jauss emphasizes that, rather than distorting the author's original intention, the narrative's "dialogicity" establishes a new subjectivity in the reader's horizon of expectations. Thus, in the act of interpretation any reading is possible and acceptable in its context.

Far from being disparate approaches to literary analysis, postcolonial studies and reception studies intersect in the entity of the actual reader.

For Francophone autobiographies, the reader's nature has been complicated by the realities of colonialism and postcolonialism. The works analyzed in this study were written in former colonies in Africa and the Caribbean, and yet they are commodities for their former colonizer, France, where most of them have been published. In this way, the reader's horizon of expectations and consequently his or her interpretation of the text can be evaluated through postcolonial studies. Further, using comparative analysis as well as the combination of postcolonial and reception theories (a transnational reception framework) allows for the discovery of more complex relationships. Using this transnational reception framework, I demonstrate that the manner in which the French public and its literary filter, the press, have received Francophone African and Caribbean autobiographies reveals not only a fracture between the autobiographers and their local community, but also the mixed reaction of a French audience in search of ethnographic information.

The reader inside the text and the reader outside the text are not so discreet as to have no influence on each other. The author's projected imagining of the reader outside the text influences his or her construction of the reader inside, the narratee. The narratee's qualities and characteristics can influence the actual reader's reception of the text.

Postcolonial Francophone Autobiographies: From Africa to the Antilles, then, is concerned with multiple readings: personal, sociopolitical, and economical. The first involves a close reading of the texts with my own expectations; the second addresses the reader inside the text; and the third looks at the various actual readers reached by the commodification of Francophone autobiographies. A reader-oriented study reveals the different collaborative and often conflictive forces that shape the message of the "subaltern" postcolonial Francophone autobiographer. However, this book is not a survey of Francophone autobiographies: its geographical focus on Africa and the Caribbean aims at revealing the reception process as a cultural production as well as a center of power politics and (mis)reading in communication between the Third World and the West through the circulation of books. The readings of Francophone autobiographies posit them as a signifier with many signified(s) according to the various readers; the author's intended meaning is often ignored as other meanings are assigned to his or her discourse as it becomes a product in local, Parisian, and global landscapes. This book shows these transformations at work within, without, and around contemporary Francophone autobiographies as they are marketed in different locations.

"THE AUTOBIOGRAPHICAL PACT"

Any study of autobiography must be indebted to Philippe Lejeune's *The Autobiographical Pact* (1989),[3] in which he defines the genre as a pact between the writer and the (actual) reader through the mediation of the text. The pact is made to ascertain the narrative's authenticity, to recognize that it is true to life as it relates to the author and the events, implying that the reader may also deny this authenticity. Similar to an oath of certainty, this somewhat legal pact involves both the autobiographer and the reader in telling and receiving the "truth." The interchange differs from what occurs in other literary genres and enables autobiography to escape the plight of "the death of the author," which Roland Barthes and other structuralists attributed to other literary genres. In autobiography, the communication game is open and clear: an author speaks about his own life, directly addressing a reader. In such a situation, the possibility of misanalyzing the text by considering the author's purpose in terms of the author's psychobiographical data, as formalists William Wimsatt and Monroe Beardsley cautioned against in "The Intentional Fallacy,"[4] becomes a moot point. Autobiography is essentially a pact of truth that binds the author and the reader: one's existence is legitimated and reciprocated by the Other. The study of such a genre requires in-depth knowledge of the author and, more importantly, an understanding of the reader(s) whom the author addresses, keeping in mind that different groups of readers may produce divergent texts. Nevertheless, despite the generic pact, the reader, who brings his or her own expectations to the text, may still mistake the author's intention. These potential "mistakes" provide the occasion for what is known in reception studies as a "misreading."

As instrumental as his definition is, Lejeune fails to insist on the reader's expectations and importance in the dynamic of the genre. In *Lecteur et lecture dans l'autobiographie française contemporaine* (1993),[5] Hélène Jaccomard makes the point that Lejeune restricts the horizon of autobiographical studies by failing to insist on the influence of publishing houses in establishing the genre. My study aims to fill in this gap by examining the critical role played by the readers and promoters of postcolonial autobiography.

THE FRANCOPHONE AUTOBIOGRAPHY

In the early 1900s during the early colonial period, French colonial authorities inculcated and demanded the need for Francophone auto-biography. Their colonized subjects, educated through their colonial schools, were required to become cultural translators of themselves and their community in order to increase the French colonial administrators' knowledge. Thus, prior to the formal literary practice of the genre, there was a tradition of written self-narratives in Francophone Africa in the form of journals, travelogues, and other self-writing during the colonial era, as Hans-Jürgen Lüsebrink illustrates in his excellent article "Autobiographies fragmentaires d'auteurs africains dans la presse ouest-africaine à l'époque coloniale (1916–50)" (1996).[6] Lüsebrink shows that colonial masters used self-narrative as a device to better understand "l'âme nègre," the "black soul," of their subjects for the sake of dominating them. His study thus demonstrates that the French colonial system has had ongoing control of autobiographical production.

Francophone autobiography as a genre has taken various forms and has origins that predate even Bakary Diallo's *Force Bonté* (1926), the first literary autobiographical production by a Francophone African, written well before the classic Francophone African autobiography *L'Enfant noir* (1953) by Camara Laye. Lüsebrink illustrates that the genre, even in its earliest fragmental forms, posed from the start the dilemma of audience that postcolonial African autobiographers face today as subjects writing in the former colonizer's language. In colonial times, the fragmented self-narratives that appeared in colonial presses were aimed primarily at a French colonial audience and secondarily at African "évolués" who, like the producers of these fragments, had gained reading proficiency by attending French schools.

Written Francophone autobiography is a genre that formerly and currently colonized subjects of France borrowed from the long literary tradition of this Western nation. As a consequence, African and Caribbean Francophone autobiographies are the hybrid result of the encounter between two respective "subaltern" entities and France, the latter being both the common denominator and the dominant factor. This type of autobiography also manifests a tension in which the autobiographers wish to express themselves to a local community, but at the same time they are confronted with their choice of a French reading audience and the publishing policies of the French press. Thus, two constraints await these writers: self-censorship as they negotiate their target audiences and censorship from the French publishing houses that control the ways in which their works become a commodity that is palatable and marketable to a French audience.

Francophone autobiography is a record of a collective historical experience; this type of autobiographical production, unlike Western bourgeois, autobiography has been studied and distinguished as community centered and nonindividualistic. Some critics have gone so far as labeling self-narratives by colonial/postcolonial peoples as "autoethnography."[7] The highly suspicious term *autoethnography* implies that the "ethnic" autobiographer is expected to write for the enlightenment of the West and its ethnologists and anthropologists. The dilemma of audience is thus already set from the start. At the same time, it is revealing that Western critics have coined such a term. No Francophone African or Caribbean would accept the labeling of another formerly colonized person as "ethnic," let alone use this label for a fellow compatriot.

Viewed from the perspective of comparative postcolonial studies, the very form of the autobiography brings with it complex history and meaning. The language in which an autobiographer chooses to write also carries similar connections to and echoes of the past. French is both the symbol of the former colonizer's presence in the colonized world and a tool for the formerly colonized to "write back" to the colonizer.

Although in terms of genre the two geographically distinct groups of texts discussed here share similarities, they also offer a major contrast: the African autobiographies follow a "traditional" style (first person, linear chronology, unity of subject, narration), whereas the Caribbean autobiographies by Chamoiseau and Confiant take a more "postmodernist" perspective (broken chronology, instability of subject, play on multiple subjectivities of the Self, modernist narration). The Guadeloupean writer Maryse Condé, although not strictly "traditional," offers an autobiography that is more sophisticated in its awareness of the theoretical problems of writing a self-narrative. All three Caribbean autobiographers show a high level of consciousness of the theories of autobiography, which they either challenge or play with. Mudimbé's autobiography, with its poststructural (postmodern) perspective, is the only African autobiography that is "nontraditional." The African autobiographies' serious tone contrasts with their Caribbean counterparts' lighter, more humorous tone—especially that of Confiant and Chamoiseau, although the "humour Créole" they use in order to make their narratives of childhood more digestible does not escape a form of "exoticism" because it may be what a metropolitan audience eager for the "exotic" expects.

A CLOSER LOOK AT THE READER INSIDE THE TEXT

The reader inside the autobiographical text is the projective creation of the writer-narrator and is detectable through signals or hints in the text. As Gerald Prince puts it in "Introduction to the Study of the Narratee":

> The signals capable of portraying the narratee are quite varied and one can easily distinguish several types that are worth discussing. In the first place, we should mention all passages of a narrative in which the narrator refers directly to the narratee. We retain in this category statements in which the narrator designates the narratee by such words as "reader" or "listener" and by such expressions as "my dear" or "my friend." In the event that the narration may have identified a specific characteristic of the narratee, for example his profession or nationality, passages mentioning this characteristic should also be considered in this first category. (13)

This list of signals is not exhaustive, and the Francophone autobiographies supply a few more, including but not limited to direct address of potential "Western readers." According to Prince, other signals of the narratee include the "inclusive 'we,'" negative statements that are responses to a narrator's (anticipated or) given question, extratextual references known to both the narrator and the narratee, comparisons or analogies that express a shared experience by the narrator and narratee, and, finally, overjustification provided by the narrator. Although the autobiographer may address primarily one narratee, traces in the text may allude to a secondary potential audience.

In addition to the narratee, there is another reader inside the text who may or may not coincide with the narratee: the implied reader. The implied reader is an ideal reader whom the writer envisions as he or she writes the text. This inside reader can also be constructed through some intra- and paratextual clues.

Unlike any other genre, autobiography has a clear agenda of communication between the author and the reader. Because the Francophone autobiographers are supposed to write for someone, there is a legitimate expectation that their main addressee is their own people. As early as 1966, the African critic Mohamadou Kane, in his seminal "The African Writer and His Public,"[8] portrayed African writers in general as trapped in an audience dilemma, being forced to write primarily for a French audience and secondarily for an African one because of the lack of an African reading culture. However, Francophone African autobiography offers a different situation, especially in the timeframe of the 1980s and 1990s.

Francophone autobiographers bring to the text a testimony that emphasizes the colonial dimension of their experiences. At least in the African context, the testimony is that of the older generation that has endured French colonialism and now writes about it for a younger African audience as a historical duty. Although the autobiographies from Martinique and Guadeloupe in the French Caribbean do not offer the same agenda as their African counterparts, they too show a concern with expressing a still-lived collective experience of entrapment in the colonial—some will say postcolonial—situation while proposing creative solutions. In their manifesto *Eloge de la Créolité* (1989), Chamoiseau and Confiant (along with Jean Bernabé) set out to advocate a "literature by us and for us," thereby positing the primacy of a Francophone Caribbean audience. A foreign reader (including a Francophone African reader like myself) of those autobiographies is faced with the "opacity" (à la Glissant) of a text written with an abundance of Creole language and structures.

It is unsurprising that the texts considered here engage a plurality of audiences because postcolonial autobiography exists in a hybrid position, historically addressing two or more audiences. The target audiences for the works under discussion are Francophone African or Caribbean, French, and American. An example of the complexities presented by the target audience is Confiant's *Ravines du devant-jour* (1993), which as an illustration of the tenets of the Créolité movement necessarily includes Creole speakers as a target audience. However, Confiant is especially careful to provide a glossary of Creole terms for the foreign reader, his other target audience, at the end of his book.

By mechanisms beyond the autobiographer's control, the message that he or she may have intended for his or her people may actually reach more foreigners than those people. What is at stake here is ideological, especially when self-censorship and editorial censorship are added into the mix. A strongly determining factor for African writers is the fact that they are writing primarily for a French audience. This reality may also influence African autobiographers to shape their discourses to meet the target audience's expectations rather than their own people's.

A CLOSER LOOK AT THE READER OUTSIDE THE TEXT

With Lejeune's concept of the autobiographical pact and Jauss's horizon of expectations, the characteristics of the reader outside the text (the actual reader) can come into focus. In the autobiographical pact, the author and reader have separate horizons of expectation: the author expects to persuade the reader, whereas the reader expects to accept the authenticity of the discourse he or she is reading. The autobiographer brings to the text a set of expectations that can be met or disappointed in the process of publication and reception. The autobiographer's expectations may be unrealized if he or she has to abide by the rules of the publishing house, thus altering certain aspects of the autobiography, or if the actual audience proves *not* to be the one envisioned by the author, thereby creating a different reception than what was anticipated. Autobiography is not a neutral discourse; more so than fiction, it involves both the author's and the reader's responsibilities. In the postcolonial context, the pact between the author and reader seems additionally burdened by the history of colonialism. One can argue that writing postcolonial autobiography is a political act because what is being represented is also political. Although this political act is apparently close to *littérature engagée* (committed writing), it differs from that genre by its pact of authenticity and confession: whereas many *littérature engagée* productions were fictional, perhaps to better soften and hide the identity of the author and the narrator, autobiography does not in general play such games.

As Jauss rightly notes in "The Identity of the Poetic Text in the Changing Horizon of Understanding":[9]

> Literary understanding becomes dialogical only when the otherness of the text is sought and recognized from the horizon of our own expectations, when no naïve fusion of horizons is considered, and when one's own expectations are corrected and extended by the experience of other. The recognition and acceptance of the "dialogicity" of literary communication brings into play in more than one way the problem of otherness: between producer and recipient, between the past of the text and the present of the recipient, between different cultures. . . . The question, to which literary hermeneutics must address itself, when faced with the otherness of a text, is how to bridge the gap between otherness and speechlessness. (9)

One distinction of importance that Jauss makes is the "otherness" of the text. As a German critic and scholar, he approaches medieval French texts such as *Le Roman de Renart* as constructions of medieval myths and other older genres and thus as forgotten or strange for the modern scholar. Cultural difference—that is, otherness—is a major motivation in studying a given text's horizon of expectations. As Jauss writes, "My initial incentive to examine the problem of the horizon of expectation of the reader for whom the literary text was originally written was the result of my study of a literature that is very distant and strange to us" (17).

The act of interpretation, as Jauss has described it, exists in history, involving a dialogue between past and present. As one actual reader of these autobiographies, I must be aware of my own horizons of expectations as I approach the works I discuss, taking into account each book's past as well as my own present. The past of these Francophone autobiographies is the 1980s or 1990s and earlier; their present is my act of reading and interpreting them now (in 2008) with my own set of expectations. That the African autobiographies under study were published after independence in 1960 is important because other autobiographies were published during the colonial era, when French authorities fully controlled the demand for their production. The African autobiographies published in the 1980s are not theoretically part of the control of the French authorities because African nations are no longer French colonies and because most autobiographers focus on the colonial era they grew up in as a way to share their testimony of that period with an African audience. Caribbean autobiographies published in the 1990s also break away from former autobiographical traditions, such as Mayotte Capécia's *Je suis Martiniquaise* (1948), which Frantz Fanon used as the example of the Caribbean woman's alienation from her own race in her desire for a white male.[10] Confiant, Chamoiseau, and Condé's autobiographies are different from Capécia's not only because they were written after Martinique and Guadeloupe became overseas departments of France in 1946, but also because the Créolité movement tries to distance itself from such alienation and seeks to cater to a Martinican audience. Condé, Chamoiseau, and Confiant dwell on depicting their childhoods in the 1930s and 1950s. My act of interpretation of these autobiographies must take into account each author's past.

My personal reading is a valuable hermeneutic approach to autobiographical productions from two culturally different groups: one familiar to me (Francophone Africa), and one foreign to me (the Caribbean). I bring to these texts a set of expectations fed by my background as a postindependence African trained as a literary scholar in both Africa and the United States. Born in the postindependence era, I grew up in two West African countries, Burkina Faso and Ivory Coast, before continuing my graduate education in the United States. The African autobiographies may seem closer to my African cultural background, although there remains a level of otherness in them because they were produced by Africans foreign to my native land of Burkina Faso and also because the authors describe a historical period that I did not experience. A different set of expectations arises for me with regard to French Caribbean autobiographies because I am not from the culture and did not grow up there. Yet the shared racial and historical bond between Africa and the Caribbean through the slave trade allows an African outsider to the island culture to have a grasp of certain similar cultural experiences. In addition, my Francophone African background and my three stays in Martinique in 2001, 2007, and 2008 help me understand the Creole language used in these autobiographies and the realities that they describe. Although Confiant's autobiography depicts life in rural Martinique in the 1950s, I can comprehend this epoch's social dynamic, with its strong communal and rural bonds, because it is close to my African background. My parents were colonized subjects of France, and I, too, carry the legacy of French cultural heritage and domination, so I can understand Chamoiseau and Confiant's ambiguities regarding the French language. Because of my own experiences, I expect an African text by people who experienced colonialism to be more critical of historical and political domination, and I expect the message to be written for Africans first. I expect Caribbean texts to speak to their immediate audiences while also acknowledging that the reader from France will be reading over the Martinican or Guadeloupean's shoulders or probably may even be forcing the latter to read over his or her shoulders. I often noticed while I read particular African and Caribbean texts that they were written primarily for a European or French audience. Amadou Hampâté Bâ's *Amkoullel* is an illustrative case because he indulges in many cultural explanations aimed at a European readership. I also found that although Chamoiseau and Confiant theoretically advocate a literature aimed at a Martinican readership, they are also entertaining a French readership fond of the exotic dimension of the Créolité movement.

AUTOBIOGRAPHY AS COMMODITY

When Francophone African and Caribbean autobiographies become commodities in the world market of publication, what are the issues at play? Literary theorist and postcolonial scholar Graham Huggan believes that Third World literature is established as a popular or successful commodity through its "exotic" appeal and through the popularization of postcolonial studies, a theory he explores in *The Postcolonial Exotic: Marketing the Margins* (2001).[11] Although I concur with Huggan, I also believe that the commodification of Francophone autobiographies presents another complexity because entities such as Martinique or Guadeloupe cannot be considered Third World. Nevertheless, Huggan contributes to our understanding of the field by proposing an intelligent distinction between *postcolonial* and *postcoloniality,* two confusing terms. He shows how they are interdependent and how they have become promotional commodities in academia:

> Postcoloniality, put another way, is a value-regulating mechanism within the global late-capitalism system of commodity exchange. Value is constructed through global market operations involving the exchange of cultural commodities and particularly culturally "othered" goods. Postcoloniality's regime of value is implicitly assimilative and market-driven: it regulates the value-equivalence of putative marginal products in the global marketplace. Postcolonialism, by contrast, implies a politics of value that stands in obvious opposition to global processes of commodification. . . . It is not just that postcolonialism and postcoloniality are at odds with one another, or that the former's emancipatory agenda clashes with the latter's; the point that needs to be stressed here is that postcolonialism is *bound up with* postcoloniality—that in the overwhelmingly commercial context of the late twentieth-century commodity culture, postcolonialism and its rhetoric of resistance have themselves become consumer products. (6; Huggan's emphasis)

A look at the paratextual devices that package postcolonial Francophone autobiographies shows the mechanism of control of Francophone subjects who engage in literary production. The capitalist and ideological dimensions play on both surface and deeper levels. *Packaging* is a term that I borrow from Richard Watts's excellent book *Packaging Post/Coloniality: The Manufacture of Literary Identity in the Francophone World* (2005).[12] Watts, following Gérard Genette's analysis shows how paratextual devices such as prefactorial endorsement and book covers frame the reception of Francophone texts in the colonial and postcolonial eras. In any paratextual study, the book becomes a "text-object" considered for the rhetorical effects that it is intended to have on readers. Unlike Genette's synchronic paratextual study, Watts shows how those devices surrounding the text influence readers diachronically—that is, at different times and in varying cultures. A diachronic perspective reveals a variety of readers and problematizes the reception of books written by (formerly) colonized peoples.

There is unequivocally a Western demand for autobiographies written by peoples that were or are under French hegemony. In *The Post-Colonial Exotic,* Huggan discusses this demand:

> Ethnic autobiography like ethnicity itself, flourishes under the watchful eye of the dominant culture; both are caught in the dual processes of commodification and surveillance. . . . This might help explain why the work of writers who come from, or are perceived as coming from, ethnic minority backgrounds continues to be marketed so resolutely for a mainstream reading public as "autobiographical." . . . Ethnic autobiographies, in this context, signal the possibility of indirect access to "exotic" cultures whose differences are acknowledged and celebrated even as they are rendered amenable to a mainstream reading public. (155)

Exoticism seems to be the incentive that allows African and Caribbean autobiographical discourse to be in vogue in French literary circles, not only for cultural and ideological reasons, but also for commercial ones. The exotic still sells even though the empire has collapsed (in Africa) or is still questioning its role in the colony (in the Caribbean). Beyond France, the Western world (in particular the United States and Germany) is curious about what writers from "indigenous" cultures have to say about themselves, their society, and their history. Huggan is right in saying that African literature in particular suffers from the "anthropological exotic": in reading literature by "indigenous" authors, Western readers expect and look for anthropological information. This mode of discovering the "other" was itself conditioned by anthropologists and ethnologists who undertook the study of the peoples of Africa during colonial times. The danger is that in reading African literature and autobiography in particular, Western readers may focus only on the works' documentary aspect and thus overlook their artistic dimensions. African autobiography in particular offers Western readers a direct entry into a foreign culture through a personal and "authentic" life narrative.

Huggan warns us against "the narrow identification of 'target' audiences, or more specifically in this case, the monumentalisation of a *metropolitan* readership, implied or not, for postcolonial texts" (30; emphasis mine). I disagree with Huggan here, though: in the case of Francophone autobiographies, it is right to identify target audiences and to infer that the autobiography's original intention or message is knowingly or unknowingly influenced by market constraints both in France and global communities. Against Mohamadou Kane's lament in 1966 that Francophone writers wrote for a metropolitan (French) audience, today it is even more valid to assert that they write also for the world community governed by the capitalist book industry and cultural exchanges controlled in large part by the West.

The West has always dominated the Francophone world, mostly to the West's advantage and with little interplay. This seems to be the case also in the literary field, where Francophone autobiographies are for the most part exhibited, promoted, and sold for their cultural otherness (value). *Postcolonial Francophone Autobiographies: From Africa to the Antilles* is therefore also a socioeconomic study of Francophone postcolonial autobiography, taking into account how it is received in its production because reception also involves a production of meaning that we assign to the work. Here the term *production* is ambiguous, meaning both the making and the interpretation of the book.

AUTHENTICITY

Behind the politics of publication and target audiences lies the issue of authenticity. For instance, paratextual and intratextual analyses show that *Kesso, Princesse peulhe* (1988) was written mostly for a French audience and that the author's testimony may be questioned in regard to the socioideological forces that influenced the production of her autobiography, which was written during a ten-year period. How authentic is Kesso Barry's *Kesso,* and for whom? Her underlying defense of the Fulani (Peulh) people helps her settle accounts with Sékou Touré, the revolutionary and first president of Guinea, said to have persecuted the Peulhs during his regime. An analysis of the two receptions of this autobiography in Guinea and in France reveals the forces that assign authenticity to the autobiographical discourse, a genre concerned primarily with telling the truth about oneself. Who should tell the truth, and to whom?

Can the autobiographer narrating his life, including his community, be regarded as betraying his people when he is writing primarily for a French metropolitan audience? The discomfort raised by this question can be seen in the angry reception of Amadou Hampâté Bâ's memoir

Amkoullel, l'enfant peul by his fellow countryman, Yambo Ouologuem, the famous and controversial author of *Bound to Violence* (1968). The issue may be that of responsibility vis-à-vis one's own people; Ouologuem's reported discontent in essence argued, "You cannot talk to *them* about *us* in such a way." This example poses the problem of the (individual) freedom of the writer in a community-oriented African context. It also raises, through the concern for audience expectations, a question regarding the mode (version) in which the self-narrative should be written. In the Bâ–Ouologuem situation, we note that there are two sets of expectations: how Bâ should write for his own people, and how he should write for a foreign (European) audience in search of ethnographic information. Without siding with Ouologuem, an intratextual analysis shows that Bâ wrote primarily for a European audience, as evidenced by the multiple interpellations to a "lecteur européen." The Self and the Other are in conflict in Bâ's case, and one may wonder if the sharing of a collective experience with a foreign audience is authentic in itself.

As Huggan suggests, African writers are aware of and sometimes resistant to this duality of cultural representation: "Are postcolonial writers persuaded to represent their respective cultures, and to translate those cultures for an unfamiliar metropolitan readership? . . . Postcolonial writers/thinkers, it could be said, are both aware of and resistant to their interpellation as marginal spokespersons, institutionalised cultural commentators and representative (iconic) figures" (*Postcolonial Exotic*, 26). Bâ's case contradicts Huggan's general assertion: in Bâ's autobiography, there seems not to be resistance, but rather compliance with the requirements of a foreign readership and the exigencies of a genre with which he was unfamiliar. One senses that African autobiographers cannot escape their "mission" as the spokespersons of their communities, and the message they deliver must be sanctioned or censored by those communities. Are we here evidencing a self-regulating authentic discourse? At any rate, can the reception by the community from which the autobiographer originates be the test of authenticity? In most cases, yes, although the truth, the representation of peoples and events, may also be relative because there may be dissenting or differing versions of that truth inside the same community.

Must Francophone Caribbean autobiographers also pay their dues to their community audience? Two of the Francophone Caribbean autobiographers under consideration, Confiant and Chamoiseau, belong to the literary school of la Créolité, whose agenda is to give a truer representation of the French isles through the revival of the Creole language. Does this agenda make their work more authentic? There have been claims that Creolité is just a fashionable device to promote Confiant and Chamoiseau in their literary endeavors but does not ring true to their own people.[13] In order to ascertain the truth of these claims, we must see how Confiant and Chamoiseau's autobiographies were received in Martinique and in metropolitan France. Were their narratives unanimously accepted as true to the realities of the Caribbean? Some divergences show that the best authorial intentions may not be best served in a market economy.

WHY AFRICAN AUTOBIOGRAPHIES? WHY CARIBBEAN AUTOBIOGRAPHIES?

In the 1997 special issue of *Research in African Literatures* devoted to autobiography and African literature (volume 28), Patricia Geesey, the guest editor, asks the question "Why African autobiography?" and offers the following answer:[14]

> Why African autobiography? Because the autobiographical texts (fictional, nonfictional, or somewhere in between) discussed in the essays collected here represent what may be the most vibrant element in African literary (and oral) corpus. In 1973, Olney wrote that "the shape" of African autobiography is "determined by the especial African-ness of the writer" (52). Today, after nearly 25 years of postmodern and postcolonial critical theory questioning national identities and subject positions, we now know that autobiographical writing is definitely *not* a text that reveals a unified, monolithic African identity. (1–3; Geesey's emphasis)

There are multiple answers to this question. What Geesey is implying but not saying is that African autobiographies become an "excuse" for Western academics to map Western theoretical and critical frames onto them. The answer to Geesey's question "Why African autobiography?" is that autobiography as a self-referential tool is an excellent place where identity construction—the dominant characteristic of African literature—is at work through a "transparent" discourse: it offers direct entry into a community through the life story of one of its members. Postcolonial literatures and African literatures in particular have been studied through the theme of identity construction or negotiation as a result of the colonial experience. Autobiography, the mirror of the Self and, more importantly, of the autobiographer's community, is the site where this process is at work in all its facets. "Why African autobiography?" Because one dominant African cultural value is the community, so the African autobiography offers different readers an entrance not only into the author's private world, but also into that of her or his community. And because autobiography has a special place in African literature and still enjoys that position. As noted earlier, an autobiography, more specifically a memoir, Diallo's *Force Bonté,* gave birth to Francophone African literature. This tradition has continued to the point that many critics have labeled African literature as being overtly autobiographical. How can it not be? Coming from a colonial experience and its sequels of psychological trauma, political subordination, and transformation, who else can Africans speak about other than themselves and their communities? What appears as a weakness is in fact a strength because the autobiographical "cachet" in African literature shows the transformative machine that was the colonial experience for Africans while also revealing how much the Africans have struggled to maintain the "African-ness." The same applies to Francophone Caribbean autobiography, which is also community oriented and which is still negotiating and settling its accounts with France.

Western academics see postcolonial African autobiographies as sites of identity creation and resistance. They therefore cast a set of expectations on these works depending on their own point of view. Some Western scholars apprehend the African autobiographical voice through a feminist agenda (whether shared by the author or not) or through postmodern notions of cultural resistance. Is the writer's "African-ness" the "anthropological exotic" that Western readers expect? The answer is most likely yes.

As a follow-up to Geesey's question on African autobiographies, it is apropos to ask the homologous question, "Why Francophone Caribbean autobiographies?" Several answers may be given. For one thing, like the Africans, the Caribbean writers come from a colonial experience with France (which continues today), yet their society is more Westernized, which has provoked questions of identity and political positioning and given birth to literary movements such as l'Antillanité and la Créolité. One might argue that identity questioning and construction, represented as conflicts, are major components of Martinican and Guadeloupean writers' works. More exposed to Western education than the average African, the Francophone Caribbean peoples and their writers in particular perceive autobiography as a direct way of expressing their identity crises.[15]

The Creole identity crisis is more acute than the African crisis and is experienced as a trauma. Thus, Chamoiseau and Confiant see the need to return to their childhoods in order to situate the origin of that crisis of the Creole in their lives. In contrast, Condé, although using the return to childhood to reclaim her identity, is suspicious of the Créolité movement and has a different agenda: to create for herself an "autobiographical space." It can be argued that the globalized Guadeloupean writer, at odds with critics who have always made connections between her iconoclastic heroines and her own provocative personality, finally decided to make peace with the literary world by publishing her only acknowledged autobiography, *Le Coeur à rire et à pleurer* (1999). By doing so, Condé confirms critics' assertions that her fictional works contain autobiographical aspects, but at the same time she claims her "autobiographical space," the freedom for a writer to blend fiction with her personal life and experience. Yet, like Chamoiseau and Confiant's works, Condé's autobiography shows the trauma engendered by a Francophone Caribbean family trapped in their identity crisis as black bourgeoisie, rejecting their black Africanness even as they are rejected by the white French. How does the last born of the family deal with this dilemma? The recollection of childhood as a preferred focus of these autobiographies undoubtedly goes deep into the turmoil experienced by Francophone Caribbean writers and their people.

Postcolonial Francophone Autobiographies: From Africa to the Antilles offers a warning that exotic postcolonial Francophone autobiographers, when promoted to foreign readers, risk becoming foreign to their own people. This book is ultimately about value: What is Francophone autobiography worth and to whom?

CHAPTER ONE

Hampâté Bâ

Equilibrium and Ambiguous Reception

Unlike the many Francophone African autobiographers who practiced autobiography at a relatively early age, Amadou Hampâté Bâ came to first-person narrative at the last stage of his career as a writer. Bâ was well known as a "traditionalist" for his endeavor to preserve African culture and traditions through his writings. He published many folktales and essays about identity in the African context, defining himself as a "man of culture." *Amkoullel, l'enfant peul* (1991) is the first of his two autobiographical writings, the second being *Oui, mon commandant!* (1994). In this chapter, I show that even when attempting to practice the Western tradition of writing about the Self, Bâ did not merely copy the model; rather, he struggled with it, interrogated it, and integrated some African elements as well as elements uniquely his own. My study contradicts Kusum Aggarwal's claim that Bâ, in his later work, had evolved into a more autonomous, independent author, in contrast to Bâ's earlier role as informant and collaborator with the French anthropologists whose authority weighed heavily in his first productions—*L'Empire peul du Macina* (1955), *Thierno Bokar, le Sage de Bandiagara* (1957), and *Kaïdara: un récit initiatique peul* (1962).[1] Although Bâ had been equally popular in Africa and France, a contrasting analysis of the reception of *Amkoullel* in both areas reveals that Bâ became even more popular in France because of political and religious extremist activities in Algeria, whereas his memoir passed unnoticed in Africa because of other political events there.

Bâ is the author of the famous saying that when an old man dies in Africa, it is as if a library has burned down. He served the French administration during the earlier times of colonization, filling several posts in exile in the neighboring country of Upper Volta (present-day Burkina Faso). He became a researcher in 1942, working for the Institut Français d'Afrique Noire (IFAN), which specializes in ethnological and anthropological collection and analysis of oral traditions. After Mali gained its independence from France, Bâ represented his country at the Executive Committee of UNESCO. He later took an active part in UNESCO's prestigious publication, *A General History of Africa*. In 1974, he received the Prix de l'Association des Ecrivains de Langue Française with the publication of *L'Etrange destin de Wangrin*, the biography of one of his compatriots. He became a member of the Académie des Sciences d'Outre-mer, and on May 15, 1991, Bâ passed away. Before the publication of his autobiography, Bâ was known as the defender of African traditions, both in Africa and in the rest of the world, through publications and media performances (radio, television, colloquia, and so forth). So far as his publications are concerned, he wrote many essays, folktales, mystical accounts, and two biographies: *Thierno Bokar, le sage de Bandiagara* (1957) and *L'Etrange destin de Wangrin* (1973). Bâ's account of his own life, *Amkoullel, l'enfant peul*, was published posthumously in September 1991.

Looking at autobiography as one distinct subgenre of life narrative, Bâ's first-person narrative is a memoir rather than an autobiography in the strict sense of those terms. Sidonie Smith and Julia Watson differentiate the memoir from autobiography in *Reading Autobiography*, defining memoir as:

> A mode of life narrative that historically situates the subject in a social environment, as either observer or participant; the memoir directs attention more toward the lives and actions of others than to the narrator. . . . In contemporary parlance *autobiography* and *memoir* are used interchangeably. But distinctions are relevant. As Lee Quinby notes, "[W]hereas autobiography promotes an 'I' that shares with confessional discourse an assumed interiority and an ethical mandate to examine that interiority, memoirs promote an 'I' that is explicitly constituted in the reports of the utterances and proceedings of others." (198)

Since Bâ makes abundant references to historical events, his text is better viewed as a memoir that covers the time periods of early French colonization in West Africa around 1900. Smith and Watson's distinction is especially useful because memoir and autobiography are confused in English whereas the distinction is made clear in the French, especially thanks to Philippe Lejeune's definition of the genre.

Historically and geographically, Bâ refers to his early life in the West African country Mali (formerly French Sudan) during the French occupation of that territory. *Amkoullel, l'enfant peul* tells the story of the adolescence of the young Bâ from 1900 to around 1920. The title *Amkoullel* is also the autobiographer's nickname meaning "Little Koullel"; the young Bâ was nicknamed after one of his uncles, Koullel, because he shared his uncle's talent for storytelling.

Born during the earlier stage of French occupation in Africa around 1900, Bâ is proud to call himself one of the eldest sons of the twentieth century, "les fils aînés du siècle" (67). Thus, Bâ positions himself legitimately as someone who has enough experience to tell the story of this time period. My interpretation is that *Amkoullel* can be read as the self-narrative of *métissage*, or how to keep one's identity while accepting another one imposed by the colonizer. The whole narrative appears metaphorically as the Self's spiritual victory over the colonizer's efforts at depersonalization, a victory which is major accomplishment for the author, since this was during the French domination of African peoples with its agenda to uproot Africans from their identities. For Bâ, writing autobiography is not a mere satisfaction of life; it is a demonstration that he was one of the Africans who succeeded in maintaining his soul without being annihilated by the French colonial system. Nevertheless, as we shall see, Bâ maintains a dialogue with French culture, indicated in his memoir by his references to an imaginary French audience.

As a whole, Bâ's first autobiography can be divided into two main parts: the first narrates his ancestry and his parental histories, and the second is devoted to his own development under French colonization. The story in *Amkoullel* is a blend of many oral genres: myth, epic, and storytelling. Both the mythological and the historical parts have an impact on the flow of the narrative. The beginning of the book develops slowly due to the narrator's lengthy description of the origins of his tribe, the "Peuls," who are also called "Fulani" (etiological myth), and of his family tree with historical and epic accounts.

One issue faced by an autobiographer recounting historical facts is the reliability of memory. Bâ seems to have solved this problem, writing in a Western tradition of autobiography, by pointing out the oral dimension of his education. For Bâ, the accounts that he narrates have to be trusted because his memory has been trained by oral tradition and practice. He therefore challenges the European dependence on written documents rather than oral reports. It is not surprising that the first element of his *Avant-propos* (foreword) is devoted to "la mémoire africaine" (the African memory):

> Several friends who read the manuscript were astonished that the memory of a man over eighty years old could remember so many things, and especially with such meticulousness in detail. The reason is that the memory of people of my generation, and more generally of people of oral tradition who could not rely on writing, is of an almost extraordinary fidelity and precision. Since childhood, we were trained to observe, to look, to listen, so that any event was imprinted in our memory as in a virgin wax. All was there: the setting, the characters, the words, even their clothing down to the last detail. When I describe the uniform of the first *Commandant de cercle*, which I saw closely in my childhood, for example, I do not need "to remember," I see it on a kind of interior screen, and I only have to describe what I see.[2]

Among all the self-narratives in my corpus, this is the only one that justifies itself so openly and with such conviction. Bâ portrays himself as belonging to a generation of people of oral tradition raised and immersed in the language and power of storytelling. Thus the autobiographer, fully aware that he is writing in a different (Western) tradition, has to justify the reliability of the source to the European audience.

That Bâ is uncomfortable talking about himself and using a Western tradition of writing is illustrated by Bâ's discussion of the order in which he chose to narrate the events. Bâ confesses that it was for writing purposes that he opted to conform to European chronology in conflict with African etiquette, which instructs one to talk about the mother first, before mentioning the father (61). Through all these justifications, one senses the uneasiness of someone from an oral tradition obliged to adopt conventions of a different tradition, European writing. Bâ felt he had to submit his narrative to a European rule. Bâ's narrative is struggling between two influences: his ancestors', and the French.

Bâ's memoir is like a story that evolves from suffering to liberation, with his father escaping the liquidation of his family and his foster father Tidjani Tall's release from unfair imprisonment. Bâ tells in detail how Tidjani Tall destroyed Bâ's royal family, the "Hamsalah dynasty," all who were killed with the exception of Bâ's father, Hampâté. Later, in an effort to make amends, Tidjani decides to adopt Bâ's father and his children. What follows his foster father's imprisonment is the positive side of the narrative: the liberation of Tidjani, and the development of the narrator's character. Thus, the narrative progresses from a slow-paced account cluttered with historical references and anthropological details to a smoother and lighter text when the narrator concentrates on his own personality and his childhood activities. It is when Bâ ceases to tell the story of others and rather tells stories in which he is a participant that the text becomes more readable. It is only starting from page 225 that the voice of the narrator becomes a strong "I" affirming itself: "I did not have any memory of the adventures of our return voyage. Was this a period of sleep of my spirit, an infantile amnesia? I do not know. On the other hand, I remember perfectly our arrival in Dokoumbo, approximately seven kilometers from Bandiagara."[3] Even if in the preceding chapter Bâ tells of his and his mother's reunion with his imprisoned foster father, and thus portrays himself as a participant in events, it is clearly and definitely at the time of their return to Bandiagara that he becomes a full autobiographer because he centers the story on himself.

In her brilliant study of Bâ's self-narrative, Christiane N'Diaye draws an interesting parallel between the personal story of Bâ and his family and the plot of the fairy tale. She does a structural analysis that illustrates that Bâ's story progresses from Hell to Heaven; after encountering and overcoming many ordeals and challenges, the hero finally triumphs and wins the object of his quest (in Bâ's story, his identity).

> If we reread Hampâté Bâ's text in the light of these configurations that are typical of the Oral genres, it appears that the experiences of travel that are lived and narrated in the XXth century are in fact represented according to the "initiation model" of Oral tradition. . . . Thus, events surrounding the first voyage of Amkoullel easily present themselves on the mode of the tale. Indeed, like the orphans of the tales, like Soundjata, Hampâté Bâ and his foster father, Tidjani, are on their way to "exile" following an injustice that shakes family and community balance.[4]

However, simply reading Bâ's memoir as a tale could be limiting because it restricts him to the theme that has defined him and that is loosely applied to many African textual productions: oral literature and the tale. Such a reading may imply a lack of originality in Bâ's memoir. Moving beyond this structural approach to examine the linguistic, anthropological, and narrative dimensions of his text reveals the originality of Bâ's narrative.

When a man in his eighties tries to remember his past, it may be difficult to connect with a generation that did not experience the same events. Bâ seems to be aware of this difficulty and is "readership conscious," since in his memoir he is very careful to clarify certain points about the past. At the linguistic level, Bâ revives the remote era he is referring to by using linguistic and anthropological information to help the reader understand the context. In using these two elements, Bâ succeeds in presenting a vision of the world from the African perspective under French colonization. Linguistically, Bâ recreates the atmosphere of the era by letting the characters of his story speak in their natural voices. For instance, to make the reader aware of the complexities represented in the colonized subject's use of the colonizer's language, he writes in the original syntax used by African people who did not learn French. They used a sort of French mostly borrowed from the African soldiers, vassals of the French, which was called *Forofion naspa*. He reproduces the way Gonfin, the guard who watched his foster father, used to talk to the prisoners: "Et il ajoutait dans son 'français des tirailleurs' (appelé français forofion naspa): Allez, travadjé travadjé! (Travaillez!) Sinon mon cochon, moi cochonner vous comme il faut!" (148). Bâ's rendering shows the reader the actual vulgar or abusive tone of an uneducated African trying to speak the colonizer's language to other Africans: not only is he using the language improperly but his vocabulary is also exclusively made of bad words. Besides the humor, there may be some irony about the use of French by some Africans. This snippet of conversation also represents a linguistic classification of the colonial "fauna." Here again, Bâ excels by giving us an African classification based on race and associated with the power structure of the colonial era. He does that by translating into French these classifications that were originally in African languages. Thus, the European is referred to as "Blanc-Blanc," the African who has been educated through the French school is referred to not as merely African, but as "Noir-Blanc," and the African who is under French rule and has not had access to their education system is called "Noir-Noir."

The anthropological dimension is rendered by Bâ in answer to the question: How does an African perceive a white person? This is a question that has not been very well addressed in African autobiographies of the colonial times such as Camara Laye's *L'Enfant noir* (1953), the classic of all African autobiographies. To my knowledge, Bâ is the only one who gives us this anthropological view of the Other by the Self. He does that through the eyes of Bâ as a young boy, encountering for the first time a "Blanc-Blanc":

> His clothing was of a remarkable whiteness but, instead of floating
> to let the air circulate freely around the body like African clothing, it
> married the shapes of the White man strictly, as if it were for him a
> carapace of protection. . . . As for the carapace of the lower extremities,
> it was the strangest: it went down to the ankles along the two legs that
> it enclosed narrowly. As for his feet, they were hidden in black shoes,
> closed, which glittered like ebony oiled well. Obviously, these shoes
> were nothing like those of the Blacks, normal inhabitants of the earth.[5]

This is the young boy's innocent perception of what a white man is, and all the anthropological details given by Bâ are very important in many respects. In addition to the irony in the description (which makes the white man appear funny and ridiculous through comparison with animals), the narrator offers the reader the African perception of the colonizer, a perception made of myth and legends: the white man seen as a creature from the sea, a depiction that is certainly associated with the first contacts between Europeans and Africans. At another level, the irony can be more subtle: I believe the author is giving a phenomenological description of a white man to an audience that is largely European.[6] According to Jean-François Lyotard in *Phenomenology*, "This is no accident: in the investigation of the immediate data prior to all scientific thematization, and the justification of such, phenomenology lays bare the fundamental manner, or essence, of the consciousness of this data, which is intentionality" (33). By bringing to his consciousness his first and innocent perception of a white man, Bâ performs a phenomenological description of both the white man's physical appearance and his clothing through the candid eyes of an African child. One may ask the question: For what purpose did the author indulge in such meticulous details in this description? My interpretation is that there is an irony behind this innocent presentation. Bâ wrote primarily for a European audience, and he wanted to let the European reader know that he or she may be perceived as an "other" too, meaning that Europeans may be "read" by the African "Self" as being "different." The narrator points out that the Africans think of themselves as "les habitants normaux de cette terre" (the normal inhabitants of this earth). This phenomenological description may be thought of as a "reverse-anthropology" in which the colonized subject makes himself as a "naïve eye," an anthropologist observing a different creature and describing it as exotic. The irony undermines the Eurocentric assumptions of the European reader. Such technique has already been used by some African autobiographers, such as Bernard Dadié, who describes the Parisians as exotic characters in the eyes of his African narrator in his semiautobiography *Un Nègre à Paris* (1959). Even if the technique is not new—it dates back to the French writer Montesquieu's eighteenth-century text *Les Lettres persannes*—its use by a former colonized subject to depict the former colonizer as he appears in an African's eyes--is significant in that it establishes the relativity of the point of view and the hegemonic discourse between the colonizer and the colonized. Because Bâ, in his dialogue with different civilizations, has always claimed to be expressing a relativism in the perception of the Other, the irony in this passage may be a "wink" toward the European audience.

The importance of identifying the audience for whom the autobiographer is writing has been pointed out by Emmanuel Ngara in *Stylistic Criticism and the African Novel*:

> The relationship between the writer and his audience is important in a number of respects. A writer writing for children should be conscious of the level of sophistication and linguistic attainment that is expected of that kind of audience. An African writing about Africa with an African audience in mind will have a different orientation from a European writing about Africa with a European audience in view. Two critics of African literature may be cited as examples. Charles Larson in *The Emergence of African Fiction*, and Harold Collins in *Amos Tutuola*, are writing about Africa but with a European audience in view and so there is much in what they say which is revolting to an African readership. Indeed, an African writer writing about Africa with a European audience in mind is likely to adopt a different attitude and a different style from an African writing about Africa with an African audience in view. (21)

Even though Ngara's criticism was intended for the novel, it applies very well to the genre of autobiography, and more specifically in the case of Hampâté Bâ. I contend that when dealing with autobiography, the writer's construction of the audience is very important. It is not surprising that Philippe Lejeune stressed the importance of the audience when defining autobiography in *The Autobiographical Pact*. Indeed, the title speaks for itself: Lejeune affirms that there must be a tacit pact between the writer-narrator and the reader of autobiography. Although Lejeune did not emphasize the issue of readership in this seminal book, he did point out its importance. As such, Lejeune's work supports my assertion that the narrative and the facts of an autobiography are dependent upon a particular readership. In the case of Bâ's memoir, a European audience is primarily targeted.

As I have stressed the importance of identifying the autobiographer's audience, it is fair to say that the reader of Bâ's memoirs may be struck by the amounts of explanatory detail and by the numerous addresses he makes to a potential non-African reader, a European audience. We see this when he mentions the Peuls for the first time: "'Pas si vite!' s'écriera sans doute *le lecteur non africain*, peu familiarisé avec les grands noms de notre histoire. 'Avant d'aller plus loin, qu'est-ce donc, d'abord, que les Peuls, et que les Toucouleurs?'" ("Not so fast!" *the non African reader*, little familiarized with the great names of our history will undoubtedly exclaim. "Before going further, what is this then, to start with, the Peuls [Fulani], and the Toucouleurs?") (20). He refers to a non-African reader again when he tells of the divorce between his father and his first wife. "Voilà qui est sans doute bien difficile à concevoir pour *une mentalité moderne*. Comment admettre qu'un ami puisse de son propre chef 'divorcer' la femme de son ami et que ce dernier accepte la chose sans discuter? C'est que jadis, le véritable ami n'était pas un 'autre,' il était nous-même, et sa parole était notre parole" (Here is something undoubtedly quite difficult to conceive for *a modern mentality*. How does one allow that a friend can, of his own will, pronounce the "divorce" between his friend's wife and his friend and that the latter would accept it without any discussion? This is because in the old times, a true friend was not an "other," he was yourself, and his word was your word) (59). Speaking of the multiple talents of his foster father Tidjani and imagining that a European reader must find this incredible, Bâ writes, "Mais revenons à Tidjani. Il n'avait pas seulement appris, dans son jeune âge, à manier pelle, pioche, hache et houe de cultivateur, il n'était pas seulement—on l'a vu à Toïni—un tireur émérite et un cavalier expert, il savait aussi, chose plus inattendue pour le lecteur européen, coudre et broder à la manière des métis arabes de Tombouctou" (But let's go back to Tidjani. He not only learned in his youth to use a shovel, a pickaxe, an axe and a hoe for farming, he was not only—as we saw it in Toïni—a sharp shooter and an expert horse rider, but he also knew, a most unexpected thing for a European reader, to sew and to embroider like the descendants of Arabs in Timbuktu) (153). Anticipating that his European readers would find it unbelievable that an African child was so multitalented, Bâ comments, "Certains s'étonneront peut-être qu'un enfant aussi jeune (il devait avoir autour de six ans) soit capable de faire tant de choses. C'est que les enfants africains étaient extrêmement précoces, leurs jeux consistant le plus souvent à imiter les travaux des adultes, qu'ils aidaient d'ailleurs très tôt dans leurs tâches"

(Perhaps some will be astonished that such a young child [he was probably six years old] was able to do so many things. It is because the African children were extremely precocious, their play generally consisting of imitating the work of adults, whom they helped, besides, in their tasks at a very early age) (176). Addressing a European readership who would not understand the way an African youth group was so well organized, he explains, "Certains lecteurs occidentaux s'étonneront peut-être que des gamins d'une moyenne d'âge de dix à douze ans puissent tenir des réunions de façon aussi réglementaire et en tenant un tel langage" (Perhaps certain Western readers will be astonished that kids of an average age from ten to twelve years could hold meetings in such an orderly manner and by speaking in such language) (247). Bâ also explains for his European audience the way in which Africans indirectly express their love toward their children through their relatives:

> The king, preceded by his only chamberlain, passed in front of his son without even looking at him. Nobody was surprised; the fact of not expressing his feelings towards his children belongs to African customs *that Europeans understand rather poorly.* In our customs, it is the duty of the uncles and of the aunts to openly express their affection for their nephews and nieces whom they regard as their own children. (482; emphasis mine)[7]

"The non African reader," "the European reader," and so on are all evidence that Bâ's autobiography was written primarily with a European audience in mind. Bâ's narrative considers or depicts such an audience in a dynamic fashion: through all these references to a potential European reader, Bâ is, in fact, using a pedagogical approach for this purpose.

In a relatively recent commentary, Yambo Ouologuem, the famous author of the controversial *Le Devoir de violence*, also suggests that Bâ's autobiography addresses a potential European reader in a pedagogical manner. Ouologuem, an oral tradition specialist who is from Bandiagara, the same village as Bâ, attacks the vision of the world presented by Bâ in his memoirs. Let us note that this is an African reader reacting against the vision of the world and the facts in a self-narrative by his fellow countryman. Ouologuem's reaction is reported in an interview between Christopher Wise and Sékou Tall, another compatriot of Bâ's, in *Yambo Ouologuem: Postcolonial Writer, Islamic militant.* When Wise asks Tall to "say more about Yambo's relationship with Bâ," Tall replies:

> Amadou Hampâté Bâ and Yambo are from the same village. They come from Bandiagara, and so they have worked together on oral lit-

erature, as well as many other subjects and themes. On the outside, Amadou Hampâté Bâ has published two books that did not please Yambo, *Amkoullel, l'enfant peul* [Paris: Babel, 1991] and a second book. This was because Amadou Hampâté Bâ told of things that weren't really true and because they had at one time developed their ideas together. Yambo was disappointed in Amadou and was unhappy with his writings. This is what he told us. Bâ failed to include what Yambo told him in his book [*Amkoullel, l'enfant peul*]. In other words, there are explanations of certain things in this book that they had once agreed upon together, and that Yambo had himself contributed, but Bâ left them out. Instead, Bâ described things that are not true. He misled his reader. He wrote according to his own ideas, rather than those of his townsmen. He wrote for himself, but not for the people of Bandiagara, whom he disregarded. So there was a disagreement between them. Yambo and Bâ disagreed on what had been said earlier. (237–38)

As this interview shows, Ouologuem reproaches Bâ for twisting certain details—details never explicitly named in the interview—instead of speaking from an African perspective. Bâ wrote for a different audience, which I suspect to be European. This may be explained by some narrative constraint or the exigencies of a genre that Bâ, an African storyteller, was not used to. This may also explain the reason why the vision of the world he puts forth in his autobiography is not shared by his compatriot. Ouologuem's reported reaction indicates that Bâ had to struggle between collective autobiographical writing (including his community) and a singular autobiography (excluding his community and Ouologuem). One could argue that, despite Ouologuem's anger, he failed to see that Bâ had to make a choice that was motivated by the genre he was writing in: his audience being primarily European, he had to write in this singular form of autobiography. Ouologuem's *Le Devoir de violence* (1969) has met with a lot of criticism for plagiarism of famous European authors. Since the controversy about his book, Ouologuem retired in his village and devoted himself to religion and mysticism. He was said to have lost his mind, but this does not hinder his reaction to Bâ's depiction of realities that are not foreign to him. In addition, this reaction can be taken seriously, as Ouologuem has been disappointed and frustrated about publication in the European press. His reaction may as well be interpreted as a frustration that Bâ oriented his narrative to a European audience primarily, which might have led him to leave out or add up things that could be frustrating for an African reader like Ouologuem himself.

Understanding the genesis of Bâ's autobiography can also clarify the issue of his intended audience. As an afterword to the second volume of Bâ's memoirs, *Oui, mon Commandant!*, Hélène Heckmann describes the circumstances under which Bâ came to write the two volumes of his memoirs, following the publication of *L'Etrange destin de Wangrin*. As a posthumous legatee, Hélène Heckmann describes the origins of the two memoirs:

> Finally, his close friends and I encouraged him to act, since for years, he had entertained us already with the majority of the tasty anecdotes which appear today in his memoirs. He thus again took pen and paper, and started to write. It was, I believe, around 1975 or 1976. As it was the day before he returned to Africa, he carried his manuscript to continue to work on it there, and a few months later, when he returned to Paris, he gave me the beginning of what he had done. According to our practice, I asked him to read again aloud. Rather than an account of personal life, it was a kind of collection of anecdotes, without a real discussion thread and without really involving himself in the account. Generally, he overlooked his own feelings or reactions in front of the events. In fact, he devoted himself, in writing, to a work of an "African traditionalist storyteller" for whom to tell about himself was rather indecent and who hides himself to let the things he wants to share speak. This is a kind of reserve to which can be added Fulani traditional decency. Each anecdote, taken alone, was a small jewel but, as it was, the piece was not easily publishable. I called friends to my rescue. During a conversation, one evoked the need for the modern reader (Western or African), to be able to identify with a central figure whose emotions and reactions he/she can feel, which was, besides, what Bâ did in *l'Etrange destin de Wangrin*. In this case, this central figure, could only be Bâ himself. . . . At the end, he said: "I understand." And what is admirable is that this man of more than seventy-five years went back to work and started again from the very beginning! In a few years of writing (which he stopped around 1979 or 1980, when he devoted almost all his time to fight illiteracy among the Fulani), that gave these marvelous memoirs whose continuation remains to be published. In this new version, the child Amkoullel, then the young man Amadou Bâ, came to life before our eyes, but the author remained faithful to his Fulani decency all the same: the confidences stop at the door of his intimacy.[8]

What is interesting about Hélène Heckmann's account is that it reveals to us the difficulty Bâ had in adjusting to a new genre.[9] Beyond this difficulty, we also have proof that Bâ was asked to write his memoirs by his European friends, and he viewed them as his first readers, as he submitted his manuscripts to them and they served as mentors to him. This aligns with the fact that *Amkoullel*'s narrative is full of addresses to a European audience, for whom many of the facts are culturally foreign.

Even if Lejeune did not develop the issue of the audience of autobiography any further, his *Récits de vie et institutions* shows that the institutions of the readership control the production of autobiographies:

> Under the ingenuous label of "authenticity" life narratives—oral biographies, autobiographies, testimonies—serve the finalities only revealed and interpreted by a pragmatic study. Examination of conscience, confession, psychic investigation, consecration of a reputation, political argument, mode of social advancement, or, on the contrary, act of accusation, even of self-accusation, life narratives, always, are part of the functioning of an institution: a church or sect, a representative of the political or judicial power, medicine, a cultural institution, a media. Is it the institution which institutes testimony, and which organizes its discourse? Isn't the rhetoric of life narratives, in the full meaning of the term, a strategy which consolidates the good conscience of the institution? (7)[10]

The institutions of readership that affected and shaped the production of Bâ's memoirs include his European friends as well as his French publishing house, as will be observed in greater detail.

As Hélène Heckmann's afterword to *Oui, mon Commandant!* verifies, institutional control did play a part in the genesis of Bâ's narrative: Heckmann confirms that Bâ was reluctant to write his autobiography and that he only did so after receiving encouragement from his European friends. To answer Lejeune's question in the above quotation about whether the rhetoric of autobiographies confirms the good conscience of the institution, it is fair to say that the French literary circle controlled the production of Bâ's memoirs, and they had a vested interest in perpetuating his image as a man of culture. Their idea, to have Bâ write his autobiography, reinforces their good conscience while at the same time supporting Bâ's legacy.

The same can be said of the publishing house: *Amkoullel, l'enfant peul* was purged, at the instigation of the publisher, of other details that Bâ had included. Their control of the production can be seen as a move to make the work more accessible to the modern reader. The publisher admits as much in a note at the beginning of the memoirs: "Amadou Hampâté Bâ's manuscript contained many developments on certain aspects of African culture or sociology. Because of the importance of the work, it was decided, in agreement with the author, to privilege the narrative and to remove most of these developments. The reader will be able to find them in other more specialized works by the author."[11] The publisher's note confirms Ouologuem's claim that Bâ omitted certain things, and it also elucidates the reason for the cultural and sociological developments being cut from the manuscript: to bring it into conformity with modern narration and to cater to a European audience.

My contention is not that Bâ wrote his autobiography just for Europeans, but rather that the Europeans constituted his first and essential readership; this does not exclude the fact that Bâ also had an African audience in mind. However, in this case, the European readership comes first and the African readership second. He uses a pedagogical technique to educate his foreign readers through the use of rhetorical questions to get their attention at the beginning of his autobiography. The imaginary dialogue between the autobiographer and a European audience reveals that Bâ was conscious of the difficulties of telling his life story to an audience that was not familiar with his culture. The merit of the autobiographer is not only to acknowledge the problem, but also and above all to solve it by answering the questions he thinks the audience may have. This proves that Bâ is a complete storyteller who anticipates the audience's expectations and reestablishes the contact with the addressee. This is a performance in the true sense of the term, worthy of the storyteller in the African sense.

At a more ideological level there is a progression within the narrative characterized by the author's increasingly critical view of the colonial world dominated by the French. Even though Bâ's references to the French are very cautious in the first part and show his leniency toward a potential French audience (which may cast him as a collaborator with the French), toward the end of the memoir, Bâ takes a more critical stand against the French colonial system. At this point, the narrative becomes more historical and factual. Interestingly enough, the level of criticism becomes more and more acute as the autobiographer grows up and becomes especially pronounced when he is seventeen. Bâ's autobiography shows greater or changing consciousness of the colonizers and their relation to his people.

I distinguish in the text of *Amkoullel* three stages in the progression of Bâ's consciousness of colonizers and his own people. The first level of consciousness Bâ presents in his memoir can be viewed as the "innocent stage." This period is distinguished by the perception of the colonizer as the "bon blanc," a person who can be defined, in the colonial system of oppression, as a white colonizer who is atypical in his kindness or generosity toward the colonized peoples. Bâ uses this term "bon blanc" in his encounter with Commissaire Monnet. After Monnet has shown him some kindness, the narrator gratifies him with, "— Merci mon bon blanc, merci beaucoup!" (416). This episode occurs during the period of Bâ's childhood when he tries to make sense of people around him. When the autobiographer refers to this time of his life, the colonizer, usually represented by an administrative authority, is portrayed as a different and strange other, but a nice fellow, anyway. This is noticed in the child Bâ's initial encounter with the first white man in his life, Commandant de Courcelles, in the long passage quoted earlier. After the first emotions of apprehension and fear, the narrator becomes more acquainted with de Courcelles and begins to like him: "Au fur et à mesure que le Blanc-Blanc parlait, je m'apaisais. Je sentis même naître dans mon coeur un élan de sympathie pour lui" (190). Even when the author is told about the circumstances that led to the captivity of his foster father, Tidjani Tall, Bâ portrays the white man who sent Tidjani to jail, Charles de la Brétèche, as a "bon blanc": "Non seulement le commandant refusa de lui passer les menottes, mais il lui permit de monter à nouveau Kowel-Birgui et le garda auprès de lui jusqu'à la fin du voyage" (98). This is after Tidjani, in a desperate attempt, tried to overrun the Commandant's horse to avoid going to jail by getting killed for his act.

The second phase of Bâ's involvement with the French colonizers is what I have deemed the "critical stage": as the author grows up, his view of the colonizer becomes more critical. As a matter of fact, in Bâ's narrative, the French colonizer is ridiculed with irony or with criticism, either directly from Bâ or in the recounted words of other Africans. The criticism by some colonized people can be noticed in the names they give to the whites. This could be considered a counterdiscourse, a subtle way used by the colonized to reduce the colonizer to a name, usually a degrading one. The Commandant in charge of the prison where Bâ's foster father is imprisoned is nicknamed "Coumandan danjenje kloti" (Commandant bouche-tordue-éclate-cris) in reference to a sickness that made him yell loudly. The Africans refer to the rude M. Monnet in a similarly manner: "Attention! Attention! crient les marchands en Bambara. M. Ventripotent s'amène, entrainé par sa bedaine" (411). M. Monnet's person has been reduced in the ironical eyes of the Africans to a big belly.

Bâ's third stage of interaction with the French colonizers is marked by a relativistic approach to various points of view. According to Bâ, one should never give up on the humanity or goodness of another person despite a negative first impression. This applies to the colonizer as well as the colonized. This relativism is highlighted in Bâ's treatment of M. Monnet, the manager of the boat who, despite his brutal appearance, will later show that he can also be a kind person, especially toward the narrator. "It was an era when the White man, whether wrong or right, was always right, at least in general. And yet I will have the opportunity, a little later on, to note that even at the bottom of a rowdy man there can be a spark of kindness, and that one should never despair of man" (412–13).[12] Earlier, in the context of the rivalry between the two families Tall and Thiam, Bâ had also expressed a view of this sort of reconciliation, or midway philosophy: "When I think of what certain Talls did to my family, I remember the very noble behavior of a Tall like Alpha Maki, and I think that one must close one's eyes on men's bad sides and take from them only what is good. What is good in us is common; as for our flaws, we all have ours, and I also I have mine" (318).[13] Bâ advocates the forgiveness of others' wrongdoings and the retention of their good side as a way to find peace with himself and with others. This midway philosophy evolved out of the ups and downs in the autobiographer's and his family's lives. Bâ's memoir is centered on the development of a philosophy of life: he proposes a sort of dialectic by which he puts together two facts to show their contradictions. Still, he does not stop at this stage, but rather moves on to a synthesis; his analysis of life's events tends to prove that nothing is black and white. This is why he came to see goodness in the rude and harsh Mr. Mollard. The autobiographer stands here as Bâ "le sage de Bandiagara" (the wise man from Bandiagara) with perspective on life, drawing wisdom from experience. Bâ devotes an entire chapter to prove his philosophical view of life in the section of *Amkoullel* titled "Vanité et poursuite du vent" (472–91), in which he depicts the grandeur of the absolutism of king Mademba Sy, a ruler who is feared and respected by everybody, even the colonizers. He then shows the king's wealth through his son Ben Daouda Mademba and the palace where the king lives. Against this "tableau," Bâ then presents the contradictory reality of the same people and the same palace, twenty-eight years later:

> It was approximately 5:00 p.m. when, one afternoon, the boat docked in front of Sansanding. I left the deck house where I rested. The spectacle which was then offered to my sight made me doubt my boatmen. "Are we yet in Sansanding? —Yes, they answered. —Sansanding, the city of king Mademba? —Without a doubt, it's Sansanding." I could not

believe my eyes. The entire river bank was degraded. The palace was in ruins and seemed to be swallowed by the ground. The beautiful plaza of fine sand, which once was cleaned only by hand, was nothing more than an abandoned field where a miserable little village market stood with its lame stands, poorly maintained, often half reversed by the north wind. (484)[14]

After the vision of the decayed kingdom of Mademba Sy in Sansanding, the autobiographer experiences a greater shock in his second meeting with Ben Daoud Mademba, the son of the king, who has so degenerated that he has become one of the poorest people in Sansanding. The necessary conclusion or synthesis that Bâ draws from the two contradictory visions, is a new attitude in life: "This day, in this moment, I divorced the world and took the firm resolution to comply all the remainder of my life, with the advice of my Master: to be helpful, to be helpful always, but to seek neither honors, nor power, nor command" (490).[15] Bâ's memoir is structured around this philosophy of bringing contradictions to harmony: he shows the gray side of life. This is why the characters portrayed in his self-narrative, from the colonizer Charles de la Bretèche who imprisoned his foster father, to the Commissaire Monnet and to the other Africans, are never totally good, never totally bad. Bâ's development of his life philosophy, which is itself an element of his identity, acts as a rejection of the colonial system built on the concept of "dépersonnalisation." Toward the end of his memoir, Bâ attacks the "mission civilisatrice" (civilizing mission) of the colonizers by pointing out its key instrument of brainwashing: the European school. By his philosophy of life, Bâ decides not to abide too much by the European way of life or way of thinking. He shows the danger of Africans who mimic Europeans' thoughts or way of life to the point of losing their essence, their Africanity, their soul. This is what he calls "dépersonnalisation." He attacks the subtle depersonalization of the Africans, implemented by the colonizer in their schools, by giving the example of Bouyagui Fadiga, who excelled in mimicking French language, culture, and mannerism to the delight of French officials:

> Mr. Assomption was particularly proud of Bouyagui Fadiga, whom he called a "pure product of French culture." And it was this, actually, which with the best intentions in the world they wanted to do to us: to empty ourselves in order to fill us up with the colonizer's ways of being, of acting and of thinking. One can only say, in our case, this policy almost always worked. At a certain time, the depersonalization of the "French subject" duly educated and trained was such, indeed, that he

asked nothing more than this: to become the certified copy of the colonizer to the point of adopting his dress, his culinary habits, often his religion and sometimes even his mannerisms. (499)[16]

Therefore, one can say that the memoir expresses a pledge for a new attitude resulting from the confrontation of two cultures: the African and the European. The reader cannot miss two main points of focus in Bâ's memoir: his insistence that the oral tradition and the European school had equal influence on his character. The book is full of many explanations of how he met masters of oral traditions and how he became interested and involved in the collection of oral texts, experiences paralleled by his Western education. Rather than seeing a contradiction, the autobiographer seems to strive for a synthesis of both, the sort of *métissage culturel* promoted by Leopold Sedar Senghor, one of the fathers of Négritude.

Yet this conciliatory element seems to be again contradicted at the end of the book when, in the last scene, Bâ parts from his mother after the Administration decided that he was to be deported to a remote post in Upper Volta (present-day Burkina Faso). The autobiographer, dressed like a colonizer, imitates the master giving the command for his guards to depart:

> I do not know how automatically to my lips came a phrase which I had heard many times in the mouths of the white officers in Kati and which I pronounced with a serious tone, emphasizing it with an energetic gesture: "All right, if everyone is ready, let's go!" The sad thing was that, suddenly, I felt stupidly proud of myself. Wearing my tropical helmet, forgetting for one moment my status of *temporary writer in an essentially precarious and revocable position*, I thought of myself as a chief officer. (518; emphasis mine)[17]

Yes, there is room for irony, but the truth remains that the temptation is great to imitate, to be somebody else, and to be someone else in a position of domination especially. Bâ shows that he himself does not escape criticism in the colonial system as he embodies the very depersonalization and the impersonalization he criticized earlier.

THE AMBIGUOUS RECEPTION OF BÂ'S
AMKOULLEL, L'ENFANT PEUL IN AFRICA
AND IN FRANCE

In this section, I conduct an analysis of the transnational reception of Bâ's *Amkoullel* to show that external political events dictated its ambiguous reception in Africa and in France. I also reveal a series of misreadings by French readers and reviewers about childhood and about how to list Bâ's memoir in the French education curriculum.

Amadou Hampâté Bâ passed away on May 15, 1991, in Abidjan, Ivory Coast, where he was also buried. In Ivory Coast, this piece of news was announced in the main official newspaper, *Fraternité Matin* (no. 7984), on Friday, May 17, 1991, with the headline, "Décédé mercredi: Hampâté Bâ inhumé hier" (Deceased on Wednesday, Hampâté Bâ was buried yesterday). On page 8 of the same issue, there are pictures of (then current) President Houphouët Boigny attending Bâ's burial. On the same page, there is a retrospective of Bâ's life and his major cultural and literary contributions. It is also mentioned that Bâ's memoirs are scheduled to be published posthumously in September 1991.

In Mali, Bâ's country of birth, the main governmental newspaper *L'Essor* issued a short front-page notice announcing the death of Hampâté Bâ in a hospital in the Ivory Coast. The notice says that Bâ's memoirs would be published in September 1991 by Actes Sud (*L'Essor,* May 19, 1991). The notice in the Malian newspaper is a concise summary of the major facts reported from Ivory Coast. It is striking to note that, in his home country, only six lines were devoted to Bâ's death, while he received national honor and coverage in the press in the Ivory Coast. The reason is that Mali in 1991 was experiencing political turmoil that overshadowed Bâ's death: in March of that year—only three months before Bâ's death—the former president of Mali, Moussa Traoré, was deposed by a coup d'etat after civilian riots and government massacres. The military government that seized power vowed to organize elections for the establishment of multiparty democracy.

However, in *Fraternité Matin,* from September until December 1991, there is no mention of the publication of *Amkoullel, l'enfant peul,* even though the memoir was released as announced in September 1991 by the French publisher Actes Sud. The Malian newspaper *L'Essor* also does not mention Bâ's memoir. This may be due to simple neglect and legitimate distraction: after the death of the author, the Ivory Coast lacked enough interest to cover Bâ's childhood memoirs while in Mali, political turmoil was at the forefront of national interests and Bâ's memoir passed unnoticed. It should be added that Ivory Coast's President Houphouët Boigny himself, a close friend of Bâ, was facing the first year of democratic elections in a multiparty system, and he was much more concerned with a turbulent political arena as he came under many attacks that year after having ruled over Ivory Coast uncontested for thirty-one years. Houphouët Boigny honored the burial of Bâ, but he was much more concerned with personal political issues than with the publication of Bâ's first memoir. This is even telling, as Bâ's reception in Ivory Coast until 1991 had been strong, for he was given the same amount of respect as President Houphouët Boigny, even being called "Le Sage" (the wise man), as Ivorians fondly called their own leader. Bâ's previous publications had enjoyed popular success in Ivory Coast as well, and his collection of African folktales, *Petit Bodiel*, was integrated into the primary-school curriculum. On the whole, turbulent political events contributed to a poor reception of Bâ's *Amkoullel, l'enfant peul* after its immediate publication in both African countries.

In France, *Amkoullel, l'enfant peul* received the French award Prix Tropiques de la Caisse de Coopération économiques only four months after its publication, as announced in *Le Monde* (December 20, 1991) in its section "Monde des livres." The ambiguity of the reception of Bâ's autobiography in Africa—specifically Mali and Ivory Coast—and in France is that, while he was a popular author in Africa during his lifetime, it is only after his death that Bâ achieved outstanding recognition in France, after the publication of his memoirs. The popularity of Bâ's first memoir in France is evidenced by the fact that, despite a semester marked by declining sales in the French publishing world, "Monde des Livres" notes in June 1992 that the publisher Actes Sud made excellent sales with *Amkoullel, l'enfant peul*, which sold twenty-five thousand copies. In addition, in 1998 Actes Sud published *Sur les Traces d'Amkoullel, l'enfant peul*, a book with photos by Philippe Dupuich, and text selected and coordinated by Bernard Magnier, director of the African collection at Actes Sud. This is a book with quotes from Bâ, including photographs of him at various stages of his life and photos of the places described in *Amkoullel, l'enfant peul*. There are some references to Thierno Bokar, Bâ's koranic and spiritual master with pictures of his tomb. Pictures of daily life in Mali are shown, especially places such as Mopti and Bandiagara, which are mentioned in *Amkoullel*. Pictures of Bâ in his study in Treichville (Abidjan) and as the ambassador of Mali in Ivory Coast also appear (134). There is also a short biography of Bâ at the end of the work (179–83). The quotations in the book, which feature Bâ's proverbs, didactic tales, mystic poems, and his original documents, are borrowed from various sources: interviews with Bâ, his own texts, newspaper statements, and so on. This is an example of an editorial effort to promote a great author posthumously, going out of its way to publish, or repackage and republish, documents about him in connection with *Amkoullel*. This may also be another way of ascertaining the authenticity of what was described in *Amkoullel*: as Philippe Lejeune notes, autobiography can be distinguished from fiction because autobiography establishes a pact of authenticity that can be verified by the reader. This justifies the use of the photographs in *Sur les Traces d'Amkoullel, l'enfant peul*. The reader is then cast as a detective; as the title can be translated as *On the Footsteps of Amkoullel*, it is fair to say that Dupuich's photographs serve the purpose of authenticating Bâ's life narrative by giving its French readers actual photos of the places trekked by the young Bâ in Africa. In an article entitled "Sur les traces d'Amkoullel," published in the French newspaper *Sud Ouest* in May 1999, the photographer Philippe Dupuich confides that he was inspired to undertake such a work after reading *Amkoullel, l'enfant peul*. Dupuich presented the idea to Bernard Magnier and the latter agreed to the project.

In the review posted on the Web site Africultures on January 17, 2002, Fayçal Chehat writes: "This excellently designed book, with a great iconography by Philippe Dupuich, has only the ambition to encourage those who do not know the Wise man from Bandiagara to catch up by going back to consult at least a portion of his work."[18] Chehat correctly points out that the main objective of *Sur les Traces d'Amkoullel, l'enfant peul* is to revive the interest of French readers who had not been acquainted with the other works by Bâ and to immerse themselves in his former publications and the interviews he gave. This supports the claim that the popularity of Bâ in France needs to be maintained and continued. This continuation is assured by the publisher and Bâ's posthumous legatee, the institutions of readership that support the continued publication of Bâ's work.

Another example of Bâ's popularity in France is the movie made by Bernard Mounier entitled *Amadou Hampâté Bâ, maître de la parole* (Amadou Hampâté Bâ, master of words), which aired on the French television channel France 3. In the *Sud Ouest* newspaper article dated November 28, 2002, in the section "La Rochelle; Culturel," Mounier declares that Amadou Hampâté Bâ had long been in the shadows in France and that Mounier had the desire make Bâ known to the (French) public: "Hampâté Bâ est très longtemps resté dans l'ombre, explique Bernard Mounier. Et nous avions le désir de le faire connaître auprès du public. C'était un diseur, un conteur, et son œuvre est symbole de la sagesse africaine." Mounier's declaration seems far-fetched in light of Bâ's popularity in France subsequent to the publication of his memoir.

It may be that Mounier means that he wants to deepen the French audience's understanding of Bâ by exposing them to audio and audio-visual archives; in this respect, he is building on Bâ's popularity rather than bringing him out of the shadows.

André Velter's review of *Amkoullel, l'enfant peul*, "Une enfance africaine" (An African childhood), published in *Le Monde* on September 28, 1991, portrays Bâ as a born storyteller ("conteur né"), but Velter is quick to add that Bâ, with the publication of the first volume of his memoir, shows an exceptional gift as a writer. Ironically enough, Velter's positive reception of Bâ is a consecration of him as a writer, although Bâ had already written many books prior to that. Velter distinguishes the oral-tradition narrator and storyteller from the creativity that he sees in Bâ's memoir. The irony is more telling because memoirs and autobiographies are distinct from novels, and in the memoir the author-narrator tries to stick to reality and facts, refraining as much as possible from using fiction. Velter also notes the historical and ethnological dimensions of the book. He also commends Bâ's usage of a delightful language that is precise and powerful at the same time. Velter presents Bâ as the man that understands and archives all the epic oral history of the peoples of the West African Savannah. Velter concludes by casting Bâ as an exceptional man stating that there is no longer any room in Africa or elsewhere for a man of his stature.

In *Le Figaro*'s edition of June 21, 2007, Olivier Delcroix interviewed Fabrice Luchini and Erik Orsenna (a member of the French Academy) about the danger of decay in style facing the French language. Orsenna's response reveals how much he admires the creativity that enabled Bâ to smoothly transpose oral narrative into a written document without altering the vitality of the narrative: "In writing, it was necessary for him to employ a terrible language to retranscribe and find this kind of natural vibration among the thousand and one African dialects. Because, when one passes from the oral speech to writing, one must change everything, without changing the meaning. All solidifies on paper. It is an immense artist who can make this solidification not an impoverishment, but a rebound."[19] When a writer acknowledges the accomplishments of another writer, it is double praise. Bâ has joined the elite circle of artists and writers; even though Orsenna did not mention it, his comments on Bâ's artistic accomplishments apply mostly to his memoirs, especially *Amkoullel*, and not to his previous works. As mentioned earlier, the memoirs signaled the entrance of Bâ into the realm of writers in the French reception. The effect and influence of Hampâté Bâ is strong even in literary circles.

The positive reception of Bâ's memoirs even extended to the religious circles in France. Shortly after the publication of the second volume of Bâ's memoirs, *Oui, mon Commandant!*, Julia Ficatier wrote an article for the November 21, 1995, edition of the Catholic newspaper *La Croix* entitled "Figures spirituelles du XXè siècle Islam" (Spiritual figures in twentieth-century Islam), in which she declares that Bâ has a large reading public in France: "In France, there are many readers of the great Malian writer: they discovered with *Amkoullel, l'enfant peul* and *Oui, mon Commandant*, two memoirs, the flip side of the decoration of French colonization, seen by a child of West Africa, who has become as an adult, a great master of the oral tradition of the black continent" (8; as noted on the excerpt).[20] In her review, Ficatier celebrates Bâ as a man of faith who is open to other faiths and to dialogue among people from diverse religious backgrounds, a man who advocates tolerance.

I strongly believe that Bâ's popularity came at a moment in history when Islamic integration was a fear both in Algeria and in France. French people remembered Bâ as a practicing Muslim advocating religious tolerance, which was in contradiction with the religious extremism in Algeria. This instilled in the French a desire to rediscover Bâ's thought and writing, and thus made his first memoir popular. In the early 1990s there was a resurgence of extremist violence led by the Front Islamique du Salut (FIS) and the military groups Groupe Islamic Armé (GIA) and Armée Islamique du Salut (AIS) in Algeria, and there were serious concerns in France, which has a prominent population of Algerian immigrants. The French authorities were concerned that the violence would spread over their country with acts of terrorism, as Algeria is very close to France. The violence perpetrated by the FIS, a Muslim-based political party, was perceived as a threat to democracy—although ironically enough, on December 26, 1991, the FIS reportedly won the first round of democratic elections in Algeria—as well as sign of intolerance of other faiths, instilling the fear that Algeria under the Islamic Front would become an exclusively Muslim country living by the law of Sharia, and not democracy. In the midst of such religious intolerance by Islamic groups and the elimination of Algerian intellectuals by Islamic militias, the publication of *Amkoullel, l'enfant peul* made the French (re)discover with new eyes a man deeply rooted in his Islamic faith, yet who is also open to dialogues with other faiths. Bâ was then perceived as a Muslim advocating tolerance and interfaith dialogue. The French people were reminded that he had even published a book about Jesus, *Jésus vu par un musulman*, which was reissued by Stock in 1994.[21] Julia

Ficatier portrays Bâ as the man who wrote the best pieces from a Muslim about Jesus:

> We are indebted to Hampâté Bâ for the most beautiful pages of a Moslem on Jesus, who, he says, is "the Spirit of God." He reminds Catholics but also Moslems that they both share the essence of an often forgotten religious fraternity. In Islam, writes Hampâté Bâ, "Jesus, Moses and Mohammed are regarded as highest in the hierarchy of the communion with the unity of God. That is to say, he emphasizes, on which esteem Islam places Jesus-Christ. Besides, it is canonically forbidden for any Moslem to utter against Jesus words, which would not be appropriate for Mohammed. Any bad word against Jesus must be punished as a blasphemy against Mohammed himself. There is no doubt, in Islam, that he who blasphemes against Jesus is destined to hell." (8)[22]

In the same issue of *La Croix*, many excerpts of *Amkoullel* are reproduced where Bâ speaks of the cohabitation of the animistic faith of the Bambara and the Islam of the Fulani, both of which he studied. In these excerpts, Bâ portrays his act of learning about both faiths as an example of "good neighbors" advocating tolerance.

THE "CANONIZATION" OF BÂ IN FRANCE

It is not far-fetched to think that the convergence of Bâ's life with his writings—especially his posthumous memoirs—in the context of Islamic political groups rejecting Western values in Algeria and France, contributed to the "canonization" of Bâ. I am using canonization here in a literary as well as a religious sense. Bâ acquired both religious and literary acceptance: he is perceived by French officials as well as French Catholics as a man of faith with whom a dialogue is possible. He is cast as a "holy man," a spiritual guru, as his religious books—*Vie et enseignement de Thierno Bokar* and *Jésus vu par un musulman*—were read extensively by a growing French audience. Metaphorically, Bâ was canonized by the French scholarly world as his position shifted from a "grand conteur" (great storyteller, oral traditionalist) to a "grand écrivain" (great writer) after the publication of his memoir. The memoirs, and especially *Amkoullel,* revealed to the French public that Bâ was a man of faith, a man of culture, a man of religious tolerance, and finally a gifted writer: his literary canonization broadened from orality (storytelling) to include writing.

We may as well speak of a "Hampâté Bâ effect" in France because his dual canonization in France made the French realize how important it is to listen to the "Other," and that an ex-colonized subject may teach them lessons about themselves and others while still retaining his own identity. Bâ's life and work lead to a perception of him as a "Humanist" (a Renaissance man) in the French tradition, a multitalented man who reflects on and writes about the role and the interrelations among diverse human beings. He is often portrayed in the French media as an oral traditionalist, a historian, a storyteller, a religious person, and a philosopher. Such a rich background enables Bâ to be regarded as worthy of the French. Bâ is a product of the French colonial system, which he helped by working in the administration and by collaborating with the Institut Français d'Afrique Noire under the anthropologist Théodore Monod. Despite the harshness of colonialism for an African, Bâ remained rooted in his faith and traditions—he collected oral tales and epics—and he continued a dialogue with the former French colonial masters. He contends that he could never be molded by the French, as he only came to France when he was already fifty years old (see *Sur les Traces d'Amkoullel*). Bâ, in the eyes of the France of the 1990s, is a "success story": a formerly colonized subject trained by the French who is still deeply centered in his faith and culture and who is willing to share it with his former colonial masters without any resentment. This position of the postcolonial subject who does not subvert or overtly criticize the French colonial situation is agreeable to the French and contributed to Bâ's successful reception in France. The Bâ effect has continued up to recent times: there is still a thirst for Bâ in France, as evidenced by an article in the French newspaper *Ouest France* (June 29, 2007) entitled "Un air d'Afrique va souffler sur Vitré" (An African wind blows over Vitré), which announced a retrospective on Bâ's works at the Media Center in Vitré.

The Bâ effect can also be seen in the adaptation of a portion of *Amkoullel* targeting a young French audience. The publishing press Syros published *Le Petit frère d'Amkoullel* in 1994, featuring illustrations by the Cameroonian-born Christian Kingué Epanya. This children's book, the title of which can be translated as "Amkoullel's Younger Brother," builds upon Bâ's account of how as a child he earned his reputation as a good storyteller and was compared to his uncle, the great storyteller and master Koullel.[23] The Bâ effect goes even deeper into French society: *Amkoullel* is used as a pedagogical and sociological tool to teach young adults and is catalogued among the books for social reinsertion, mostly directed at helping troubled young children.[24]

Bâ's popularity moved beyond the realm of the literary and into the domain of sociology when his memoir was adapted for the stage. Théâtre Sans Frontières, in collaboration with Atelier International de Recherche et de Création Théâtrale, staged a play adapted from *Amkoullel* called *L'Enfant peul*, which toured France and England in 1999. The presentation on the Théâtre Sans Frontières Web site reads: "Théâtre Sans Frontière collaborates with Paris based Atelier international de Recherche et de Création Théâtrale to bring you a rich tale of Africa, bursting with colour song, movement and epic storytelling. An international ensemble of actors come together for this first ever stage adaptation of Amadou Hampâté Bâ's acclaimed autobiography."[25] The play *L'Enfant peul* was once again adapted for the stage in 2004 when the playwright Catherine Levy-Marie transformed the tale into a play, as reported in the magazine *The Stage* (October 4, 2001). In *Aperçus culturels*, an online magazine that gives an overview of cultural and artistic events in the Franche-Comté region, it was announced that the group L'Allan would stage a production called *Amkoullel* in 2004, created by the musical group "Le Nine Spirit." Showcasing actors, musicians, singers, and "improvisateurs," *Amkoullel* blended the spiritual dimension and jazz.[26]

Another book by Bâ, the biography of his spiritual master, *Vie et Enseignement de Thierno Bokar*, was staged by the renowned playwright and British director Peter Brook and was performed all across France (Paris, Lille, Tourcoing, and so on) and some parts of Europe. Peter Brook's staging of *Thierno Bokar* in France is a continuation of the Bâ effect in France and, by honoring his spiritual master, an homage to Bâ. The life and wisdom of Bokar were revealed by Bâ, and it is only after the publication of *Amkoullel* that there is a renewed interest in Bokar. Because Thierno Bokar was the master and mentor of Bâ, French readers were curious to go to the source to discover how Bâ received his wisdom. Performances were scheduled from October 26, 2004, to January 15, 2005, according to the Web site.[27]

In the December 13, 1999, edition of *Le Monde*, Thérèse Marie Deffontaines published an article entitled "La Mémoire et l'écrit: Amadou Hampâté Bâ" (Memory and the writer: Amadou Hampâté Bâ). This article is a retrospective of Bâ's life and accomplishments, and it also reviews an episode of the French television series "Un Siècle d'écrivains," broadcast on France 3, which featured Bâ. The series is dedicated to showing connections between an author's life and works; it aims at giving a "century" overview of International Letters by drawing portraits of selected writers from around the world in the time span of five years.

In the episode that featured Bâ, the former president of Mali, Alpha Omar Konaré, and Hélène Heckmann, Bâ's literary legatee, were interviewed. Thérèse Marie Deffontaines laments in her article that the forty-five minutes of the show were not enough to capture the multiplicity of Bâ as a linguist, historian, ethnographer, sociologist, and so on.

BÂ IN THE FRENCH SCHOOL CURRICULUM

The Bâ effect can also be perceived in the French school curriculum, which has incorporated his books, especially *Amkoullel, l'enfant peul*, into its teaching programs. At the Lycée Européen de Villers-Cotterêts, there was a special class for first-year middle school students who had to read two texts by Bâ. The objective of the course was to revive students' reading habits and train them to read effectively. They read the opening chapter of *Amkoullel, l'enfant peul* and *Le Petit frère d'Amkoullel*, an adaptation of Bâ's first volume of the memoirs for a younger audience. The opening chapter of *Amkoullel, l'enfant peul* is read for its sociological information. The final objective was to assess how two passages from the same work could be read differently by various readers (here, adult and child audiences), and to answer questions about why people should read the memoirs and about Bâ's intended audiences.[28]

On the official Web site of the French Ministry of Education, Éducnet, in the pedagogical sequence suggested by the Académie d'Amiens for second-year high school students, under the subtitle "genre narratif," *Amkoullel* is the first text on the list followed by *La Dot* by Maupassant. This attests to the Bâ's popularity: his memoir is integrated into the French school curriculum. Nevertheless, *Amkoullel* is wrongly classified under the rubric of "Le récit: le roman et la nouvelle" (Narrative: the novel and short story). Bâ's memoir has fallen into the dominion of mere narration and worse, fiction.[29] *Amkoullel, l'enfant peul* is also on the Academie de Nancy-Metz's select list of nineteenth- and twentieth-century novels for second-year high school students; yet, it is only described as capable of arousing students' interest and curiosity.[30] According to the Web site, this list is extracted from the first- and second-year high school list of September 2001. The same list of books was selected by the Academy of Amiens.[31]

The Web site of the Collège Jean Moulin Le Pecq reproduces the official reading list suggested by the National Education Ministry, where *Le Petit frère d'Amkoullel* appears on the section for first-year middle school students (sixième in France, equivalent to seventh grade in the

United States) under the rubric "Romans et récits centrés sur la vie affective" (Novels and narratives centered around affective life).[32] The
same description is given by the Web site Savoirs CDI, which provides
professional resources for teachers and librarians.[33]

On the Web site weblettres.com, Christian Raseta compiled a list of
short stories and novels from Francophone Africa. According to Raseta, the objective is to suggest a diversity of readings for French students,
to introduce them to neglected authors, and to expose them to different
usage of the French language by Francophone writers. "It was a matter
of finding novels and stories written by authors of Francophone black
Africa, in order to propose to the students different readings, with these
objectives: the discovery of mainly unknown authors, the discovery of
the francophonie (the language can present notable differences with
the one to which our students are accustomed), the discovery through
these novels of human realities far from the usual stereotypes."[34] The
Web site is dated Thursday, April 16, 2005. There is a note that this is
an unofficial site maintained by a teacher and that this list was gener-
ated by a chat-room question and that this compilation by Christian
Raseta is a result of contributions by French professors in the chat room
Profs-L. *Amkoullel, l'enfant peul* is listed under the rubric "Romans et
nouvelles." It is worth noting that, once again, Bâ's memoir is wrongly
catalogued in the section for novels and short stories. We must bear in
mind that this is a synthesis of a number of French high school reading
lists, and *Amkoullel, l'enfant peul* is listed along with *Le Coeur à rire et
à pleurer* by Maryse Condé, as well as nineteen other books by Francophone authors. The incorrect cataloging of Bâ's *Amkoullel, l'enfant peul*
suggests that despite the popularity of the book in France, the French
school did not know how to classify it. This also confirms what was
stated earlier: Bâ had to struggle to transfer his life narrative from an
African oral narrative way to a written document in the French tradition; it appears that despite his efforts, the French school does not have
a clear idea of which rubric to put it under.

In her online article "Francophonie," Christiane Chaulet-Achour
portrays the peripheral position of Francophone works in the French
school curriculum: "The French-speaking cultural space appears explicitly only in the programs of first-year high school students, as part
of "literary and cultural history." In the second year, it is replaced by
the European cultural space. This parallel clearly shows the outsider
position where it is relegated; its entry is related to what is common-
ly called cultural openness and dialogue among cultures."[35] Chaulet-

Achour laments that in the marginal section suggested as secondary reading, there are few francophone titles (6). However, despite Chaulet-Achour's lament, it is worth noting that *Amkoullel, l'enfant peul* is in a good company on that list alongside major Francophone works: Ben Jelloun's *L'Enfant de sable* and Joseph Zobel's *La Rue Cases-nègres.* This attests to the Bâ's popularity, as his first memoir is sitting next to titles by Francophone writers renowned in France.

It is also worth noting that at the Lycée Pierre Béghin in Grenoble, in the new programs for the last class in high school (the *Baccalauréat* is considered the first university diploma in the French system), Bâ's *Amkoullel* is on the list of "books of interest" for a workshop on "colonisation, décolonisation, Tiers-Monde, les Sud." In actuality, *Amkoullel* and Albert Memmi's longtime classic *Portrait du colonisé* are the only books by former colonized subjects on that list. The objective of this course-workshop is to expose French students to the history of France and her former colonies, global issues and the Third World.

> Between pessimism marked by an often condescending fate and happy optimism over the beauties of "misery under the sun," the media convey an extremely biased and incomplete image of the Third World in the spirits of the young Frenchmen of the beginning of the 21th century. Their last year of school must contribute to give them some keys to grasp diversity, complexity and the formidable dynamisms and forces of change currently at work in Third World countries.[36]

Bâ's memoirs are also represented in the university curriculum: both *Amkoullel* and *Oui, mon Commandant!* were on the reading list of a course titled "Autobiographies, Autoscopies" taught by M. Tumba Shango Lokoho at the Université de la Sorbonne Nouvelle in September 2005. This course is an advanced course for senior students getting a BA degree (a "Licence").[37]

On the National French Bibliography, "Bibliographie nationale française," Bâ's *Sur les traces d'Amkoullel* is surprisingly the only one of his books listed, not *Amkoullel* or any other book. The irony resides in the fact that *Amkoullel* is more representative of Bâ's authorial work than *Sur les traces d'Amkoullel,* since he himself worked on his memoir while the latter is the result of a French photographer and the publisher of Actes Sud's endeavor to make a compilation of Bâ's sayings, interviews, and places he had been to, as a follow-up of *Amkoullel.* Under the rubric "Biographies, genealogies," *Sur les traces d'Amkoullel* is listed in a cumulative list of books about biographies and genealogies catalogued up to the year 2001.[38]

CHILDHOOD AND ITS (MIS)REPRESENTATION/CONCEPTION

In an interview with the online Francophone literary magazine *Mots Pluriels* in 2002, the French scholar Madeleine Borgomano asked the renowned Ivorian writer Ahmadou Kourouma if he thought that the image of the African child portrayed in both *Amkoullel* by Bâ and *L'Enfant noir* by Camara Laye was still current or was now outdated. Kourouma responded that the image of that African child was outdated. "The black child, as described by Camara Laye and Hampâte Bâ, is on the verge of extinction. One has to go deep into the bushes of Africa to find Camara Laye's black child."[39] There may be a quid pro quo in the French reception of Bâ as, according to Kourouma, the portrayal of the African child in Bâ's memoir as well as in Camara Laye's autobiography is becoming obsolete in contemporary Africa. This questions the reception of Bâ's *Amkoullel* in France because the memoir is used as a representative depiction of an African child, even though this image is fading. It could be said that the French reception of Bâ's memoir is marred by its anthropological focus; French readers see the depiction of African childhood as an ahistorical fact rather than as a temporal, fading reality. The unquestioning and unproblematic aspect of the African child growing up in colonial times while keeping his own traditions meets the horizon of expectations of the French. The horizon of expectations in France from the 1990s to the present, marked with a reassessment of its colonial history, finds in Bâ's memoir a voice that would not challenge the "positive aspects" of the French colonial enterprise in Africa. Bâ's memoir, especially *Amkoullel* (and not *Oui, mon Commandant!*) meets that horizon of expectations in that it does not address colonization in a challenging way: Bâ remained barely unchanged by the colonial situation. The question posed by Borgomano is not innocent, and it is not without purpose that she associated *Amkoullel* with *L'Enfant noir* in her question to Amadou Kourouma. *Amkoullel* is equated with *L'Enfant noir*, a longtime classic and a well-received autobiography of an African, written and published during colonization, which proved to be uncritical of French colonization. *Amkoullel* met with a successful reception in France because Bâ returned to his childhood marked by French colonization and remained true to himself while establishing a dialogue with the former master. *Amkoullel*, more so than its sequel *Oui, mon Commandant!*, which depicts more confrontations between French administrators and the local indigenous populations, enjoyed a positive reception in France because it is uncritical—or at least not overtly critical—of the French, and it is set in the unproblematic time of childhood. *Amkoullel*'s reception is set in the background of the reception of Camara Laye's *L'Enfant noir*, and the work meets the expectations of the French.

Amkoullel, still a favorite book in France in the context, figured prominently in the 2005 debate over how an official history of French colonialism must be written. During that heated debate, many French officials, historians, and common people were in favor of emphasizing the positive rather than the negative aspects. Without giving the French a positive slant on colonialism, Bâ's *Amkoullel* tells them of an idyllic childhood (although with some troubled moments) under French colonialism. What is more, Bâ is perceived in France as a product of the French colonial system who does not "talk back" or "write back" in a contentious way. Bâ did not lead a frontal attack to the French colonial enterprise, but rather engaged in a dialogue, which could also be interpreted as a form of collaboration, especially given that his memoir was a product of a collaborative effort with his European friends. This contradicts Kusum Aggarwal's thesis that Bâ's later works show more independence, with Bâ as an autonomous author who distances himself from his early collaborative books. As my analysis of the work and its reception demonstrates, *Amkoullel*, one of Bâ's last works, was more collaborative than singular. Nonetheless, Bâ's position is not strictly "postcolonial," in the sense that while he does revisit the colonial era he does not challenge it or revise it in his first memoir.

CONCLUSION

Bâ's memoir shows his ambiguity in constructing his Self out of the colonial encounter; he resolves that ambiguity by remaining true to his origins and beliefs while sharing with the colonial world his Africanness through ethnological books, folktales, and so forth. Bâ had to answer pressing questions early in life: What does one become after one's dynasty was almost extinct and when one's country, after being invaded, is under the administration of new and foreign rulers who are imposing their views on Africans through their own school? The resolution of this ambiguity is the midway philosophy that Bâ developed through experience and observation. The theme of ambiguity continues even in the reception of his first memoir, which was unnoticed in Africa while it attained popularity in France. The popularity of his memoir in France is due to a number of factors, internal and external: the stature of the writer himself and political events. Bâ's attitude toward colonization appears as a personal triumph of a colonized subject who remained rooted in his African culture, whereas the ambiguous reception of his first memoir cast him as a postcolonial collaborator because his positive reception in France has staged him as an unproblematic emblem of a colonized subject coming out of the colonial experience with a positive attitude, which is agreeable to the horizon of expectations of the French. It could be suggested that this ambiguous situation of Bâ comes fundamentally from his attitude toward human beings in general as his philosophical view—the midway philosophy—or vision of the world in *Amkoullel* shows that he advocated openness to Africans and French altogether, avoiding condemning them harshly. Bâ's positive reception and canonization in France is very ironic because it shows that he could attain the status of writer in France only when he finally collaborated with European scholars on the writing of his memoirs. His work, as I have shown, is no longer a strictly individual but a collective effort, and this may explain why his reception was widely popular in France. My contention is that Bâ's last work is better perceived as a collaborative effort and brings him back to the dynamics of his earlier productions, which are tainted with anthropological collaboration with Europeans. Bâ's case shows the limits of a formerly colonized subject who is trying to write about himself and who gets caught in the problematics of the audience he should be writing for, the constraints of the publishing world, and the external events beyond his control.

CHAPTER TWO

Valentin Mudimbé

*Autobiography, Philosophy, and Exclusive
Francophone Reception*

Valentin Mudimbé is well known in the American academy for his numerous works on Africa. The publication of his autobiography, *Les Corps glorieux des mots et des êtres*, on his fiftieth birthday attests to his continued interest in Africa as well as his own academic achievements. In the present chapter, I propose that the autobiography of this African scholar who was born and raised in the colonial Belgian Congo is a site where history, philosophy, and self-narrative meet, largely because of the hybridity of the work. Second, I show how philosophy permeates and shapes *Les Corps glorieux des mots et des êtres*. Third, I analyze Mudimbé's position toward Anta Diop and Négritude as parallel to that of the theoreticians of Créolité, the French Caribbean theory that rebuts the intellectual legacy of Aimé Césaire. I demonstrate how Mudimbé's life may also be read as a metaphor for modern Africa. Finally, my study of the reception of Mudimbé's autobiography raises the question of language choice and addresses the limited transnational reception of his book.

Born on December 8, 1941, in Kinshasa in the Belgian Congo, (formerly Zaïre, currently the Democratic Republic of Congo) Valentin-Yves Mudimbé is a Francophone intellectual with multiple specialties who has made his way in the world of the American academy as a renowned scholar. Yet his intellectual career was preceded by his total immersion in religious life as a Benedictine monk in Africa. After deciding on his own to become a monk in Rwanda, Mudimbé chose to leave the religious world in order to enter the secular one as a student and scholar.

From the start, Mudimbé himself acknowledges that *Les Corps glorieux des mots et des êtres* (The glorious bodies of words and beings, 1994) is only partially autobiographical, as it is presented also as an essay on various subjects centered on the author's life: "If the first genre enables me to account for my present situation, because of my childhood, it is purposely and systematically partial for this work to be described as autobiographical in the strict sense of the word. While the second genre seems to be close to an essay, it is far too subjective, restricted, and even occasionally, doctrinaire to claim to be an essay of good quality" (II).[1] After this presentation of his work as a blend of autobiographical accounts and essay elements, Mudimbé, toward the last part of his book, paradoxically declares *Parables and Fables* to be "*le plus autobiographique* de mes ouvrages" (157–58; emphasis mine). This declaration seems ironic because the book to which he refers is a series of essays written by Mudimbé on subjects such as anthropology, politics, philosophy, and theology, with Africa as the common denominator. The only part narrated in the first person in *Parables and Fables*, and the only section that has obvious connection to the author's life is the preface, in which Mudimbé recounts his "intellectual odyssey" during the 1968 revolution in Europe, while giving summaries of seminal works by French intellectuals. Besides the preface, nothing justifies calling *Parables and Fables* autobiographical, or as the author puts it, "the most autobiographical of all [his] works." This description of *Parables and Fables* as an autobiography seems to be far-fetched, and I shall disagree with Mudimbé's definition by asserting that *Les Corps glorieux des mots et des êtres* is the most autobiographical of all his works because it is mainly written in the first-person singular and is centered around the development of the author's personality, points that are only partially true in *Parables and Fables*.[2] One should note that an author's definition of intent is not to be taken for granted because it may be used to mislead the reader, especially because Mudimbé himself was reluctant to label *Les Corps glorieux des mots et des êtres* as entirely autobiographical.

Even though there is not a neat separation between the autobiography of the author and the essays he writes, as a whole, *Les Corps glorieux des mots et des êtres* is about the life of a former monk who became an atheist intellectual. At an early age, Mudimbé was selected by his spiritual father, the Benedictine priest Dom Thomas Nève. After seminary, Mudimbé decided to become a monk, despite the warnings of other senior priests who were his mentors and professors. In August 1952, he joined the Benedictine Seminary at Jadotville-Panda and, in 1959, entered the monastery in Bujumbura, Rwanda, to become a monk. By personal choice, he renounced his vows and left the monastery in 1963, becoming a student at the University Lovanium at Léopoldville (Kinshasa) while working as a "Professeur auxiliaire" of Latin. In 1966, he met and married his fellow countrywoman Elizabeth Boyi, who was his classmate at the Université Catholique de Louvain et Paris from 1966 to 1970. In 1970, he became a professor and an administrator at the University of Zaïre. The conditions of his departure for exile and his integration in the new academic world of the United States are the last developments recounted in his autobiographical work. Mudimbé emphasizes how his religious training and discipline have influenced his whole life based on the Benedictine motto, "Ora et labora" (Pray and work!).

The essay portion of his book shows the clear influence of Marxism and French intellectuals such as Sartre, Merleau-Ponty, De Certeau, Althusser, Foucault, and Barthes, some of whom were his friends. This influence shows in the way Mudimbé analyzes his past and present selves. The essay revolves roughly around the intellectual goal of the author: to rethink African tradition and history. Among its subthemes are the place of the Christian religion in Africa; a critique and evaluation of the colonial legacy; the various forms of African socialism and the development of Africa; Euro-American versus African feminisms; and African studies in philosophy, anthropology, and politics.[3]

The narrative has a false linear or chronological appearance because the author makes many digressions in the middle of the story of his life in the form of sociological, political, or philosophical reflections. The originality of this autobiographical work is in the combination of the self-narrative accounts and reflective essays. This accomplishment questions the frontiers of autobiographical writing for an intellectual. It is as if the author could not write the story of his life without giving the story of his ideas and thoughts. This tactic may also be an aversion to the self-centeredness of telling only the story of one's life, which confirms Josias Semujanga's definition of *Les Corps glorieux des mots et des êtres* as an "intellectual autobiography." In writing the story of his life, Mudimbé seems uncomfortable about just telling his own life: this disciple of French structuralists and poststructuralists knows well how false and pretentious it is to tell the story of one's life as an absolute truth about one's identity. In French thought, such an endeavor is ironically labeled as *se raconter*, and Mudimbé's uneasiness recalls Sartre's project in writing his autobiography in *Les Mots*, which proved to be an irony against the genre, as Philippe Lejeune shows in *The Autobiographical Pact*.[4] In this context, it therefore seems logical that for Mudimbé the scholar, his autobiography should not be limited to the narrative of his social life, but rather must be continued with the story of his intellectual life and reflections.

There is an almost religious seriousness of tone in the book's narrative, and this may be due to the philosophical and existential analysis that the author makes and to the religious background of the author. Nevertheless, there are a few parts that are anecdotal and humorous, such as when Mudimbé writes of his amusement at being mistaken for a priest by various people in Africa as well as America many years after he renounced his religious vows because these mistakes contradict the proverb "L'habit ne fait pas le moine." He writes, "L'habit ne fait pas le moine, dit-on. Mais y a-t-il une allure, un je ne sais quoi d'autre qui le fait?" (Clothes do not make the man, says the proverb. But is there a demeanor or something else that does it?) (144).[5]

Of course, as in any autobiography, there is also the usual division between the younger Self and the adult. One distinctive feature of Mudimbé's autobiographical work is that it is scattered with numerous questions, which are partially or completely answered on later pages. Most of these are raised by the adult Self who questions his own identity: "Suis-je moi-même? Qu'est-ce que cela signifie de m'appréhender comme un moi-même, alors que tout me désigne comme un pour-autrui? Est-ce l'allure, la démarche, un je ne sais quoi qui l'indiquerait comme ecclésiastique?" (Am I for-myself? What does it mean to understand myself as if I really am for-myself, whereas everything shows that I am for-others? Is this the look, demeanor, or something that would reveal me to others as a clergyman?) (141). In addition to all this questioning, there seems to be a constant thread in the autobiographer's life: the quest for liberty and independent thinking. After he was chosen by Dom Nève during his childhood to serve in the religious order, Mudimbé's later decision to break away from the church appears to be a way to liberate himself from constraint and live his life as he desires. This thirst for liberty later forced him to exile himself from his country in order to avoid political constraints. Yet this search for independence, which he achieved in his intellectual life, did not isolate Mudimbé in an ivory tower. He was reminded by a French scholar that he did not exist "for-himself" only, but also "for-others," in the existentialist sense of the words:

> From this moment on, explicitly, I started to see myself, more and more, as a sign, a question mark for others. George Balandier, who came to Duke to receive an honorary doctorate was to confirm it when I was taking leave of him. After we hugged, he said to me: "Do not forget that you are an ambassador." For whom? For which mission? Again I have this feeling of seeing myself as detached, both subject and object, and subjected to the expectations of others: a pure product for-others, reified. Shall I analyze that? (127)[6]

Mudimbé is not only an individual; he is a sign read by others as representing Africa, as if he were on a diplomatic mission. This comparison could parallel his training as a religious missionary whose function is to be devoted to God *for* others. Even though puzzled by this impression of existing "for others," Mudimbé the narrator and not the historical figure now does not see any contradiction as he writes that the Benedictine way of life influenced his life and became his second nature; therefore, it seems logical that he should be called upon to serve for others, even in his secular life.

As a matter of fact, Mudimbé sees himself as on a mission when, after questioning his usefulness to Africa in his position as a university professor in the United States, he sees that all his intellectual productions were geared toward what he calls "the salvation" of his country of birth:

> My goal to act, as scholar, in the Zairean political context, could not produce any decisive action. I could not expect any spark to come out of my teachings of philology at Lovanium or Lubumbashi. Today, I say to myself: the key is there, in my childhood yet again. My painting wanted to capture the breath of life in its bareness; my poetry, like my essays, ridiculed the moods and tendencies of Bourgeois inspirations, but my university work, in spite of my country's falling apart politically, was a solid proof of our good education curriculum and its competence. My goal was a religious mission: to save. (162)[7]

Despite the serious tone of the work, Mudimbé's *Les Corps glorieux des mots et des êtres* also gives an impression of achievement and self-satisfaction. From the beginning, Mudimbé acknowledges that, by writing his autobiography, he wants to summarize his accomplishments on the eve of his fiftieth birthday. One may note that there is an obvious sense of self-satisfaction here that differs from the humble tone of the book as a whole, especially in the part devoted to his American years. Mudimbé is proud to have adapted his Benedictine training to a new environment, which won him his academic success:

> But his key to success was to have adapted, instinctively, a secular discipline, acquired during his adolescence, to the style of competitiveness and productivity of the American university. A Benedictine day is divided into three: eight hours of prayer, eight hours of work and eight hours of rest. A laicization of *Ora et labora* had enabled him over many years to re-examine the contents of the three components of the grid without changing its meaning. As a result, every day, he could count on eight hours of personal intellectual work, eight hours of teaching and administrative work, and eight hours of leisure and rest. (128)[8]

If the third-person singular is used here to reduce the tone of self-praise, it does not deny the self-satisfaction of the autobiographer. Interestingly enough, the third person serves the narrative function of diluting self-praise here as it casts Mudimbé as the object of his own discourse; it also shows how Mudimbé sees himself with a trace of satisfaction as being seen by others in the American academy, where race is a factor: "He is black, of course, and what is more, an African. That he could read ancient Greek without a dictionary, that he masters Latin, and that he speaks more than ten modern languages, that he works more than ten hours per day, was unbelievable. He had to deal with new enmities: he had become one hundred percent a member of the American academic world" (129).[9] This confirms the function of autobiography: to tell the story of an exceptional being.[10] As Mudimbé himself acknowledges, his situation was very unusual for the colonial period he was living in, when a priest chose him for the Benedictine life, at the age of seven.

In order to understand how Mudimbé analyzes colonialism, it will be useful to look at the relationship between the son and his parents in Mudimbé's autobiographical work and see how this relationship sheds light on the colonial situation in the former Belgian Congo. At first reading, the autobiographer's relationship with his parents seems to be distant, and this could well be explained by the fact that he was taken away from them at the age of seven. Still, both parents seem to be used in the text to illustrate points that the author is trying to make. His mother gets his attention, and the relationship between mother and son is an atypical one; it is a struggle for communication in the form of a game in multiple different indigenous languages:

> I am bound to be taken away from her. I cannot clearly understand
> her reservations. She suffers from my coldness. Sometimes I conde-
> scend to come down from my cross to listen and speak to her, but from
> a distance. I know, already, how to stiffen myself in my future destiny.
> For example, in order to avoid her control, well before I am eight, we
> communicate in a kind of discrete confrontation, yet an ongoing one.
> If she speaks Luba to me, I answer her in Swahili, thus indicating my
> assimilation into a cultural circle which she knows little about. If she
> addresses me in Swahili, I answer her in Luba or, more often in Songye,
> emphasizing, by this act, my patrilineage and my disapproval for her
> poor knowledge of Swahili. My game amuses her, of course. She does
> not laugh at it, however. I have a feeling of power. She, on the other
> hand, appears to find a subject for affection in it. This game is a kind of
> caress always started but never completed. A very strong bond is built
> there yet denied all at the same time. Today, I would say that my moth-
> er and I were an exemplary couple. Between the son and the mother,
> one should not speak of love but it was expressed in this type of inno-
> cent game. (30–31)[11]

This may indicate that his election into priesthood by the separation
from his mother cost him a certain form of alienation replicated in the
game he plays with his mother using various languages in order to establish a distance of status between them, thus embracing the colonial
hierarchy that makes him closer to the colonizer, superior to or different from his mother's status.

Mudimbé uses his father to give an illustration of the Belgian colonial
system. He describes his father in his duties as *ajusteur* at the Belgian mining company (127–33), and he contends that his father was proud of him
and wanted him to become an engineer, to attain the same level as his own
technical "superiors" in the company hierarchy. Mudimbé claims that he is
"the father of his father," because of his school success, which fulfilled his
father's wishes. Yet there was not intimacy between father and son, only
the sense that the father was proud of his son; as for the son, there was
no real appreciation of his father, only the strange claim that his success-
-accomplishing his dad's dreams--makes him the father of his father! His
father in his position at the mining company and his mother as a house-
wife are cited as examples of the social category of Congolese who were in
the middle ground between the Western educated middle class and the
masses in the colonial Belgian Congo. Mudimbé locates them at the center of the struggle between the Western and the African orders: "Dans la
classification coloniale, mon père n'est pas un 'évolué.' Il est quelque part, à

mi-chemin entre le villageois des ouvrages anthropologiques et l'assimilé parfait du projet de conversion coloniale" (In the colonial classification, my father is not categorized as an "African literate." He is somewhere halfway between a villager from anthropology books and the perfectly assimilated African, the goal of the colonial assimilation project) (39).

Both of his parents are distant from him, and Mudimbé explains this distance by his integration into the religious family; the church becomes his second family as he was severed from his natural family. Thus, his training as a Benedictine monk in the colonial Belgian Congo posits Mudimbé as a sign of the continuity of the colonial enterprise, which at the same time gives him a different status from his fellow countrymen.

Because of his religious training, it is not so surprising that despite his later Marxist and existentialist philosophies, Mudimbé sees himself as predestined, a chosen being: "A présent que je peux, à froid, regarder mon parcours, je me dis: l'universitaire international ou, simplement, l'homme que je suis devenu est, pour beaucoup, le fruit d'une élection" (Now that I can take a cold look at my life itinerary, I say to myself: the international scholar or, simply, the man that I have become is, for many, the fruit of God's choice) (153). He continues in more detail:

> My childhood comes back to me: a framework, an art, a vocation. I emerged from it and, since then, I have been turning around in a garden, puzzled. The die was, obviously, cast from the beginning. Even in my rebellions, I would live according to ancient standards. I will die remaining faithful to this garden-framework or, more exactly, with the habits that I acquired from it. Even my hesitations testify, as a whole, to this past. With God circumvented, the futility of Sunday's beauties forgotten and, with it, the extent of the Christian symbols reduced to illusions of faith, there still remains in me a dream foundation, a Catholic culture and its virtues. (158)[12]

Mudimbé sees himself as predestined for his later intellectual work, after being "elected" or chosen by Dom Thomas Nève who destined him to religious vows. The quotations above show Mudimbé's existential reflection using the very words of Jean-Paul Sartre's existentialist work *Les Jeux sont faits*. It is ironic that rather than sharing Sartre's existentialist theory on the dynamism of every human being to transcend history by coping with contemporary events, Mudimbé sees himself as someone who was preselected and designated from the beginning to become the person he is now. His attitude seems to be passive as opposed to the active existentialism expressed by Sartre.

In front of his parents Mudimbé appears as a totally assimilated African, the fulfillment of the colonial project at the cost of his distant relationship with his parents. This, in addition to his election into priesthood, reveals that Mudimbé was subjected to the contingencies of the moment. However, later on, the renouncing of his vows marks his existentialist commitment by making a personal decision that affects his entire life. While he adopts a sentimental tone to reflect on his relationship with his parents and his introduction into priesthood, Mudimbé becomes more analytical and cold in his reflection of the global colonization in Africa.

In the essay section of *Les Corps glorieux des mots et des êtres*, Mudimbé sees colonization as twofold: global and personal. He is critical of this period that he evaluates as alienating, and concludes with the paradox that it was not all that bad:

> This brings me back to the colonial use of the Greco-Roman lesson, specifically to the ambiguity of colonization: was it so bad, when one compares it with present times and the bloody whims of our political leaders? From the very start of the colonial conquest, the Africans experienced the occupation as a danger. It could take, here and there, forms of salvation; that was the case in East and Central Africa. Many local sovereigns chose to be part of the new order. Some of them quickly backed off when they understood the occupant's ambition, as was the case in the history of the occupation of Buganda. Others, to refer to the book by Yambo Ouologuem, played Salif, a detestable symbol. Alas it is, also a model of the general ambivalence of the history of colonization and its hypocrisies. . . . Thus, Salif embodies our sign of contradiction. He welcomes conquest, lets himself be corrupt and corrupts others. Colonization takes root. (177)[13]

Additionally, Mudimbé's analysis of Africa does not stop at the colonial period, but includes a harsh criticism of its postcolonial situation. According to him, even after independence in 1960, African leaders continued the colonial legacy, never denying the superiority of Western civilization, as they continued its same mode of exploitation. Mudimbé blames African leaders for their recourse to myth in order to deceive the people; they therefore establish a rhetorical practice of an order of discourse by giving the impression that independence was a break with the colonial era:

And Zaire could be only a metaphor. There the State appears to be in
an isomorphic relationship with a linguistic machine. With the assis-
tance of the police force paid to keep the citizens in alarm and to maintain an infrastructure that is falling apart, our African states maintain,
primarily, a rhetorical practice. It presents, in any case, clear tenden-
cies. It is, initially, a totalitarian language and claims to present an absolute beginning. In actuality, when it is closely analyzed, one realizes
that it mixes various registers, and proposes, in an incantatory rhythm,
desires and complexes of overcompensation already formulated or, at
least, outlined under the first republics. This language covers up, in an
astonishing way, the continuation of colonial policies and their practices. (191–92)[14]

To Mudimbé, African independence was a façade that claimed to break
with the colonial era, but at a deeper level, it was just a continuation
of the colonial order in its practice. The autobiographer condemns the
deceptive usage of language to represent reality whereas it does not offer practical solutions to the reality of the citizens; it is just serving as a
cover-up, a mask.

In Mudimbé's autobiography, colonization is used as a metaphor
on a personal level, when the autobiographer describes himself as
somebody who let himself be colonized and benefited from it. One
has to remember that the subtitle of Mudimbé's book is "Esquisse
d'un jardin africain à la Benedictine" (Sketch of an African garden
designed in the Benedictine fashion). In the metaphor of the Benedictine garden, Mudimbé blends the notion of nature and culture with
colonization. He defines etymologically the process of colonization
as the cultivation of nature and accepts that he was colonized in the
Benedictine way. In discussing how the Benedictine staff was used to
check on him through the watchful eyes of Dom Charlier, the director of the school he was attending, he writes, "Thus, the permanent
gaze on me causes neither resistance, nor astonishment. It colonizes
me, certainly, but what can that mean? This monitoring, it seems to
me, enters my secret games with God" (15–16).[15] Later, he returns to
the metaphor:

Colonization as the reason of the victors could thus be, at best, only an
invitation to assimilation and to grow. So I mean: a rearrangement of
a physical space, a taming of human beings according to a new code of
values; a colonization in the etymological sense of the word (*colére*: to
plow), exactly as we can decide to transform a piece of forest into a gar-

den, raised in transcendence, and which we have decided to promote to the respectability of a status. (194)[16]

Clearly, the metaphor of the garden could be interpreted on another level where Mudimbé symbolizes the colonization of Africa by Europe; the autobiographer represents a continent, and the personal and over-all colonization become a single process. Yet Mudimbé himself sees the colonization of Africa generally as a failure to reconcile the African and European traditions, while presenting his personal colonization in the metaphor of a Benedictine garden as a successful one.

Another remarkable feature of Mudimbé's autobiographical work is the recurrent use of questions, mainly existential ones, which the protagonist asks himself, clearly showing the influence of philosophy on his life and work. Here are some examples:

> Mr. E. De Jonghe, in *L'enseignement des Indigènes du Congo-Belge* (1931), complains about the Blacks becoming uprooted and starting to "believe they are equal to the Whites and even superior." Shall I think of my father or myself today? (46–47)[17]
>
> Have I ever believed in a God? I do not know. For years and years, the question appeared useless to me. I left the Benedictine life out of exhaustion. (75)[18]
>
> Nevertheless there still remains a serious problem: a problem of credibility and sincerity. Am I still a Christian? And, could I claim, without any contradiction, to be both a Christian and an African nationalist, and to live in peace with myself? (100)[19]

These questions are meditative ones and do not receive any definite answer in the narrative. They may also show the existential turmoil of Mudimbé the scholar. While a great number of these questions are open and show the doubts and fears of the autobiographer, Mudimbé does ask some specific questions, as in this passage: "That Sunday morning in September, like probably, many others to come, my life runs into a question. And, this one sticks, and is vivid, in my thought: am I, really, a connection between the African past and the modern and Christian Europe?" (53–54).[20] Four pages later, the autobiographer seems to have found the answer: "Ainsi, il est clair que les mémoires 'africaines,' les anciennes et la coloniale, loin de s'opposer se complètent plutôt. Je pense les incarner" (Thus, it is obvious that "African" pasts, the ancient ones and the colonial one, far from opposing each other, complete each other admirably. I believe I embody both) (59). Here, Mudimbé places himself at the crossroads, where he is influenced by African and

Western heritages, and this confirms what I have stated above in saying that Mudimbé can be read as a metaphor for modern Africa, an Africa bound to succeed.

While giving special treatment to his existential questions, Mudimbé also questions the religious aspect of his life, which influenced him since his childhood. Christianity as a personal belief and as a collective institutional belief for Africans is at the center of his thought. Mudimbé seems to justify his embracing the Christian faith as a conjunction of specific circumstances, yet he gives the impression that he rejects Christianity personally. This critical stance parallels the rebuke that Mudimbé gave a clergyman who asked him about his agenda for his African students. Mudimbé replied that he would like his African students to be highly critical of African traditions by using the legacy of Judeo-Christian thought, and he would encourage them to be atheistic. These existentialist and critical statements that he made during his Zairian years are later contradicted. Paradoxically, after rejecting Christianity, Mudimbé comes to think that it is the only solution for a majority of Africans confronting their human situation:

> Unfortunately what I think is simply disastrous. Yes, Christianity appears to me, for the time being, the only ideology and the only system which, in non-Islamic Africa, can help us to maintain believers' spiritual and moral integrity and, at the same time, to give them courage and reasons to persevere with a certain dignity in their human dreams and, especially, to overcome the calamities and the irrationality that African politicians are causing for us. (98–99)[21]
>
> Yes, Christianity thus means the failure of my past, of my tradition, and the beliefs of my ancestors. The vanquished almost always adopt the religion of the victors. We did it. I am one example. (100)[22]
>
> The road that I took has all the characteristics of a process of dispossession: baptized in a religion "foreign" to my Africa, introduced early into a school and cultural system whose standards came from the West, I learned, thanks to admirable teachers, to think and to experience the extraordinary resources of a complex and multicultural universe. From there, I can dream of solving the major contradictions of my belonging to two cultures: African and European, but also without claiming to develop any theories, I can reflect on the models and the structures likely to contribute to a human and spiritual promotion of the people from which I come. (104)[23]

It is in the essay part that Mudimbé makes abundant use of the first-person plural, the collective "nous" to address his fellow Africans as a whole. In these passages, he is very critical of African history, traditions, and politics. He is skeptical of the theories of the Senegalese anthropologist Cheikh Anta Diop who contended that African civilization preceded European civilization and was superior, based on studies of ancient Egypt. Mudimbé goes against such a vision:

> That philosophy, in the name of a mystifying authenticity or under the pretext of an absolute African cultural otherness, should give up the place of our modernity and our reification which in our history points to two dates (that of the beginning of slavery and the introduction of colonization) to take refuge in the illusory folds of a mythical tradition, appears to me simply scandalous in terms of urgency and of survival strategies. All things considered, I sincerely think that our future does not reside either in the celebration of glosses about Negro antiquities or in the worship of the museum-piece epics, but rather in the awareness of what we are today as women and men. We can and must oppose the neo-colonial thinking. (179)[24]

Like African politics, Mudimbé thinks that this claim is a mystification that distracts Africans from the harsh reality of their everyday life. I find Mudimbé's critical assessment of the theories of Cheikh Anta Diop to be very close to the position defended by Patrick Chamoiseau, Raphaël Confiant, and Jean Bernabé, the authors of *La Créolité*, yet different at the same time. Launched in 1989 with the publication of the manifesto *Eloge de la Créolité*, Créolité is an intellectual, cultural, linguistic, and political discourse defining an identity specific to the French Caribbean. For the defenders of Créolité, it is not a complete rejection of Négritude, a movement that promoted a return to a mythical and historical glorious Africa in order to shape the identity of Africans and the diaspora. The supporters of Créolité believed that Négritude was necessary at its time in history. The whole process is considered to be a dialectic, and Créolité serves as the synthesis to Négritude and colonial discourses allowing contemporary Caribbean people to supersede the contradiction by asserting their own being. Therefore, Créolité's founders are careful not to denigrate Aimé Césaire, their fellow countryman and cofounder of Négritude; they instead see his efforts as necessary but limited because they were not rooted in the realities of the Caribbean, since he was rather looking at Africa as a mythical source of origins. Rejecting the "Europeanity" and "Africanity" they see in Négritude, Créolité pleads for an internal vision of the Caribbean focused on the French Caribbean realities: "La vision intérieure," which can be reached by writing in Creole. Mudimbé, like the authors of *La Créolité*, wants to consider a problem or a situation (such as the Africans or the Martinicans) in their present state, and he rejects any recourse to a so-called ideal or glorious past irrelevant to the present reality. Clearly, like Chamoiseau, Confiant, and Bernabé, who consider the French Caribbean in its current state as a melting pot of races, cultures, and languages, Mudimbé is advocating that Africans take into account their colonial heritage. In this case, Mudimbé and the defenders of La Créolité are united in their opposition to the theory of Négritude. Yet, in this pragmatic stand, Mudimbé and the defenders of La Créolité are different in the sense that La Créolité reacts against a cultural movement that started in the 1930s and Mudimbé is critical of a historical theory that was claimed in the 1950s and 1960s. Nevertheless, whereas Négritude promoted the glory of African kingdoms and empires between the tenth and fourteenth centuries, Mudimbé goes back two thousand years more to attack a statement based on the glory of ancient Egypt, clearly anterior to the period in which the authors of Négritude take pride. In their reactions to Négritude and what the autobiographer refers to as "antiquités nègres," both Mudimbé and the defenders of La Créolité deal with the common theme of identity in an immediate and contemporary state. Besides his opposition to Cheikh Anta Diop's theories, Mudimbé was also very critical of the Négritude movement, especially of Léopold Sédar Senghor, one of its champions, while at the same time respecting the intellectual qualities of the earlier African thinker. On the whole, Mudimbé is against the mythical representation of the African past, which he characterizes as a mystification. Considering the defeats of Africa, he wonders if the flaws in African tradition were preexisting factors that prepared the ground for Africans to be forced into slavery, colonization, and exploitation by Europe (180). What is recurrent in Mudimbé's attack on Africa and its thinkers is that he is against their essentialist theories, promoting an existentialist position; in this case, he is very close to the defenders of *La Créolité*. Mudimbé seems to be in favor of *métissage culturel*, and this goes along with his existentialist orientation and justifies his criticism of Anta Diop's theory of the anteriority of the black civilization.

There is a philosophical dimension in Mudimbé's autobiography that struggled to position itself vis-à-vis the existentialist position of Sartre. After having described himself as a predestined person—an antiexistentialist stance—Mudimbé revealed a more existentialist commitment in his renunciation of the vows and his entry into the secular world. Yet, more than Sartre, his philosophical position is more in line with that of Maurice Merleau-Ponty.

In the "Avant-propos," Mudimbé shows his debt to Maurice Merleau-Ponty's thought as expressed in *Phénoménologie de la perception*, and he acknowledges that he borrowed the title of his autobiography from the French philosopher. Let us consider to what extent *Les Corps glorieux des mots et des êtres* contains the phenomenological legacy of Merleau-Ponty, and to what purpose Mudimbé uses such a perspective to analyze his Self. Phenomenology can be defined as the study of the development of human consciousness and self-awareness in relationship to the world, and this philosophical orientation uses description as a means to approach the Self and the objects of consciousness. Mudimbé's autobiography can be considered in this phenomenological line because the author, after becoming a renowned author and scholar, tried to reconstruct the various steps that led him to become the international scholar he is now. In search of his past, Mudimbé posited himself in the line of the French philosophical tradition, and this is clearly demonstrated in the text by the various questions (quoted above) in which the author asks himself about his Self and his existence as an African in between two conflictive worlds. The questioning of the Self and the self-critique are Western philosophical exercises, and Mudimbé has taken Western philosophers as his models. Among all these models, it seems that Mudimbé is closest to Merleau-Ponty's vision in the *Phénoménologie de la perception*. In that seminal book, the French philosopher advocates the subject's direct experience of the world through perception in opposition to the more idealistic and transcendental phenomenology advocated by Hegel and Husserl. As Mark Stephan explains in "Ricoeur and Merleau-Ponty on Narrative Identity":

> As it is well known, Merleau-Ponty went to great lengths to distance himself from the idealist interpretation of phenomenology Husserl presented in *Ideen I* and in the *Cartesian Meditations*. In the *Phenomenology of perception* and succeeding works, one sees in Merleau-Ponty the deliberate attempt to overcome the dualistic definition of meaning, truth, and self from the side of subjectivity alone. Rather, such categories are themselves mediated linguistically. In regard to the self-understanding, for example, Merleau-Ponty states that the "subject provides itself with symbols of itself in both succession and multiplicity, and that these symbols *are* it, since without them it would, like an inarticulate cry, fail to achieve self-consciousness."[25]

In *Les Corps glorieux des mots et des êtres*, the subject tries to understand himself via some symbols, such as the Benedictine garden, his role as ambassador, and the colonization of Africa. Yet what really brings Merleau-Ponty and Mudimbé closer is the method of analysis they use in their respective books, which are both highly intellectual narratives. In questioning himself and his own thoughts, it appears that Mudimbé follows Merleau-Ponty's dialectical method as exposed in *Phénoménologie de la perception*. Here it is worthwhile to turn to James M. Edie, who states that Merleau-Ponty's method in *Phénoménologie de la perception* is a dialectic one, though different from Hegel's and Sartre's:

> I believe that the root of the dialectical method in the *Phenomenology of perception* is not, however, to be found primarily in Merleau-Ponty's reflections on either Husserl or Hegel, but in his own studies of perception as these relate to the entire philosophical tradition, namely to the theories of Lagneau, Alain, Hume, Berkeley, Kant and above all in more recent gestalt psychology and behaviorism. Here his method in each chapter is to oppose intellectualism (realism, naturalism, positivism) to show in as elegant a dialectical manner as possible that both opposed theories contain a good deal of truth and to show that in some sense each is acceptable, but only when corrected by the other.[26]

Mudimbé is fond of questioning himself and others freely in his autobiography. In much of this questioning and critique, he appears to be ambiguous and even contradictory. In the middle of the narrative of his life, which illustrates the deep influence of the Benedictine order, Mudimbé the scholar asks himself whether he still believes in God while at the same time justifying that no matter how he fights it, the Benedictine way of life has shaped his nature. Mudimbé rejected Christianity, yet later claimed, paradoxically, that it is the only possible religion for postcolonial Sub-Saharan Africa. This ambiguity reaches another level when Mudimbé attacked the essentialist positions of both Senghor's Négritude and Anta Diop's "antiquités nègres," while at the same time maintaining an intellectual respect for them and the way their theories were presented. Overall, what dominates Mudimbé's autobiography is the constant opposition between African tradition and European heritage, and he uses a dialectic that is similar to Merleau-Ponty's as he opposes both entities while validating each of them. This is shown at a more personal level as evidenced by the fact that his success in one of the most prestigious American universities does not deprive him of his claim to remain African. In fact, in analyzing himself, Mudimbé states that he has become a U.S. citizen but remains deeply African: "Je suis américain sans l'être et ne suis plus de mon pays d'origine, tout en le demeurant profondément" (I am an American citizen without being an American truly, and I am no longer from my homeland yet I remain deeply Congolese) (165). What is more, the bulk of his work has always been focused on Africa. When one knows that Merleau-Ponty was seen in his time as "the Philosopher of ambiguity and contradiction," his relationship with Mudimbé becomes much clearer in the way the latter analyzes himself and others in his autobiography. Mudimbé's dialectic view seems to be that Africans should deal more with their current situation while being critical both of their ancestral traditions and of embracing the Western rational legacy. This intermediary situation does not call for a tangible synthesis, but it is an existentialist acceptance of a complex present situation in order to deal with the future.

PRIVILEGING THE FRANCOPHONE AFRICAN READERS

One may wonder for whom Mudimbé was writing. One possible answer could be for himself, and this seems to be all too evident in the autobiographer's self-praise. Another response may be that he wrote for the academic world, especially because he devotes many pages to the evolution of his thoughts and summarizes many of his previous publications in the essay portion of *Les Corps glorieux des mots et des êtres*. A third answer may be that he wrote for his former students in Africa as well as in America. Looking to the narrative, the most obvious readership consists of his former African students, as Mudimbé himself addresses them clearly and specifically toward the end of the autobiographical work:

> I turn back to you, my former students and, now, my friends, colleagues, my equals. There is a faith to transmit to the new generation. A spirit too. I know that you are fed up with naïve statements about "African traditions." I know also that you have exhausted all your stores of patience to still believe that there is a limit to the blows of your anger and of your hopes for a better Africa. You are right to hope, in spite of the general stupidity which surrounds us. I know, also, that you have doubts sometimes. How many times have I heard this alarming statement: "generosity does not pay . . . especially in Africa today." Why, my Lord, would you want to be paid for your faith? Remain what you are: believe in yourself, in your actions. You are not alone. Your faith is, to

re-use a metaphor coming from a book of which I have forgotten everything, an important and solid ring. Believe me, you are and we are numerous. Bound, tied to one another, one day, we will end up, turning ourselves into a cable capable of moving rivers and mountains, and of rebuilding Africa from scratch. (197–98)[27]

We would need a masterly study of art and society in Central Africa which could compete with the excellent works on traditional art. Why wouldn't you do it, Hélouya, Jenny, Louise? I am writing this in the Autumn of 1991. The season is splendid. Immensely, luminously beautiful. And I think of you. The leaves' beautiful lace speak to me of a style. I associate it with you. A new season is here, yours. What will you do with it? (201)[28]

Hélouya, Jenny, and Louise are a definite and clear audience in the mind of the autobiographer, and by mentioning that he wrote this address in the fall of 1991, Mudimbé indicates that they are his former students (now his colleagues) to whom he suggests another direction for further studies. In this address to both the Africans in general and his former students Hélouya, Jenny, and Louise in particular, Mudimbé appears prophetic as he encourages both groups with a vision full of optimism for Africa and African Studies. In both passages cited above, the "vous" that Mudimbé uses to address his former students becomes a collective "nous" in which the autobiographer shares his belief in the future of Africa and wants to revive the faith in his former students, and the passage achieves a somewhat prophetic dimension because the author's choice of words is not entirely innocent: Mudimbé uses some metaphors that are related to a biblical message when he speaks of moving mountains.

It is striking that Mudimbé wrote his autobiography in French and published it in Canada and France although his academic success is more prominent in the United States, where he currently resides. Since Mudimbé published all of his most successful books in English during his American years, it follows that he was quite capable of writing in English, which could just as well have been the language of his intellectual autobiography. Nevertheless, the fact that he wrote it in French and had it published in both France and Canada indicates that he was catering to a Francophone audience. Yet Mudimbé's Francophone trajectory is oblique: even though he had written many works of fiction published in France (by Présence Africaine in Paris), it is revealing that in the early 1990s Mudimbé appears not to be well known in France, as evidenced by the 1990 review by Jean Pierre Péroncel-Hugoz in *Le Monde*: "In effect, by writing these brief *Carnets de Mère Marie-Ger-*

trude, V. Y. Mudimbé has created a new and strong African character. This Zairian writer, unknown in France, was born in 1941; he currently teaches at the American university, Duke, and is much appreciated in the Anglophone world whose language he used in his fourteenth book, *The Invention of Africa*."[29] This review, dated only four years before *Les Corps glorieux*, shows the contradiction that Mudimbé was unknown in France yet successful in the United States, but chose to write his intellectual autobiography in French. One reason for this contradiction could be that Mudimbé wanted to present himself as an example to a Francophone audience. His primary audience is therefore a Francophone African audience, and his objective is to show them, through his example, that success is possible for French-speaking Africans in America, provided that they work hard at mastering the language and that they adapt to the American work environment. Yet it is not a message addressed to all Francophone Africans: it is primarily for the educated ones who have or want to have a career in the American academy, especially in the field of African studies.

The actual reader of Mudimbé's *Les Corps glorieux des mots et des êtres* is a Francophone African scholar indicating the elitist dimension of his intellectual autobiography. Through this elitist focus, Mudimbé develops a rhetoric of exemplariness that excludes other Africans but extends to the whole Francophone African community of scholars beyond the Belgian connection.

Mudimbé has an "oblique" trajectory in the Francophone world because the former colonizers of his country were not the French but rather the Belgians. He studied in Zaïre, Belgium, and France. He published many creative writings in France and finally became a superstar in the American academy by publishing his books in English. Unlike Hampâté Bâ and Kesso Barry, Mudimbé has an oblique relationship with France; this relationship is more linguistic and cultural than political. The fact that he was supposedly unknown in France is revealing, and the paradox of his attachment to French culture and thought shows that he is a particularly Francophone intellectual. Having a Francophone country (Belgium) as former colonizer makes Mudimbé a different Francophone subject than Bâ and Barry, who are both linguistically and culturally bound to France.

How was Mudimbé's autobiography received in his native Zaïre/Congo? An analysis of local newspapers shows an absence of reviews on Mudimbé. In major Zairian newspapers (*Salongo*, *Umoja*, *Demain le Congo*, and *La Fraternité*) there is no mention of Mudimbé's publication *Les Corps glorieux des mots et des êtres*. *Demain le Congo* is an opposition newspaper that regularly runs a section called "Idées" (Ideas) with some reflection on the role of the intellectual, but it does not have a cultural or literary section. Some newspaper issues did not come out in 1994, and there was no mention of Mudimbé or *Les Corps glorieux des mots et des êtres* that year. Mudimbé left Zaïre in the early 1980s for America, fleeing political coercion under a one-party regime. When he published his autobiography in 1994, his country was enjoying democracy and there was a plurality of newspapers from the opposition. This environment, which was critical of the ruling regime, should have welcomed Mudimbé's publication because it also contains a deep and harsh analysis of the Zaïrian regime. Yet the opposite was true: Mudimbé's autobiography was not reviewed in any Zaïrian newspaper from the ruling party or its opposition.

In *Le Livre littéraire: Bibliographie de la littérature du Congo (Kinshasa)*, a bibliography of literary productions by Zairian/Congolese writers published in 1995 by Mudimbé's compatriot Pius Ngandu Nkashama, there is a section on Mudimbé's publications, especially in the part "Classement par nom d'auteurs" (123–24). Nkashama is an eminent critic of African and Congolese literatures; what is more, he resided in the United States around the time of publication of *Les Corps glorieux*, and there is little doubt that he must have been aware of Mudimbé's publication. However, the listing of Mudimbé's publications does not include *Les Corps glorieux* and stops at *Shaba Deux*, published in 1989. The lack of mention of Mudimbé's 1994 publication *Les Corps glorieux* in Nkashama's 1995 bibliographic listing may be due to the delay between the completion of this bibliographic manuscript and its actual publishing by L'Harmattan in 1995. One can assume that at the time Nkashama submitted his manuscript for publication, Mudimbé's *Les Corps glorieux* was not yet released and was therefore not included; the delay between the submission of the manuscript and its actual publication may explain the discrepancy. The omission is not due to lack of reception but to the delay between the actual bibliographic work and its submission for publication.

The lack of reaction and review of *Les Corps glorieux des mots et des êtres* in local Zairian newspapers indicates that Mudimbé has endured the fate of exiled writers: unknown (or lesser known) in his country, he is more popular in the Western world, especially in the United States. One could also say that Mudimbé has transcended the narrow border of his native Zaïre/Congo to make himself readable to the Francophone world, even if only to those who have become African intellectuals and scholars.

CONCLUSION

Les Corps glorieux des mots et des êtres is an exploration of the life of an exceptional African who was destined to be a monk and made himself a star in the secular academic world. The autobiographical narrative is also the history of Africa at the crossroads between two systems of thought: that of the traditional Africa, and that of the modern West. While admiring and siding with Western thought and its rigors, Mudimbé advocates a reconsideration of African traditions in order to find a better path for this continent that has been through many challenges. It is no surprise that in his autobiography Mudimbé quotes Cheikh Hamidou Kane's *L'Aventure Ambiguë* (1962), a book that blends autobiographical and fictional narrative to explore the conflict between two antagonist civilizations. Whereas *L'Aventure ambiguë* ends with madness and death as a solution to the hero's crisis, Mudimbé is in favor of a more productive way to combine the two civilizations for the betterment of Africa's future. I would like to suggest that Mudimbé's self-narrative, though centered on Africa and African studies, could be also read as an American immigrant autobiography, and this of course contributes to further the complexity of Mudimbé's life story.

In his autobiography, Mudimbé offers himself as an example of modern Africa, once colonized and now having to construct an identity fusing African and European cultures. Mudimbé's career owes much to his Benedictine training, which he successfully transferred to American academia. His career and his autobiography also owe much to the French philosophical tradition, especially that of Merleau-Ponty, the philosopher of ambiguity, which places Mudimbé in a complex position. Now that he has become an "African American," Mudimbé's autobiography falls into the trap of the transnational autobiography written in exile from his native Zaïre. Forgotten and neglected in his home country, he is popular in the Western world, thereby confirming the saying, "No one is a prophet in his homeland." The reception of Mudimbé's autobiography poses a question of choice of language. Mudimbé, in his endeavor to reach out to his country and the Francophone African community at large, chose to write his autobiography in French despite the popularity of his previous publications in English. If Mudimbé has shown himself earlier as a metaphor of modern Africa, he is also casting himself as an example to an elitist group of fellow Francophone African scholars as a success story in yet another linguistic and cultural environment.

CHAPTER THREE

Kesso Barry

Autobiography, Masculinity, Ambiguity,
and Limited Reception

The autobiography of Kesso Barry is atypical compared to those by other autobiographers considered in this study because her autobiography is her only publication and because she declares she wrote it for a special audience: her daughter Sandra.[1] However, Kesso Barry shares the same ethnic origin as Hampâté Bâ, as she is a "Peuhle" (Fulani). In this chapter I examine how a Francophone African woman autobiographer appropriates masculine attributes in order to create a counterdiscourse aimed at criticizing a male-dominated society. I also show that the writer's conquest of masculinity is individual and does not correspond to a feminist agenda because Kesso is entangled in a series of contradictions that make her regret her choices and question her situation as an exiled African in France in an interracial marriage. Her situation of "in-betweenness" coupled with some aspects of her autobiography and sociopolitical conditions, I argue, limit the reception of her work to date.

Distinguished nomads all over Africa, the Peulhs (Fulanis) have been the object of many studies. The writer Amadou Hampâté Bâ, a Peuhl himself, describes them as a cattle-breeding people, who converted to Islam over the centuries and who have kept a strong sense of identity and nobility.[2] The Peuhls are also subjected to a highly demanding code of conduct, called *Pulâaku*, which forms part of their identity. To cattle-breeding Peuhls, certain activities are considered as masculine or feminine, as Salamatou A. Sow indicates:

> If the cow can be considered as a legacy of group identity, leading the
> herds and culturing milk can be regarded as specific cultural legacies
> of which each group takes care of: a man who churns milk will make
> everyone smile and a woman who weaves the calf cord makes herself
> ridiculous. There are thus certain acts that are perceived as specifically
> feminine and others as specifically masculine. The chain of transmis-
> sion of valued knowledge is a key to the understanding of the legacy.
> For nomadic Peuhls, the patriarchal chain of transmission is built
> with a masculine link, symbolized by the staff and the pastures, and a
> feminine link symbolized by the calabash and milk. The latter is rather
> matrilineal. (6–7)[3]

Let me emphasize here that Peuhl society is rigidly organized around masculine and feminine activities, thus establishing a social order whose transgression would be a subject of ridicule or scandal. Kesso, although she is Peuhl, is neither nomadic nor a commoner because she is the daughter of the Almamy, the king and religious chief of a settled Peuhl community. In this study, I intend to analyze not the writing style opposing the masculine and the feminine; rather, I will examine the discourse of Kesso the subject, of one autobiographical "I" casting a critical eye on the African society in which she was born and grew up. In a patriarchal and strongly Islamized society, this critique is cen- tered upon the masculine/feminine axes and ultimately shows this fe- male subject's preference for attributes associated with the male gen- der. Kesso subverts the two gender systems by showing admiration for strong women and a determined will to break social taboos. Kesso is cast as an anticonformist, a rebel; however, characterizations that por- tray her as a "revolutionary" princess are inaccurate because her re- bellion is only personal and does not aim at a structural change of her country as a whole. This study offers a socioanalysis of Peuhl society as it is described by the autobiographer, an androcentric society, to bor- row a term used by Pierre Bourdieu in his work *La Domination mas- culine*.[4] The maturation of a female "I" in search of the possession of male attributes follows a progression starting with her understanding of masculinity in the Peuhle society, her admiration and desire for mas- culinity, and finally her appropriation of "male" qualities. One could wonder about the status of Kesso between the masculine and the femi- nine: Could she be a "misovire" (a woman who cannot find a man who meets her ideals), or does she destabilize or complicate the simpler bi- nary system? Other questions also emerge: Is feminism a useful concept for reading an autobiography written by an African woman who is opposed to the socioreligious and antifemale standards of her country? Do the many contradictions in her text reveal a limitation of her goal of personal freedom via the appropriation of masculinity? These are questions that will help us to evaluate the complexity of a text that begins under a guise of simplicity.

Kesso, Princesse peuhle (1988) tells the story of Kesso, born of royal blood in Guinea-Conakry under French colonization in the 1940s.[5] Kesso, whose name means "virgin," shows a spirit of independence while very young and breaks socioreligious taboos, to the great despair of her parents. As the years go by, her sense of independence grows, and she chooses for herself a malleable husband to prevent her parents from forcing her to marry a polygamous husband. After her divorce from her first Guinean husband, Kesso uses all possible tactics to conquer the man who will become her second husband, the French industrialist Gérard Decoster. She spends the second part of her life with her second husband and their daughter Sandra in France, where Kesso works as a fashion model and accompanies her husband on his business trips. She nevertheless finds herself in an ambivalent situation as an independent African woman living in Europe who holds onto memories of her childhood that range from rebelliousness and nostalgia.

At the narrative level, Kesso's autobiography is characterized by the use of the oral tradition as a style of writing. The text's first words establish the story in this form:

> Sandra, it is to you that I am writing. It is about my life and I could begin my narration with: once upon a time in Fouta-Djalon there was a little girl who was called Kesso. She was Peuhle, Moslem, and a princess of royal blood promised to a royal marriage. I would continue a narration where the strange and the marvelous would weave a multicolored fresco to make you dream. But my life is not a tale, even if it resembled one for the length of a childhood. (9)[6]

To start with, one can note Kesso's ambivalence in the use of the tale to tell her life, which translates at the same time as a call and an embarrassment altogether. Kesso's embarrassment is explained by the mismatch between the tale that she "could have told" her daughter and the reality of her life, which forced her to develop a strong independent will and assertiveness in a highly political society ruled by tradition and Islam. In addition, Kesso Barry means the word "tale" as in "fairy tale," such as "Cinderella" or "Snow-White," in which princesses are the main characters. She thus refers to a European tradition of the fairy tale, undoubtedly because the first audience of her text, her daughter Sandra, had never visited Africa (at least, at the time Kesso was writing this part of the autobiography). As Irène Assiba d'Almeida has noted in her article on Kesso's work, "Like a tale, the objective of the autobiography is not only to entertain but also to instruct. Addressed to Sandra, the daughter ignorant of African cultures, Barry's autobiography is deliberately didactic."[7] By using the tale as a pretext—understood in its double meaning as an excuse and a prologue—Kesso Barry narrates her life, which she presents to her daughter as both exemplary and didactic. The autobiographer is then in a postcolonial paradox because, as a noble woman by birth, it was not traditionally her job to narrate her life story—that is the job of the griots, professional storytellers of low caste. However, the older Kesso has as her primary audience her biologically and culturally mixed-race daughter, the fruit of her marriage with the Frenchman Gérard Decoster. She must therefore tell her life story to her daughter, who is foreign to African cultures; thus, as an autobiographer of noble extraction, Kesso does violence to her traditional culture because of her situation when narrating.

READING THE MASCULINE AND FEMININE IN PEUHL SOCIETY

As a child growing in Peuhl society, Kesso learned how to read the cultural codes that govern the relationship between men and women. Through her observant gaze, one can understand how Peuhl society allots values of "feminine" and "masculine" to men and women, as well as to certain behaviors. We have seen the autobiographical account's false start: the fairy tale is replaced by harsh reality. Life is a struggle that Kesso had to endure to become the woman who she wanted to be in a doubly hegemonic environment, subject to the authority of her father, the king, and to the authority of Islam. Thus she gives her life story to her daughter as an example, and this example seems to be the opposite of what Kesso's own mother was for her. Very early, Kesso realized the submissive condition of Peuhl women with respect to men by observing the relationship between her polygamous father, her mother, and the other wives. Kesso takes a rebellious and critical tone when she describes the exaggerated humility of her mother in front of her father:

> In the morning, when he walked into the courtyard and the women,
> his wives, stood at their window or in front of their door to try to at-

> tract his attention in hope that he would condescend to come up to
> them to chat, I saw my mother, her body tense as the string of a bow,
> trembling from head to toe. In those moments, I read such an entreaty
> in her gaze, I perceived such distress there, that I was enraged in my
> heart. It is certainly at that time that I promised myself never to marry
> a man who would have several wives. (29)[8]

After this scene, Kesso, outraged, advises her mother to leave her husband
so that he, in accordance with custom, would come to claim her by asking
for forgiveness with the symbolic gift of ten cola nuts. Her mother's answer
is a stinging slap that Kesso does not forget. When she is twelve or thirteen
years old, Kesso promises herself not to marry a polygamous man.

In a highly hierarchical Moslem and "feudal" society (the word is
Kesso's), Kesso learns that a woman's destiny is to serve her husband
and to fulfill his needs. The feminine is defined in terms of tenderness,
entreaty, and weakness, of which her mother serves as the perfect example. Two women nevertheless stand out in this environment because,
in spite of the social codes, they have qualities that would traditionally
be characteristics of men: a certain authority and a strong expression
of independence. These are the "women-males" who have a strong personality to show and whom Kesso admires. There is the imposing Mrs.
Diala, the griotte, who is perceived as a "male" in Peuhl community,
as witnessed by Kesso's father's opinion about her: "Mon père, qui la
tolérait parce qu'elle le faisait rire avec ses histoires, disait d'elle que, si
elle n'avait pas été femme et griotte, elle serait à coup sûr devenue un
grand chef de canton" (My father, who tolerated her because she made
him laugh with her stories, said of her that if she had not been a woman
and a griotte, she would undoubtedly have become a big *chef de canton* [chief of many villages]) (47). The perception of Mrs. Diala's "masculinity" is based on her qualities of determination and power. Let us
remember that during colonization, the *chef de canton*, an exclusively
male role, had almost total command over the "natives." By contrast,
Mrs. Diala's husband is generally perceived as "feminine" because of
his lack of character, will, and authority. Kesso sums this man up with
a sentence that shows all her scorn: "C'était un être falot, qui vivait à
l'ombre de sa femme" (He was a weak fellow, who lived in the shadow of
his wife) (46). From the antithetical husband-wife pair of Mr. and Mrs.
Diala, Kesso learns that the gendered attributes are not a matter of bio-
logical sex but can instead belong to anyone.

Another person who inspires Kesso to understand masculine/femi-
nine relations differently is her paternal grandmother. Just as she re-

spects Mrs. Diala, Kesso also admires her grandmother, who symbolizes independence and a "male" character. "Unlike my mother, she had always had a strong personality and lots of character that old age had not dulled. People said that, as a young woman, she had fought with a rifle at her husband's side, against her own family, at a time when the two clans were disputing over power. I often heard the griots tell this story, which I liked particularly" (31–32).[9] In the traditions of this society, war is a noble activity reserved for men who must distinguish themselves through military exploits.[10] A woman who takes up weapons just like her husband and starts to fight valiantly both transgresses the order of things and demonstrates masculinity. It is this unusual masculinity that Kesso admires in her grandmother whom she regards as "unlike [her] mother." Kesso rejects the submissive attitude of her mother, which makes the latter the epitome of the stereotypical Peuhl Moslem woman obeying her husband's orders and who is deprived of initiative. Kesso perceives such an exaggerated submissiveness as the female condition to avoid: "Elle était l'exemple parfait de la femme musulmane traditionnelle, élevée dans le respect absolu des us et coutumes, discrète jusqu'à l'effacement, obéissante jusqu'à la soumission" (She was the perfect example of the traditional Moslem woman, raised in the absolute respect of the customs and habits, discrete to the point of disappearing, obedient to the point of submissiveness) (27).

Kesso also recognizes at a young age that the delimitation between the world of men and that of women is even expressed in the distinct spaces assigned to each of them. In describing the palaver hut, Kesso is aware that it is the public space reserved for men: "C'était la case des hommes, et aucune femme n'avait le droit d'y pénétrer, excepté pour quelques tâches ménagères indispensables. L'endroit était tabou" (It was the men's hut, and no woman had the right to enter there, except for some essential domestic tasks. The place was taboo) (25). As Pierre Bourdieu puts it in *La Domination masculine*:

> The power of male domination resides in the fact that it escapes justification: the androcentric vision imposes itself as neutral and does not need to articulate itself in discourses aiming to legitimate it. The social order functions as an immense symbolic machine system tending to reify the male domination on which it is founded: . . . it is the structure of space, with the opposition between the meeting place or the market, reserved for men, and the house, reserved for women, or, inside the house, between the male part, with the hearth, and the female part with the cattle shed, the water and the plants. (22–23)[11]

Bourdieu's analysis of the Kabyle society is applicable to the Peuhle society because of the shared values.

THE ADMIRATION FOR AND THE DESIRE
OF THE MASCULINE IN KESSO

Kesso's observation of masculine/feminine relationships brings her to
admire women who especially embody or develop masculine characteristics, and this in turn creates in her a desire to adopt such characteristics by associating herself with the male gender. Several incidents
related in Kesso's autobiography demonstrate her will to appropriate
the male behaviors of the young boys her age: "I preferred to play with
boys rather than with the girls my age, whom I found too well-behaved
and too submissive already. Over the forbidden games which I shared
with the boys there loomed the idea of fault" (73).[12] Kesso explains how
her father was even told of her bold efforts to appropriate masculine
behaviors:

> It was reported to him that I spent my time playing soccer with the
> boys, that I wore shorts and only a shirt when I was going to swim in
> the river, that I rode a bicycle and showed my legs; they also told him
> that . . . What didn't they tell him? All that was true, and I did not hide
> it. I spent most of my time with the boys from Mamou; I liked their vi-
> olent games, which I preferred to those of the girls my age, and nobody
> could have prevented me from doing what I wanted. (55–56)[13]

And Kesso continues, describing her gravitation toward "male"
activities:

> Lots of us went on these hunting trips . . . and, in the middle of all
> these men, me, the incorrigible little princess. (91)

> I wanted to be like the boys, to behave like them, and to remain wor-
> thy. (92)

> I much preferred boys' games to girls' games. (93)[14]

In a strongly hierarchical society where the roles of the gender are rigidly codified, Kesso appears a double rebel: firstly, she transgresses the
masculine/feminine norm, scorning girls' games and joining the boys';
secondly, she transgresses the political order in which the king's daughter must be reserved in conduct and should not associate with boys.
Kesso expresses social nonconformism by inverting cultural codes,
which we can readily describe as a subversive tactic, allowing her to

escape from restrictions on her freedom. Yet this subversion is specific and limited to herself; it does not promote a radical change in women's condition in her society. Kesso often carries out this subversion through clothing, and there is an abundance of references to the young princess dressing up, particularly in the scene where she insists on following her brother Alphadio to an initiation ceremony that is supposed to be secret and reserved for men:

> Tired of being asked repeatedly, Alphadio, when his turn came, agreed to take me along with him; "*Dress up as a boy*, and come with me," he told me one evening. *It was a crime*, obviously, but I was not afraid of anything, and Alphadio wasn't either. That night, *I entered this world prohibited to women*, and I watched the warlike dances and the violent fights of these boys hardly older than I. (93; emphasis mine)[15]

Later on, she says to her other brother Thierno Mamadou, who rebukes her on the liberty she takes in letting people see her thighs on the merry-go-round at a fair: "—Si ce n'est que ça, la prochaine fois, je mettrai un pantalon. Thierno Mamadou ne comprenait pas ce défi: une femme musulmane ne porte pas de pantalon!" (—If that is all it is about, next time, I will wear pants. Thierno Mamadou did not understand this challenge: a Moslem woman does not wear pants!) (77). The text does not indicate whether Kesso puts her words into action, but the reader can imagine the nonconformist little princess doing such a thing. This is a clever subversion of modesty into masculinity.

A woman wearing men's clothing in a patriarchal and Islamized society constitutes a scandal; nevertheless, Kesso's primary-school teacher Fanta Sylla encourages it. She earns sharp reproaches by inviting the girls, Kesso included, to dress in shorts during the physical education class: "The dignitaries were horrified; they came to see my father and said: 'Almamy, how can you tolerate that this woman lives among us? It is impossible to imagine what she requires of our daughters. She undresses them half-way, people see their legs, and she has them play soccer like men. When they fall down, they spread their thighs and . . . '" (104).[16] Kesso declares that her teacher Fanta Sylla, with her Marxist views and her determination to fight against men's hegemony over women, confirmed in her what she had already felt confusedly: her preference for masculinity, which gave her a sense of freedom (103).

Kesso also confesses her passion for certain activities strictly reserved for men, namely hunting and collecting taxes. At Kesso's insistence and after her other brother Thierno Mamadou describes her as a "real tomboy," he agrees to take her along elephant hunting. In this passage Kesso emphasizes the allure of this "vie extraordinaire qui m'attirait autrement plus que les palabres et les occupations casanières des femmes de la concession" (extraordinary life which attracted me much more than the palaver and the domestic occupations of the women in the family courtyard) (89). Tax collection is another male activity with which Kesso associates herself, despite customs. During colonization, Kesso's father, sovereign of his area, is to ensure the collection of taxes for the French authorities. The Almamy sends his son Thierno Mamadou to collect taxes. Once again, Kesso specifies, "C'était un domaine strictement réservé aux hommes, mais je m'arrangeais, une fois encore, pour me faire emmener" (It was a domain strictly reserved for men, but I managed, once again, to get taken along) (95). Unsatisfied with the idea of accompanying her brother, at the end of the round Kesso asserts the right to take care of the tax collection personally when she is adult. Her mother, a guardian of traditions, quickly punishes this affront to the Peuhl code of conduct: "Lorsque je revenais à Mamou, ma mère m'attendait, et j'avais droit à une correction. Pour ma fugue et pour mon insolence, car affirmer sans honte qu'un jour je prendrai la place d'un homme était de la dernière impertinence" (When I returned to Mamou, my mother awaited me, and I was in for a corporal punishment for my running away and my insolence, because to shamelessly declare that one day I will take the place of a man was the ultimate impertinence) (98). After observing the social contrast between "masculine" and "feminine," Kesso thus feels the desire to adopt roles and symbols normally associated with men.

All her attempts at transgressing the supposedly immutable order of her society not only prove the extent to which she felt the need to rebel, but also they show that the androcentric Peuhl society was ill prepared to accept such a disturbance. Kesso's male allies, her brother Alphadio, and to a greater extent, her father, let her be herself, but with the hope that "she will get over it!" Her father's silence in front of his daughter's atypical behavior is puzzling; however, it can be understood as a form of favoritism. Indeed, everything would lead us to believe that Kesso's father, described as the representative of feudalism and religion as well as the person responsible for her mother's submissiveness, would oppose his daughter's independence. On the contrary, the silence of her father testifies to a tacit complicity that Kesso acknowledges by total admiration for him because she recognizes that without his permissiveness, she would not have become who she is. The book's dedication is revealing of Kesso's gratitude: "À l'Almamy, mon père, à Gérard mon mari, les deux hommes qui m'ont permis d'être moi-même" (To, my father the Almamy, to my husband Gérard, the two men who allowed me to be myself) (7).

Conscious of the burdens imposed upon women in her society, Kesso knows that if she adopts "feminine" characteristics she will end up as one of the wives of a polygamous man. She thus marries a man of her own ethnic group, but who does not meet the standards of her royal family. Kesso's "unnatural" marriage aims at circumventing the dictates of her androcentric society, through the inversion of social codes for her own benefit: whereas customs typically allow the potential husband and the parents to choose the wife, it is Kesso herself who chooses to marry Baïlo—a modest family's junior son—whom she admits that she does not love.

THE CONQUEST OF THE MASCULINE: FEMINISM OR "MISOVIRISM"?

Kesso achieves the true conquest of masculinity only after having attracted the attention of Gérard Decoster, a French industrialist working in Guinea. Kesso now reverses the traditional roles of the male courting the female because it is she who takes matters in hand and decides to court Decoster. The second half of her autobiography shows all the tactics Kesso deploys to overcome Decoster's reserves: advances, recourse to magical practices, stalking, and so on. Kesso casts herself as a "hunter" pursuing her "prey," an image that echoes her childhood passion for hunting and at the same time confirms her appropriation of masculinity.

By studying an autobiography written by an African woman at odds with her culture of origin, one may ask if the writer performs a feminist act. In "Kesso Barry's *Kesso*, or Autobiography as a Subverted Tale," Irène d'Almeida proposes that Kesso's "subversive" behavior could be considered feminist act. However, Barry herself noted in an interview with the African women's magazine *Amina* that she is not a feminist.[17] Nevertheless, it is also possible to characterize Kesso as a "misovire," that is, a woman who "hates" men, or who does not find any to her taste. Taking up a term Werewere Liking used in her novel *Elle sera de jaspe et de corail: Journal d'une misovire*, Rangira Béatrice Gallimore defines "misovire" as follows: "The "misovire" or rather "misovirism," if we can allow ourselves here to make a concept out of it, was born from the frustration of the African woman who could not manage to find a man who met her aspirations within modern Africa. Thus the "misovirism" is distinguished from radical feminism and must be apprehended in dialectical terms" (86–87).[18] Agreeing with Gallimore's definition, I contend that the young Kesso, growing up in Peuhl society, appears to be a *misovire* because none of the men who seek to court her find any favor with her. Even her deliberated choice to marry Baïlo is more of a calculation on her part than true love. Africa in transition toward modernity does not offer Kesso a man worthy of her, which can explain her decision to marry a non-African. Thus, until her meeting with Gérard Decoster, Kesso appears as a *misovire* in the African context. This condition disappears, however, as soon as she marries the French industrialist. The irony of Kesso's initiatory quest is that as a princess of a kingdom that had kept a degree of independence from and disdain toward the French in spite of the burden of colonization, Kesso marries a representative of the much-criticized colonial power. A reason for this attraction could be the fact that since Baïlo no longer offers her a loophole to escape her highly traditional society, Kesso prefers a man who symbolizes France, not the France of the colonizers to which she is accustomed and which she scorns, but that of an "énarque" (an alumni of the prestigious French school of public administration, Ecole Normale d'Administration) recently arrived and without an immediate connection to the colonial situation. Thus, Kesso's nonconformism needs an outlet, and it is Decoster who offers her one. By proposing this interpretation of Kesso's actions, I do not mean to imply that Kesso and Decoster do not love each other; rather, I would like to suggest that in the narrative economy of the text, Decoster appears as a means for Kesso to escape from a society in which she is suffocating.

CONTRADICTORY SPEECH, USURPATION OF TITLE, AND THE LIMITATIONS OF THE PLANS

If Kesso's story stopped here, it would be that of a successful life won only through her fight in a male-dominated society by the appropriation of masculinity. However, Kesso's trajectory reveals a series of contradictions in her narrative of self-empowerment that limit its purpose as an exemplary life. As a woman author making a didactic speech to her daughter, and as a woman who prefers masculinity, Kesso offers contradictions at two levels when she speaks about a man, Iéro, and about a woman, Hadiatou, whom she admires. In the Peuhl society in which Kesso grew up, during French colonization, there were still slaves subjected to the authority of the Almamy and whom the nobility were forbidden to befriend. However, Kesso crosses the line and shows a particular admiration for one of them, whose virility and strength she admires: "Il s'appelait Iéro, il était fort, il était beau, j'étais en admiration devant lui. Avec la seule force de ses bras, il pouvait arracher un arbre ou maîtriser un jeune taureau échappé" (His name was Iéro, he was strong, he was handsome, I was in admiration before him. With only the strength of his arms, he could uproot a tree or control a young runaway bull) (39). Kesso's admiration for Iéro resembles love, but Kesso makes this distinction when explaining the feeling to her daughter Sandra: "J'étais amoureuse de Iéro, non pas comme on l'entend ici, mais comme on peut aimer un beau cheval de race" (I was in love with Iéro, not as it is understood here, but as one can love a beautiful race horse) (40). The space called "here" refers to France, and Kesso denies that she was passionately in love with the young slave, justifying her feelings toward him by comparing them with those which one could have for a horse. An explicit contradiction is established in Kesso's speech, when, after having declared to her father that she would like to marry Iéro, her father, amused, decides "to give him to her." Kesso bitterly concludes, "Aujourd'hui, je me rends compte de ce que ce mot a de terrible, car mon père me donnait Iéro comme on offre un cheval ou un objet" (Today, I am realizing how terrible this word is, because my father gave me Iéro the way one gives away a horse or an object) (40). Kesso does not seem to realize that the description of her feelings for Iéro take part in the same "terrible" attitude that she resents in her father. Moreover, because she had declared that her feelings for Iéro were akin to the feeling a person has for a horse, she should logically not be offended by the gesture of her father offering her Iéro as though the slave were a horse. One could conclude that Kesso sees in Iéro some male features that she admires, such as great strength and determination. However, her hesitation to label her feelings for Iéro as love is in conformity with her *misovirism*: although Iéro is an extraordinary man, he still remains a slave, so in spite of Kesso's susceptibility to his good looks and strength, he is not able to offer her the desired exit. Iéro is a limited version of the masculine, and she has to wait for Gérard in order to fulfill her dream.

There are also contradictions and irony in the subtitle of Barry's autobiography insofar as her nonconformist behavior deprives her of any right to be called a Peuhl princess, despite her birth rank in the eyes of her society. The true princess, according to Kesso herself, is her sister Hadiatou:

> My sister was a true Peuhl princess, a model girl, the image of what every parent wanted. Respectful of traditions, she behaved according to my mother's wishes on all occasions. She always lowered her eyes when people spoke to her, she spoke only when she was questioned and she dressed decently: never a dress which shows her knees, or trousers which mold her curves; she wore only the traditional loincloth and shirt. (84)[19]

Moreover, the more her sister subjects herself to Peuhl customs, thus remaining a traditional woman, the more Kesso Westernizes herself, moving away from the values of her society. We should bear in mind that in Peuhl society, which kept its cultural and political integrity in spite of French colonization, Westerners' clothes and their behavior were perceived as ridiculous: "On the holidays, during which we put on our most beautiful clothes, the men in white or blue *boubou*, the women in their multicolored tunics, and the *Commandant de cercle* and his friends showed up in their ridiculous attire, wearing shorts and tropical helmets, perspiring and exhaling miserably, we did not have any pity for these men who, in our eyes, did not have any class" (129).[20] This illustrates the contradictions inherent in the bicultural identity that Kesso has constructed for herself: she is the Self that (rebelliously) dresses in European clothes and also the traditional "we" of the passage above, finding European clothes ridiculous.

Kesso, then, is this contradictory hybrid in relation to Peuhl society, and her sister, Hadiatou, is the model daughter to their mother and for this reason deserves the title of princess. Logically, Kesso should show repulsion for her sister who copies her mother's submissiveness. She does not, however, and one could suggest that once she has appropriated masculinity and reorganized her life in France, Kesso is confronted with her assimilation into the French world where she is not completely accepted as a black woman who has married a white Frenchman. This existential discomfort thus leads her to regret the choices of her childhood that enabled her to have such a destiny. Her sister Hadiatou, her perfect opposite, represents to her the possibility and the nostalgia for another life that she could have fulfilled in a total integration in Africa. Kesso's insistence on the title "Peuhl princess" on the cover of her autobiography would thus testify to a desire to appropriate a title that was, to some extent, refused her. The older Kesso admits that, unlike her sister, she became too sporty and Westernized, a confession that certainly reveals her regret at having not become more of a Peuhl princess herself. Kesso also perceives the autobiographical enterprise to "speak about oneself" as an anomaly, "une maladie de Blanc, dont je suis atteinte moi aussi" (a White people's disease, that I too have caught) (36).[21] If Kesso's goal were to offer herself as a model to her daughter Sandra, these various contradictions in her text would undermine the logic and the success of her project. Finally, started as a dialogue with Sandra, the text finishes like a monologue testifying to the defeat of Kesso, who did not know how to integrate into her society of origin and who also finds herself as a foreigner in France.

KESSO BARRY'S LIMITED RECEPTION
IN GUINEA AND IN FRANCE

Identifying Barry's intended audience is problematic because her autobiography, which is ostensibly intended for the author's daughter, shows a plurality of audiences. Obviously, there are other audiences for whom this autobiography was also intended. Beginning as a pseudo-dialogue with a single clearly identified inscribed reader, the autobiography then develops into a monologue with the author herself questioning her childhood and analyzing some of the issues she faced. The pseudo-monologue at the end of the autobiography suggests a shift of audience from the daughter to the mother herself. In discussing her autobiography's progression and its intended audiences, it is worth mentioning that Kesso Barry wrote her autobiography from various journals that she kept. In *Romancières africaines d'expression française*, Jean-Marie Volet and Beverly Ormerod give the actual age of the first inscribed reader, Sandra, relative to the year in which they were writing: "De cette union naît son troisième enfant, Sandra, qui a 20 ans en 1991" (From this second marriage her third child, Sandra, who is now twenty years old in 1991, was born) (37). From this, one can infer that, at the time of publication of the autobiography in 1988, Sandra was seventeen years old. Yet, at the beginning of the autobiography, Kesso reveals Sandra's age in a direct address to her daughter: "Sandra, tu as presque dix ans et tu ne sais rien de l'Afrique" (Sandra, you are almost ten years old and you do not know anything about Africa) (10). All of this indicates that it took Kesso seven years to write the book. From Sandra's tenth to seventeenth years, Kesso Barry was trying to tell the story of her own life.

Still, since there is a clear difference between the teenager and the soon-to-be-adult Sandra, Kesso Barry may have taken her inscribed audience's maturation into account during the composition of her autobiography. Maybe this explains the difference between the first and second parts of the text: while the first part is devoted to Barry's happy childhood, the second part becomes more critical and even pessimistic, and the narrator apparently changes her audience at the end as if talking to herself in a monologue.

Beyond her daughter Sandra, the product of the union between her French husband and herself, Kesso also writes for French readers, as evidenced by her autobiography being published in Paris by a French publisher, Seghers. Given the formal presentation of the autobiography, the secondary audience after her daughter is logically a French audience. Even the wording of the title, *Kesso, Princesse peuhle*, seems calculated to attract potential French readers by emphasizing the exotic origin of the author as an African princess. The paratextual juxtaposition of the two pictures on the book's cover—one of Barry and one of her mother—serves the same purpose. At the intratextual level, in the autobiography there is an obvious reference to a potential European audience: "La structure de ma famille est difficilement compréhensive pour un Européen" (The structure of my family is very difficult to understand for a European) (54). Writing ostensibly for her daughter, it is surprising to note that Barry uses the masculine in this quotation; this indicates that she sees beyond her daughter a potential French audience named with the singular masculine generalization "un Européen."

One may therefore ask, "What about the African audience in this autobiography by a woman from Guinea?" It is possible to say that this audience is also included, although schematically and sporadically. The reference to a potential Guinean audience could be seen in Kesso's harsh criticism of Sékou Touré, a man she had admired then despised. Kesso seems to hold Sékou Touré responsible for the political and economic disaster in her country from 1958 to 1984:

> In 1958, Sékou Touré took control of a prosperous country, largely self-sufficient, and even an exporter of food, potentially rich for its mining and its infrastructure, which was known to have nurtured a cultivated elite who studied in France, England or in the United States, a country which could have been one of the beacons of Africa. At his death (in his bed, since the reign of terror that he had maintained would have foiled even any notion of an attempted assassination) he left behind a ruined, devastated, and destroyed country, whose most capable citi-

zens had been assassinated or had fled abroad, without the protection
of a social or political organization, a country rotted down to its deep-
est roots. And yet, until his death, this man kept up an illusion, his
lies worked, his boastings were listened to. By what mysterious magic?
Perhaps History will tell us one day. The Guineans, themselves, had
understood for a long time. After his death, it did not take more than
three days for all of the posters carrying his portrait or the slogans of
his era to disappear completely. (181)[22]

Whom is Kesso addressing in this passage? Her daughter Sandra seems
to be absent from this confessional speech, which takes the audience for
granted as knowledgeable about the information she is disclosing: she
appears to be restating facts that her audience already knows. It is possible that she is addressing a Guinean audience or an African audience
at large in this negative evaluation of Sékou Touré's legacy. It is obvious that this passage was added after the death of the Guinean leader
in 1984. Yet her relationship with the socialist leader and her criticism
may prove ambiguous because Sékou Touré admired her as much as she
admired him. As Kesso Barry herself confesses in her autobiography,
Sékou Touré had personally helped her in securing her father's agreement to her wedding with her second husband, Gérard Decoster.

The readership of a written message is instrumental in understanding the narration and its purposes because writing is about the selection
as well as the suppression of information, processes which may fluctuate
depending on the particular audience the author has in mind. Therefore,
Kesso Barry's autobiography, intended for various inscribed audiences
whose identities are revealed explicitly in the text, is complex. The variety
of audiences in the narrative also points to a lack of consistency in Barry's
stated intention to cast herself as an example for her daughter. Since she
also has in mind other audiences (herself, French, and Africans) her discourse deviates from exemplification and touches on aspects that are remote from her daughter. In her interview with *Amina*, when asked about
for which public she wrote, Barry declared that it was not up to her to
choose an audience: "J'ai fait ce que j'avais à faire, mais ce n'est pas à moi
de me choisir un public" (I did what I needed to do, and it does not fall to
me to choose an audience) (66). Such a statement is contradicted in her
autobiography where she does address a multiplicity of audiences. Yet she
can also concede that there is a difference between inscribed audiences
and the actual readers whom she cannot control.

HOW WAS *KESSO, PRINCESSE PEUHLE* RECEIVED IN GUINEA AFTER ITS PUBLICATION?

When Kesso published her autobiography in 1988, Sékou Touré had already passed away in 1984. There was a new military government, Comité Militaire de Redressement National, led by Lassana Conté, which ruled Guinea. The legacy of Sékou Touré had been contested, as evidenced in Kesso's quote, which alludes to a greater tendency of Guineans to accept any criticism of their previous leader. *Horoya* was the official and only Guinean newspaper published weekly; its subtitle was "Organe National d'Information: Comité Militaire de Redressement National." In all the issues from 1988 there is absolutely no mention of Kesso Barry's *Kesso*, although the newspaper consistently provided occasional coverage of Guinean authors: issue 436, published in August 1988, reads, "Rencontre avec . . . Ahmed Tidiane Cissé: poète, écrivain, dramaturge guinéen" on the publication of his play *Le Tana de Soumangourou* (6). In issue 426, published on May 7, 1988, there is coverage of prizes given to Guinean writers: "Union Nationale des Ecrivains de Guinée: Remise de prix aux lauréates du concours de poésie, de nouvelle et de conte" (8). There is evidence that the official Guinean newspaper was not only attentive to literary productions but was also aimed at promoting emerging Guinean writers. The lack of coverage of *Kesso* by the Guinean press may be due to the fact that as an expatriate, Kesso Barry did not have the recognition in her home country that would justify her literary reception there; moreover, her autobiography was her only publication. These reasons do not diminish the constant focus of the book on Kesso's Guinean roots, which she emphasizes. It is noteworthy that in her autobiography she is very critical of Guinea's first president, whom she met as a youngster. Political reasons do not sufficiently explain the autobiography's limited reception because Sékou Touré had died and the new regime was critical of him.

There are also some aspects of Kesso's autobiography that make it unpalatable to an African audience and that limit its reception. One aspect can be inferred from the *Amina* interviewer's questioning of Kesso's realistic and detailed description of female circumcision. Because genital mutilation is a taboo subject in African culture, even the African women's magazine finds it shocking, and this embarrassing content limits the popularity of the autobiography in African circles. It is revealing that, twelve years after the *Amina* interview, Kesso was interviewed in *Littérature féminine francophone d'Afrique noire* by another

African woman critic, Pierrette Herzberger-Fofana, who asked Kesso about circumcision:

> Your book is a fictionalized biographical work which gives one the impression of reading a fairy tale intersected with some rather tragic events e.g. I think of the event which is included in the press and which makes the fortune of the popular media: the female circumcision. You yourself report the circumstances in which you underwent this operation. Is this only a faint remembrance forgotten in the limbs of your memory? (393)[23]

To which Kesso replied:

> This operation marked me a lot because it traumatized me. With the passing of time, I came to reconsider all my past life. I reflected much on it and do not see the utility of such an act that, in my opinion, does not have any *raison d'être*. I wrote my story in order to draw the attention of the authorities so that they should help to eliminate such a practice, which I consider a mutilation. (393)[24]

In choosing the subject of female circumcision as the opening question of the interview, Herzberger-Fofana shows how central it was to the reception of Kesso's autobiography. Through Herzberger-Fofana's comments preceding the question, it becomes clear that at the time of *Kesso's* publication Kesso's description of circumcision attracted the attention of the press and was also talked about in popular circles. Since this is a taboo subject in African circles, especially among African women, Kesso's description of that traumatic experience seems to have provoked repulsion from part of the African audience. Kesso's answer reveals that she wrote about circumcision in order to reach out to authorities who could help stop this female genital mutilation, as she calls it. This adds another dimension to the writing and reception of her book because she is adding another special audience beyond Sandra, the French, herself, and the Africans: the sociopolitical authorities, although it is not clear whether these authorities who may help stop this mutilation are Africans or French. As a whole, in this interview, Kesso is claiming a level of militancy in advocating for better treatment of women in society despite her sustained claim that she is not a feminist.

It is noteworthy that another African woman autobiographer, Ken Bugul, had already broken the barriers of sexual taboos with *Le Baobab fou* (*The Abandoned Baobab*). Yet Marietou Bèye (the author's real name) had to resort to the tactic of using the pseudonym Ken Bugul.

For Kesso, whose name appears on the cover, the task is more difficult as she does not operate in anonymity. Her autobiography reached
a level of scandal that Bugul avoided by using a pseudonym. The reception of Kesso and Bugul's respective works reveals how the reception of
an African woman's autobiographies in a conservative African context
can become problematic.

KESSO'S RECEPTION IN FRANCE

Apart from the Paris-based African women's magazine *Amina*, there
was apparently no attention given to Kesso's autobiography by French
newspapers or periodicals when it was published. In the *Amina* interview, Kesso reveals that she was also interviewed on French television:
"Après mon passage à la télé, j'ai une fois surpris une conversation entre
deux personnes qui se demandaient si j'étais vraiment l'auteur de mon
livre" (After I appeared on TV, I once overheard a conversation between
two people who wondered whether I was the real author of my book)
(66). Although no trace of Kesso's television interview remains today,
it shows that an effort was made to promote Kesso's autobiography to a
wider audience. Nevertheless, there is not enough evidence to indicate
that Kesso's autobiography was well received in France and in African
circles. This limited reception is odd given that Kesso was a model in
Paris in a part of her life (her picture on the cover shows her in a gown
she wore for the French designer Ted Lapidus) and that the "exotic"
title, *Kesso, Princesse peuhle*, catered to a French audience. Herzberger-Fofana's 2000 interview with Kesso in *Littérature féminine francophone d'Afrique noire* revealed that the discussion of circumcision was
what the press had retained from her autobiography, yet traces of such
media reports are lacking. What remains is the idea that at its publication, *Kesso* was met with a "scandalous" reception that focused on female circumcision, an act that is not practiced in France and that, even
though practiced by some Africans, remained a taboo subject then.

CONCLUSION

The appropriation of the masculine by a young "princesse peuhle"
starts with a reading of the codes in her society and is guided by models, both negative (Kesso's submissive mother) and positive (Mrs. Diala
and Kesso's paternal grandmother). An autobiography that avowedly

seeks to be exemplary, *Kesso, Princesse peuhle* is the story of a fight for personal assertion against the risks one faces when one is born as a woman in a traditional and Islamized African society that is already undergoing full transformation under the effect of French colonization. It is also the story of the rise to power of a woman who knew from the start how to distinguish the cultural codes of her society and who affirmed the desire to oppose them by her appropriation of the masculine. Kesso, "the virgin," is at the same time a dishonor to and a scandal for her parents, who are religious and traditional authorities and whose hopes she does not fulfill. Her writing project is an extension of her childhood desire to break the taboos and restrictions that governed the relations between men and women in her community of origin. The autobiography of Kesso, presented in the form of the voice of a woman who gives a progress report on her life and her testimony on life in an Africa in transition between colonization and independence, raises several questions. Talking to Sandra, her daughter, as an interlocutor at the beginning of her autobiography, Kesso wants to show her through her example that a broad place is granted Sandra in the world. This pseudo-dialogue of assertion of herself and her daughter eventually winds up as a monologue on the condition of an African woman in "exile" in France and of regret at having left behind a traditional communal life in Guinea. The objective of the project, that is, to offer herself as an example to her daughter, is not reached because of Kesso's various contradictions in connection with her mother, her sister Hadiatou, and even her presence in France. Kesso could have been also a contradiction for those who affirm that African autobiography worries too much about the community. Kesso Barry gives the example of an individuality that developed in a constraining collectivist context; however, her autobiography, which could have been the exception, vacillates toward the end between the individualism to which she has aspired and the regret of losing the communal life she had rejected. As such, her autobiography is a borderline case of exception to the communal label assigned to African autobiography as a genre. Her project of appropriating the masculine in order to assert herself in an androcentric society is also limited by Kesso's focus on acquiring her own freedom rather than alternatives for Peuhle women in general, a characteristic that separates Kesso from any feminist initiative and that establishes her as a rebel rather than as a revolutionary. To use a distinction suggested by Michel de Certeau, I propose that the appropriation of the masculine by Kesso is more of a tactical project rather than a strategic one, with tactics being an art of the weak who have neither "la possibilité de se donner un projet global ni de totaliser l'adversaire dans un projet distinct, visible et objectivable" (the possibility of designing a global project nor to size up the adversary in a distinct, visible project, able to be seen objectively). [25] It is undoubtedly the reason for which Kesso's success—and the critical reception of her biography—is limited.

Kesso Barry's autobiography, initially a discourse of empowerment told by a mother to her daughter, proves to be more complex as she addresses many other audiences, including herself. The reception of her autobiography is also a complex one, as it is mainly gathered through echoes of the two interviews she gave to *Amina* and to Herzberger-Fofana. The lack of newspaper reviews in her country of birth indicates that Kesso has become foreign to her own country and suffers the fate of exiled writers facing anonymity at home while they may receive some literary recognition abroad. Published in France by the Editions Seghers by a somewhat public figure (Kesso was a model), what seems to have remained of her reception in France and in Africa is limited to the scandal she caused by the realistic description of female circumcision, which she experienced and denounced in her autobiography and in interviews. It is striking that her 1988 autobiography is the only book that Kesso Barry published, which raises some questions. Could it be that the immediate reaction to her book may have caused the writer to retire from writing? This is a possible explanation as Kesso appears to have faced misunderstanding from part of her audiences. If the discussion of female circumcision was too descriptive to have been addressed to her daughter Sandra, but, as claimed by Kesso, was instead written to alert sociopolitical authorities to this mutilation in African society, the reactions of the African audiences show that she did not accomplish her goal of awakening consciousness, since most of them were shocked to see such a taboo subject discussed in such vivid detail. This misunderstanding may have caused her to stop writing lest she should create more scandals. Kesso's best intentions were not best served, especially by the media, which saw in her description of female circumcision a piece of sensational news. That sensationalism may have contributed to the limited reception of Kesso Barry's *Kesso*. The study of the reception of Kesso's autobiography shows, mainly through her interviews, that she catered to different audiences and that once released, she could no longer control opinions about and the reception of her autobiography.

CHAPTER FOUR

Patrick Chamoiseau

The Theatrical Self and a Paradoxical Reception

Patrick Chamoiseau was born in Fort-de-France, the capital of Martinique, in 1953. He studied law both in his country of birth and in France, and he served as a probation officer in Fort-de-France before working as a librarian with young prisoners in France. Chamoiseau collaborated with his fellow countryman Raphaël Confiant and Jean Bernabé on the literary manifesto *Eloge de la Créolité*; the three authors are considered the primary partisans of Créolité, the theory of French West Indian literature, culture, and identity. In this chapter, I demonstrate that *Antan d'enfance*, one of a series of autobiographies by Chamoiseau, uses orality to display a theatrical performance of the Self while it defends Creole and Créolité elements thematically. I also show that the autobiography was fairly well received in France and in Martinique, where favorable press coverage created a supportive audience, even though some Martinican commentators criticized the work. The critical Martinican reactions are aimed not only at the autobiography but also at the Créolité movement itself, which it exemplifies.

Chamoiseau is a prolific author, playwright, and essayist who has won numerous prizes. His novels include the Prix de l'Ile Maurice-winning *Chronique des sept misères* (1986); *Solibo Magnifique* (1988); the Prix Goncourt-winning *Texaco* (1992); *L'Esclave vieil homme et le molosse* (1997); *Biblique des derniers gestes* (2002); *À Bout d'enfance* (2005) (reedited as *Une Enfance créole III, À bout d'enfance* by Gallimard in 2006); *Un dimanche au cachot* (2007); and *Les Neuf Consciences du malfini* (2009).

He also wrote a play in the form of Creole folktale (1981's *Man Dlo contre la fée Carabosse*) and a collection of Creole folktales entitled *Au Temps de l'antan* (1988), winner of the Grand Prix de la littérature de jeunesse.

Chamoiseau is also the author and coauthor of numerous essays: *Eloge de la Créolité* (1989); *Martinique* (1989); *Guyane, Tracés-mémoires du bagne* (1994); *Lettres créoles: Tracées antillaises et continentales de la littérature: Martinique, Guadeloupe, Guyane, Haïti, 1635–1975* (1991, in collaboration with Confiant); *Ecrire la parole de nuit: La Nouvelle Littérature antillaise* (1994, in collaboration with Ralph Ludwig); and *Ecrire en pays dominé* (1997) which is part-essay and part-autobiography.

Antan d'enfance, the first of a trilogy of childhood autobiographies that also includes *Chemins d'école* (1994) and *À Bout d'enfance* (2005), was first published in September 1990 by Editions Hatier. *Antan d'enfance* was renamed *Une Enfance créole I: Antan d'enfance* when Editions Gallimard published a 1993 edition of the book to keep in line with the series of autobiographies by Chamoiseau, which became *Une Enfance créole II: Chemins d'école* (1996) and *Une Enfance créole III: À bout d'enfance* (2006), respectively. In 1990, Editions Hatier created a series called "Haute Enfance," for which selected authors were asked to write about their childhood. "Haute Enfance" was under the directorship of René de Ceccatty, a writer who worked as a journalist and literary critic at *Le Monde*. At the end of December 1991, when Editions Hatier closed, Gallimard inherited the "Haute Enfance" collection. In 1999, Carol Wolk translated *Antan d'enfance* into English as *Childhood* for the University of Nebraska Press. In this chapter, I will be using both the 1993 edition of *Antan d'enfance* and Wolk's English translation.

Chamoiseau's novels usually take place in the Caribbean and are marked by a search for an oral literary perspective in the written text. Most of his essays are centered on the problem of literature in the French Caribbean and revolve around the notion of Créolité. *Antan d'enfance* is a narrative of the autobiographer's childhood in Martinique in the 1950s. Chamoiseau's first autobiography initially focuses on himself and his family; later, it expands to include the immediate community of Fort-de-France. The autobiography opens with a foreword establishing the relationship between fire and the family house in Fort-de-France. As a fire destroys the family home, one part of the autobiographer's life is going into oblivion. The Creole childhood that Chamoiseau wants to depict is full of nostalgia, and telling his story is also a way to recapture or revive the past that burned with the destruction of the house, a symbol of his family's memory and space. The narrative focuses on the early years of his childhood with a special concentration on his senses, the games he played, and his first perception of the human and natural environments. The young Patrick is fond of destroying bugs of all kinds and admires his mother, who is the center of all the activities in and around the house. As he grows up, he ventures out of the domestic sphere to which he was restricted before, and he then gives a picture of his outings—following his mother to the market and going to the movies with his friends. These are not only glimpses of his childhood but also of Martinique and the situation of the Creole language in the 1950s.

Chamoiseau divides the first part of his childhood autobiography into two sections: "Sentir" (sensing) and "Sortir" (going out). "Sentir" depicts his early years of childhood when he experienced the world on his own; it is limited to his nuclear family and has the house as the center of his operations. "Sortir" is devoted to the young Chamoiseau's first experiences with the outer world, in different spaces such as the marketplace and the various shops he was commissioned to go to, not to mention his theater experiences with his playmates. Later on, I will show that there is also an internal division within the "Sentir" section.

What is remarkable about Chamoiseau's autobiography are the different levels of creativity. Like Raphaël Confiant, a codefender of Créolité, Chamoiseau is fond of juxtaposing a standard French with a form of "Creolized French." One example is the description of the cure for a sick pig:

> Il y avait des années difficiles. Malgré tout *le manger* distribué, *le cochon-planche* demeurait épais comme l'ombrage d'un fil-crin. Man Ninotte augmentait les doses avec du lait de vache, puis consultait en désespoir de cause les expertes de la campagne descendues *filer du commerce* au marché. On examinait les yeux de la bête, l'épaisseur de son poil, la couleur de sa langue. *On tenait considérants* sur les diamètres de ses déjections et cela finissait toujours par une accusation en règle contre les vers. Le cochon passait alors ses journées à ingurgiter des touffes d'herbes jaunâtres qui dénouaient les boyaux, des fleurs de nettoyages. (64–65; emphasis mine)

> [Some years were hard. Despite all the food it received, the pig remained as thin as the shadow of a strand of hair. Ma Ninotte augmented its portions with cow milk, then in despair consulted the country experts who came down to do business in the market. They examined the animal's eyes, the thickness of its coat, the color of its tongue. They considered the diameter of its dejections, and it always ended in a ritual accusation against worms. The pig then spent its days ingurgitating tufts of cleansing flowers and yellowish herbs that unclogged the intestines.] (31)

"Le manger," "le cochon-planche," "filer du commerce," and "On tenait considérants" are Creolized expressions of French; Chamoiseau substitutes this usage for the regular usage of French. This is not a new strategy, as Confiant also makes an abundant use of "français créolisé" in his autobiography, *Ravines du devant-jour*, and it is well known that Haitian authors have been using this dialect in their writings since the 1930s. Like Confiant, Chamoiseau prefers to interject "français créolisé" into passages of regular French to keep a tone that is specific to Martinique.

Another remarkable stylistic element of Chamoiseau's autobiography is his incorporation of brief stanzas of poetry, used as transitions:

> First communion Chocolate
> to write it is to salivate
> to think of it is to suffer
> to commune is chocolate. (49)

> The capsule
> flattened
> elongated
> sounded the thread and cut sharp
> thumb sliced open
> fingers bandaged
> yo-yo season of beautiful battles. (77)[1]

Better said, these are prose poems that serve as pauses in the body of the autobiography. They usually summarize what the author had previously said and prepare the transition to another topic.

The multiplicity of genres employed within the text is also made evident in an interchange Chamoiseau witnessed between his mother, Man Ninotte, and a trader in the market; the autobiographer recreates this conversation as if it were a scene from a play:

Ma Ninotte:	Someone told me stuffed tomatoes are to die for this year. . . .
The Merchant:	Someone told me that too. If you want a pound, I can give you such and such price. . . .
Ma Ninotte:	Really, huh?
The Merchant:	Yes, really. . . .
Ma Ninotte:	Give me those *dachine* things, honey. . . . I'll try to eat them after all. . . .
The Merchant:	There're so much. . . .
Ma Ninotte:	That's for the tomatoes?
The Merchant:	For the *dachines*, yes.

Ma Ninotte:	Well, I won't be eating *dachines* either, my dear. . . .
The Merchant:	How much you want to pay for the *dachines*?
Ma Ninotte:	I'll try to make a salad of *christofines*. Where can I find them?
The Merchant:	Take the *dachines*, sweetie.
Ma Ninotte:	Weelll, I don't need them anymore. . . .
The Merchant:	Do me a favor, take the *dachines*, sugar. . . .
Ma Ninotte:	What's your price, honey? (81–83)[2]

It is my contention that this dialogue, which covers three full pages, is a way for Chamoiseau to put an emphasis on the oral tradition of his culture and to point out the strategy of bargaining, which is a performance as well as part of the practice of shopping in his country. Man Ninotte is portrayed here as a clever and smart bargainer who obtains the goods at the price she wants; there may also be a focus on her as a go-getter who manages to acquire everything the family needs by using her social skills.

Chamoiseau's autobiography constantly refers to a particular audience, and this is likely a narrative strategy that Chamoiseau borrows from the folktale, especially in its performance or delivery; since the tale is delivered orally, the connection with the audience is very important, and this is why the reader has the impression of a "dialogue" or different "dialogues" with various audiences. The traces of these audiences are to be found in Chamoiseau's "calling outs." The references to "frères" (brothers) and "partageurs" (sharers) not only evokes aspects of the Creole "conteur" by establishing a connection with the audience, but these direct addresses in the text may also point to a specifically Martinican audience. This audience seems to be the most important one since it is mentioned in the beginning, the middle, and the end of the autobiography:

O sharers
You know how childhood is!
(there is nothing left of it but we keep it all). (ix)

In our shared memory, brothers, there was Matador. (32)

Then began a long wait, o brothers, the most terrible, I believe, of our collective childhoods. (34)

O my brothers, it [the house] is dying in its dust. It is suffocating in memories. The stairway has shrunken. The hallway has become narrow, and a warehouse has reduced it by three-fourths. . . . O my brothers, I want you to know: the house has closed its windows one by one, quietly detaching itself from the world, gradually closing around its guardianship of an era—the fragile archive of our childhood yore. (111–12)[3]

Unlike many other autobiographies I studied, including Confiant's, Chamoiseau's autobiography seems to have only one addressee, namely, the people referred to as "frères" and "partageurs." Contrary to the other autobiographies, there is no apparent reference to a possible European audience; only the autobiography is dedicated to René de Ceccatty, the director of the "Haute Enfance" collection at Editions Gallimard, the publisher of Chamoiseau's autobiography.

Yet it seems as though there is still another addressee interpellated by the autobiographer: his own memory. Throughout the book, Chamoiseau calls out to his memory as if establishing a "dialogue" with it. This so-called dialogue is used to make a pact and to interrogate his memory:

Memory ho, this quest is for you. (3)

Memory, let's make a pact long enough for sketch, lower your palisades and pacify the savages, reveal the secret of the traces that lie at the edge of your brushy borders. I bring neither sack for kidnapping nor knife for conquest, nothing but intoxication and a mighty docile joy at the rhythm (flow of time) of your flow. (4)

O selective memory. You no longer remember his disappearance. In which attic did you store his death? Did you see him floating belly-up in the courtyard tub, or do you retain a vision of his hunched body on one of the steps? Do you remember him emerging into the daylight, his brain shipwrecked without a compass, standing bewildered beneath the mamas' brooms? It's possible he never died, that he simply decided to change houses. I can't picture him dead, floating in the mucky stream of a canal. Perhaps he set up camp between two dreams and remains there, mummified in an eternal insomnia. Memory, that is my decision. (29)

Memory, I see your game: you take root and form in the imagination, and the latter blossoms only through you. (35)

There is the image of Papa-the-shoemaker. It's hazy. Who's talking memory? What prowler remembers? (62)

To the little boy he recited La Fontaine, and the fool is hungry for more. Oh memory, is there mink oil in the beatings of the heart? (63)

Memory, are you taking off? (105)[4]

The autobiographer's memory becomes a companion throughout the book, and after interrogating his memory, in the last citation toward the end of the autobiography, the autobiographer seems to have come to an understanding of its nature by proclaiming that it is just a structure and that the imagination fills the gap left by memory when writing an autobiography: "Il n'y a pas une mémoire mais une ossature de l'esprit, sédimentée comme un corail, sans boussole ni compass" (179). (There is no memory but a skeleton of the spirit, sedimented like coral, with neither chart nor compass [107].)

There is a clear indication that Chamoiseau is making a theory about autobiography that establishes as its premise the unreliability of memory when writing autobiographies. Chamoiseau, in the middle of the dialogue with his memory, calls it "mémoire sélective" (selective memory), implying that his memory keeps certain things and forgets others, insisting thus on the unstable nature of his own memory. Among all the autobiographers in my corpus, Chamoiseau is the only one who really constructs a theory about autobiography through the act of writing about his personal experience. The progression of his dialogue with his memory and the conclusion that memory is not entirely reliable show that he used the practice of writing autobiography as a means of arriving at a theory about autobiography. The theory is based on Chamoiseau's interaction with his memory and implies that any attempt to write an autobiography is bound to unreliability because of the unstable nature of memory. To Chamoiseau, fiction is a necessary tool in writing the story of the Self. Of course, Chamoiseau is not breaking new ground here, as the points he is making have already been asserted by other theorists. What is new, though, is the experimental dimension of his investigation; the act of writing his autobiography is lived as an experiment after which the autobiographer draws the necessary conclusions.

This tendency to theorize about autobiography as a practice reaches a level of specificity when, throughout the book, Chamoiseau also establishes a theory about childhood autobiography:

> You never leave childhood, you hold it tight inside. You never detach
> from it, you repress it. It's not a process of improvement that leads to
> adulthood, but the slow sedimentation of a crust around a sensitive
> state that will be the core of what you are. You never leave childhood,
> you begin to believe in reality, what is said to be real. Reality is firm,
> stable, often drawn at right angles—and comfortable. What is real

(which the child perceives in close proximity) is a complex, uncomfortable deflagration of possibilities and impossibilities. To grow up is to cease to have the strength to perceive it. Or else to erect a mental shield between this perception and the self. That's why poets never grow up, or so little. (50)

Where does childhood end? What is this dilution? And why do you wander in this dust, whose scattering you cannot contain? Memory, who remembers for you? Who fixed your laws and procedures? Who keeps inventory in your thieving caves? (106)[5]

The autobiographer becomes a theorist about childhood autobiography and proves to be the most theoretical of all the autobiographers in my corpus, even more so than Amadou Hampâté Bâ, who devoted a particular chapter to memory and its reliability in the African context. Even though both authors share the oral tradition, Chamoiseau, unlike Bâ, does not believe in the total reliability of the memory to recollect childhood events. Chamoiseau uses experiment in order to build a theory, therefore using a deductive approach; in contrast, Bâ uses an inductive approach by theorizing on the reliability of his memory in the early chapters of his autobiography. I am borrowing the terms *experiment,* *deductive,* and *inductive* from the natural sciences. An experiment is a research carried out to draw conclusions in order to set general rules or build a theory. Deductive is the adjective related to "deduction," and it means a conclusion reached by some observation and logical reasoning; it is the opposite of induction, which is a mathematical or scientific undertaking with the purpose of demonstrating a theory or a rule that was set before the experiment.

At the linguistic level, Chamoiseau is a master of orchestrating multiple grammatical subjects. Most autobiographies are written using the first-person singular pronoun "je," thus establishing a stable identity of the autobiographer. Chamoiseau, however, alternates his use of the first-, second- and third-person singular pronouns, *je* (I), *tu* (you), and *il* (he, in this case), to represent three distinct aspects of his "Self." Chamoiseau most frequently employs the third person, *il,* also referred to as *le négrillon* (the boy), to indicate the young self that was present for the experiences recounted. The second person, *tu,* is used by the autobiographer to call out to his memory: "Peux-tu dire de l'enfance ce que l'on n'en sait plus? . . . Mémoire ho, cette quête est pour toi" (21). (Can you tell of childhood what is no longer known? . . . *Memory ho, this quest is for you* [3; italics in translation only].) The first-person singular pronoun, *je,* is used only sparingly: "The melancholy boy then knows the world and silently questions his life (it was a matter, *I* believe, of a child's unexpressed anxiety; but it is also possible that these were simply hours of stupor connected to the idiocy of which certain other little boys—his very closest enemies—suspected him)" (22; emphasis mine).[6] The first person refers to the autobiographer, the adult Chamoiseau, to be differentiated from *le négrillon* of his childhood. While the "dialogue" is established between the *je* and the *tu*, in reality the topic they are discussing is *le négrillon/il*. An ironical tone may be noticed in the autobiographer's reference to himself as *le négrillon*, and later on as *le rôdeur* (the prowler); this shows also the distance that the autobiographer wants to set between his adult and younger selves. This trinity of autobiographical subjects in Chamoiseau's autobiography establishes a tone of objectivity while showing some originality over other autobiographies on childhood narrative.

Although in the autobiography there is the plurality of subjects *je/tu/il*, one may ask if there is a plurality of perspectives as well. The play among the three subjects seems to be centered on the initial point of view of the adult Chamoiseau identifiable with the subject *je*, whereas *tu* and *il*, while referring respectively to the autobiographer's memory and his younger Self, do not show a different perspective. Clearly, it is the adult Chamoiseau who is organizing the discourse of his autobiography.

In observing this, I have to partially disagree with Suzanne Crosta when she declares in her article "Marronner le récit d'enfance: *Antan d'enfance* de Patrick Chamoiseau et *Ravines du devant-jour* de Raphaël Confiant":

Mais dès qu'on lit les premières lignes d'*Antan d'enfance* de Chamoiseau, le lecteur est surpris de constater l'emploi de la troisième personne. L'alternance des deux voix, celle de la première personne et celle de la troisième personne, privilégie une lecture axiologique de cette plage temporelle que représente l'enfance. Le narrateur adulte, qui se souvient de son enfance, s'exprime à la première personne lorsqu'il intervient dans le récit pour faire des jugements de valeur, ou pour s'interroger sur les prémisses de son projet mnémonique. Le recours à la troisième personne est utilisé plus souvent quand le narrateur décrit les événements du passé à travers les yeux du "petit négrillon." Ce jeu de la modalité narrative accuse l'écart temporel qui sépare le narrateur-adulte du personnage-enfant, et a pour effet d'insister sur la situation de dépendance qui caractérise leur mise en relation dans les conventions du récit d'enfance.[7]

Surprisingly enough, Crosta forgets to mention the use of the second-person singular pronoun, *tu*, which is the second word used in the introductory sentence of the text and by which the author interrogates his memory and, more importantly, by which he establishes an autobiographical contract with himself. Yet she is right in emphasizing the modernistic connivance between the adult-narrator and the child-character through the use of the third person.

While the originality of using three grammatical subjects is modern, at a deeper level, the autobiography is conservative due to the lack of real interaction among the said subjects. If Chamoiseau's memory is his companion in the recollection of his childhood years, and if *le négrillon* represents his younger Self, there is actually no real dialogue among these subjects, as they do not reply to the questions asked by the *je* of the text. Rather than a dialogue, it seems that Chamoiseau is having a monologue with himself. At first, there seems to be a sense of dialogue, but at a deeper level, it is just a monologue. Still, what is interesting about the use of the three subjects is that it reinforces the idea of modern autobiography as the fracturing of the Self into many entities: as Rimbaud famously asserted, "Je est un autre."[8] Even at this level, it is fair to liken Chamoiseau's use of autobiography to theater, as he stages his three subjects while calling out to a potential Martinican audience; the autobiography becomes therefore a performance of the Self or Selves, a play in the skillful hands of the author. This linguistic aspect contributes much to the literary dimension of Chamoiseau's autobiography, which is definitely modern in its form and content.

More remarkable is the autobiographer's good-natured transparency in showing the potential dubiousness of his recollection of his childhood memories. In fact, there are many occurrences where the author casts doubt on his own statements:

> A fine victory, but he had to learn to sleep while continuing his fanning motion. It's possible he succeeded, but no one has ever come forth as a witness. (21)

> Another version of the genesis of the chicken coops is possible. (23)

> Ma Ninotte's only fear as she ran after her own was that it would be stolen, but as I write this, I suddenly remember that nothing at the time was stolen. (30)

> Ma Ninotte never had enough room. She ended up running laundry lines on the roofs of the kitchens; the man of today still doesn't understand how she managed to get up there. (54)[9]

In the recollection of his childhood, Chamoiseau goes beyond the objective tone by using his imagination to reconstruct an event he did not actually witness: he evocatively describes the mothers cooking outside collectively with other housewives. His imagination fills in the details that he had not directly observed:

> The little boy never saw the day when the mothers cooked side by side in these rooms, separated by wood dividers. . . . *He imagines* the disturbing spicy steam that pervaded these rooms where the mamas showed the world their culinary talents. They competed in audacity in order to scent the pickled fish, send wafting odoriferous fricassees, better transmit to the universe that there was, in their part of the world, on that day, not a miserable cod sauce, but a slice of beef. *He supposes* that they also sang, or chatted through the dividers, before hauling their big pots up the creaking stairs to a pack of starving children, home from school, and to the men busy drinking punch in the company of the midday boozer, expert in timing his visit. (22; emphasis mine)[10]

The first chapter, "Sentir," which recollects Chamoiseau's childhood curiosity of the outer world, is comprised of several subdivisions. This chapter can be seen as three stages (somewhat corresponding to the staged evolution of prehistoric humans): a period of hunting, a period of acquiring fire, and a period of mastering iron.

The period of hunting, or "L'âge de la chasse" (28–29), refers to the autobiographer's endeavor to catch flies in order to feed the spiders. The period devoted to the acquisition of fire is called "L'âge du feu" (31–33), and it is in this period that he proceeds to destroy the spiders by burning them alive with matches. The period of iron is referred to as "l'âge de l'outil" (34), and also as "l'âge de la lame" (35); this period corresponds to the destruction of spiders and worms with a razor blade. The story of the development of Chamoiseau's Self is central to "Sentir," which covers half of his autobiography.

This classification in three stages could be considered a "mythical" representation by the adult Chamoiseau of the young Chamoiseau in his progression toward a more "evolved" young man, on the path to becoming the writer he is now. The author dissociates himself from his younger Self as if asserting that he is a product of an evolution (prehistorically and historically). Chamoiseau's focus on this evolution aligns with Lejeune's definition of autobiography as the history of the development of the author's personality. Chamoiseau dissociates himself from his younger Self, by calling him sarcastically "le négrillon." In contrast, he will later refer to his adult Self by a different nickname, "l'homme d'aujourd'hui" (the man of today), and the transformation between the two selves is very striking, as one is used to explain the other under the pen of the autobiographer:

> Around these measly trophies the little boy organized pagan ceremonies. The man clutches them today somewhere in his shadows. (27)
>
> Beneath the killer lay the makings of someone who today is incapable of doing the slightest harm to the most despicable of the green flies. (29)[11]

After all the killings he committed in his childhood, the adult autobiographer seems to have learned a lesson and dissociates himself from such an activity; from a killer he has become a pacifist in the time period referred to as "aujourd'hui." This change of personality, demonstrated by a change in behavior, carries even into the domain of taste, when Chamoiseau confesses his current dislike, as an adult, for seafood which his mother always fed them: "Aujourd'hui, l'homme qui a tant donné supporte malement dans son assiette les produits de la mer." (145) [Today, the man who's paid his dues can barely stand the products of the sea in his plate (85).]

In the history of the development of his personality, Chamoiseau does not credit only personal experience; he also gives credit to the influence that others had on him, especially the doctor and the pharmacist who used to take care of his family:

> Neither one practices any more. They live in slow motion somewhere, among children and grandchildren who may not even know the heights of their devotion. I see them as immortal, as everlasting as certain trees. It is from them that the man of today gets his inclination toward open hands and his inability to say no to what is asked of him. He knows—happily, out of weakness—how to give. (62)[12]

The autobiographer explains how he became a generous person who is fond of giving presents due to the influence of these two practitioners.

As with Confiant, there is a tendency to defend the Creole language and heritage in Chamoiseau's autobiography; many references to Créole or Créolité are scattered all over the autobiography, and they touch on various areas. The general tone of his autobiography seems to convey the idea that Chamoiseau misses the spontaneity and creativity of the Creole language in its old usage. Chamoiseau expresses his regret for the disappearance of Creole traditional medical practices under the pressure of modern medicine, which the autobiographer sees as a loss for dominated nations:

> Thus Creole medicine was losing its paths of transmission. The man of today knows that there are now broken peoples who have to be re-taught the elementary principles of medicine and hygiene, who are out of touch with their own genius, and whom others try to "develop" to the rhythm of another genius. A people becomes feeble and dies when its traditions are invalidated even to itself, when it freezes them, grasps at them, perceives them as archaic without ever adapting them to the changing times, without absorbing them and moving into modernity, armed with their wealth. So it is for us in places. (57)[13]

In this militant statement, Chamoiseau goes beyond the case of Martinique to address all colonized people who are uprooted from their traditions due to Western colonization and civilization. One finds in this statement almost the same activist and militant tone as in his semiautobiographical essay Écrire *en pays dominé*. Chamoiseau places Western medicine in opposition to the infusions and herbs that his mother used to give her family when they got sick. His mother is a guardian of Creole medicine; Chamoiseau refers to her as "la haute confidente," and he lets her speak in the first person, *je*, her voice distinguished by italics in the body of his autobiography (although the italics were not maintained in the English translation): "I knew how to measure my fevers and where the pain was; my intestines, my stomach, and my heart were familiar with Guinea grass, the flavors of the good-for-everything herbs, and the cha cha herbs. But since I didn't know the new bodies of you children, I had to let the doctor man with his medicine do his work" (57).[14] The Creole folktale is the main representative of oral literature, and Chamoiseau makes a point in his autobiography to highlight his first childhood encounter with the folktale, linking it with the concept of Créolité that he coined with Confiant and Bernabé:

> City storytellers were rare. In any event, the little boy had never seen one. He encountered the Creole folktale with Jeanne-Yvette, a real storyteller, which is to say, unfathomable in memory and unbeatably cruel. Scared you to death with two words, a hint, a meaningless song. She played on silence, on language. She splattered death with laughter, gathering this laughter from terror alone. She led us along to the rhythm of her tongue's squalls, making us believe anything. We watched for Mama Dlo in the shadow of the stairs. We ran-for-it at the smell of a zombi she sniffed. She forced us to undress at the mention of

a she-devil who hated clothing. She taught the little boy the astonishing richness of Creole orality. A universe of canny resistance, of salva-
tional cruelty, rich with several genies. Jeanne-Yvette came to us from
Caribbean memories, from the swarming of Africa, from the diversi-
ties of Europe, from the festering of India, from the quakes of Asia,
from the vast touch of the peoples in the prism of the open islands, the
very sites of Creolity. (70)[15]

In this important passage where the author relates the creativity and
richness of Creole folktales to the very fundamentals of Créolité, the
reader notes that the idea of "diversalité" already mentioned in the
manifesto *Eloge de la Créolité* is evident in Chamoiseau's autobiography. It is also very interesting to notice that the publishing date of the
former corresponds to the date of the final touches in writing the autobiography, 1989. Moreover, Chamoiseau points out an element that
is very important in oral literature: the theatrical or dynamic aspect of
its delivery, emphasized in the above passage by the power of Jeanne-
Yvette's words on their imagination.

In his eulogy of Creole's creativity, the autobiographer goes so far
as to obliquely rebuke the renown Césaire in this revealing quotation:
"Par-dessus, la consternation criarde des premiers arrivés découvrait
ce que les vieux-nègres appellent (ou plus exactement crient): an tÿou-
manman, et Césaire: un désastre" (120). (Above it all, the shrieking
dismay of the first arrivals discovering what the old-folks call [or more
exactly cry] "an tÿou-manman"; what Césaire would call "a disaster"
[67].) This passage is worth analyzing in light of the theory of Créolité.
In *Eloge de la Créolité*, Chamoiseau and his cowriters had called for a
new literature grounded in the Creole language, and even if they did
not criticize Césaire directly, they did reproach him for not using the
Creole language in his seminal work *Le Cahier d'un retour au pays natal*. In his autobiography, Chamoiseau finds fault with Césaire for identifying a typical Martinican reality, not by its local Creole phrase, but
by a French word. Even though the attack is oblique, the mention of
Césaire's avoidance of Creole is a sharp judgment against the leader
of Négritude; here the "vieux-nègres" in the quotation represent the
older Martinicans who use Creole language in its spontaneity whereas
Césaire symbolizes the sophisticated intellectual out of touch with the
common people. Autobiography seems to be a locus where personal as
well as ideological matters are addressed.

The status of the Creole language is a major point in Chamoiseau's
autobiography as, when recounting the situations in which the colo-

nized Creole language is in use in its spontaneity, he refers to a scene in the movie theater and expresses his regret, nowadays, for the disappearance of certain aspects of this language: "The talkers and jokers stood straight in a jovial circus we encouraged. At the time there was no such thing as applause, but there were precise modulations of the throat, which the Creole language of today has lost" (99).[16] There is a regret of the loss of the Creole language as the autobiographer makes himself the accountant of Créolité by contrasting Creole usage during his childhood in the 1950s to its current usage in Martinique.

Identity, of course, is an important subject for both Créolité and for Chamoiseau in his autobiography. In a remarkable passage set in a movie theater, the autobiographer illustrates the complexities surrounding identity when dominated peoples gaze upon their representation in movies. Chamoiseau confirms the general tendency of colonized people to identify with the white colonizer rather than the dominated people when there is a representation of both types; Chamoiseau confesses that because of this misidentification, he later had to learn how to become "créole," assuming his own identity of dominated being:

> The Chinese laundrymen repeated mechanical servilities with a nasal twang. The blacks were half idiots, with big roving eyes, constantly in terror. They filled the landscape with zealous domestics, blissful bartenders, jazz statues, savages endlessly gesturing and jagged. Their appearance elicited widespread laughter from the audience, which grew nervous. The little black boy perceived no commonality between himself and this representation. Indigenous meant black, wild, and often mean. We were Tarzan and never the half monkeys he defeated. The mechanisms of film functioned full stream. We identified with the strongest, who were always white, often blond, with eyes of celestial innocence, forcing us into internal ruin without our realizing it. It would take a major revolution for the little boy to subsequently consider himself black and obstinately learn to be so. Later, he had to learn to be Creole. (101)[17]

This passage summarizes the development of the autobiographer's consciousness of his identity, first delusive when identifying himself with the white colonial master, then with the African during the period of Négritude, and later by finding the definition of his own identity as a Creole from the Caribbean. The movie theater becomes a mirror that helps the autobiographer reflect on his identity by way of the different races represented, allowing himself to build his own identity. Of course, one senses automatically the influence of Chamoiseau's fellow countryman Frantz Fanon, who had already mentioned the complex of the colonized in front of his own representation in the presence of a white man, in *Peau noire, masques blancs*.[18]

Despite its innocent appearance, Chamoiseau's autobiography seems to bear a subtext of subversion that parallels his opinion as the defender of *Créolité*; of course, all this is subtly expressed "in passing" in the middle of an autobiography that looks like an experiment on the writing of autobiography, as I showed earlier. The whole project of this autobiography seems to be the revalorization of the Creole language. As a coauthor of *Eloge de la Créolité*, Chamoiseau is faithful in illustrating the aesthetic dimension of Créolité. His autobiography is a good example of this, especially at the linguistic level, and the scattered remarks on the current decline of the Creole language go in this direction. The oral dimension is very obvious in Chamoiseau's autobiography, and he makes it the key aspect of Creole culture. As he declares in an interview with James Ferguson:

> The basis of this culture's literature, it follows, is oral rather than written, for slaves and labourers were not encouraged to read or write. Instead, they transmitted their myths, stories and poetry by speech, and the storyteller became a key figure in the cultural life of the community. "Créolité" tries to restore to the modern-day writer that status of storyteller by breaking down the barrier between the written and the spoken, French and Creole.[19]

The status of the modern storyteller or "conteur créole" was made obvious through the numerous interpellations to a potential Martinican audience referred to as "frères" or "partageurs," through the use of the three narrative subjects, and through the mixture of genres within the body of the text.[20]

Already in *Lettres Créoles: Tracées antillaises et continentales de la littérature*, Chamoiseau and Confiant had defined the Creole storyteller as serving four distinctive roles: one who speaks on behalf of others; one who guards the collective memory; one who seeks to entertain; and one who puts resistance into words.

> En attendant que des chercheurs s'y intéressent, on peut déjà profiler quatre fonctions de l'oraliturain créole que l'on retrouvera par la suite et sous des formes diverses, souvent partielles, dans nos tracées littéraires. Quand on ne les retrouvera pas, leur absence se fera lancinante. Le conteur est d'abord celui qui donne voix au groupe. Il n'est pas un créateur en suspension, mais bien le délégué d'un imaginaire collectif auquel son art s'ajoute. . . . L'oraliturain fut aussi, dans les premiers

temps, gardien des mémoires. . . . Distraire fut aussi une de ses fonc-
tions. A Marcel Lebielle, les conteurs disent souvent que leur tâche est
de "faire goûter un bon bocal de miel," de "faire passer le temps." . . .
Enfin, verbaliser la résistance, selon les modalités déjà vues.[21]

The authors of *Lettres créoles* declare that these four functions can be
more or less evident in modern Caribbean literature, and thus it will be
worthwhile to ask if Chamoiseau's autobiography complies with these
criteria. The answer seems to be a vibrant "yes" because Chamoiseau's
autobiography is structured around the use of oral literature. Chamoiseau himself, as a writer and coauthor of the theory of Créolité, plays
the function of delegate; he fulfills the first criterion by speaking for
the Martinicans through his autobiography, which has a subtly subversive nature. Chamoiseau in some way also guards the collective memory of the Martinicans through his own autobiography by his depiction of childhood in the Martinique of the 1950s; he even calls out to
his "frères" and "partageurs" when he speaks of "mémoire commune"
(shared memory) and "communes enfances" (collective childhoods).
With respect to the third criterion, although it may not be obvious, the
entertaining level of Chamoiseau's autobiography can be seen through
the play among the three narrative subjects and the theatricality of his
writing, which employs various genres. Finally, addressing the fourth
criterion, the resistance aspect was already present in the ideology of
Créolité, and it is made manifest in the autobiography's use of Creole
within the text as well as in its various pleas concerning the status of the
Creole language and culture.

Another consideration with Chamoiseau's autobiography is the vari-
ation of dates and how it relates to the act of autobiographical writing.
As mentioned at the end of his autobiography, Chamoiseau complet-
ed the work in "Fort-de-France, [on] 3 octobre 1989" (the same year
Eloge de la Créolité was published), and it was published by Hatier in
1990 and then again in 1993. More importantly, a "préface inédite de
l'auteur" was written by Chamoiseau himself for the Edition Gallimard
publication in 1996.

In view of its publication history, one should infer that when Chamoiseau finished writing the manuscript of his autobiography in 1989, his
house had not yet burned down—the fire broke out in 1993. Therefore,
the preface of 1996 gives an additional tone of nostalgia that was absent
from the beginning, namely, the emphasis on the recreation of this past
moment. With the writing of his autobiography coinciding with the
publication of the literary manifesto *Eloge de la Créolité*, it is not far-

fetched to say that the influence of the manifesto is echoed in the autobiography, though it is more understated.

The first part of Patrick Chamoiseau's autobiography is devoted to
the earlier years of his childhood, but bears the traces of the adult's
perspective on his childhood. This appears through the usage of three
grammatical subjects that create distance as well as through the various
applications of oral genre techniques such as the interpellations and
the mixture of genres. More important is the autobiographer's subtle
endeavor to break the innocent tone of an autobiography that was supposed to describe his childhood, through several critical remarks on
the status of the Creole language, medicine, and culture in Martinique,
which are in direct line with the more militant project of the *Eloge de
la Créolité*.

ANTAN D'ENFANCE'S RECEPTION IN FRANCE

A few reviews attest to a fairly positive reception of Chamoiseau's first
autobiography in France. *Antan d'enfance* was among the first books
to introduce the "Haute Enfance" collection, which featured childhood
narratives and was initiated by Editions Hatier in 1990, and which
was later picked up by Editions Gallimard under the directorship of
René de Ceccatty. On August 31, 1990, "Monde des livres" from the
prestigious French daily newspaper, *Le Monde*, estimated that *Antan
d'enfance* sold between twenty and thirty thousand copies, whereas titles with top sales ranked in the one hundred thousand to two hundred
thousand range (J. M. G. Le Clézio's *Onitsha* was among those with top
sales). This represents a relatively good performance for Chamoiseau
since it was only his third noncollaborative work after *Chronique des
sept misères* (1986) and *Solibo Magnifique* (1988). Considering that he
was competing as an outsider in the French literary market at the time
when La Créolité was at the introductory stage, his reception is more
remarkable. Most of the French reviews were replicated in Martincan
newspapers and magazines.

ANTAN D'ENFANCE'S RECEPTION IN MARTINIQUE

In an October 1990 issue of *Antilla*, there is an article by Serge Médeuf
(no. 405, October 19–26, 1990, pp. 40–41). Although it is not clear in
which newspaper the article originally ran, it appears that Serge Médeuf is a metropolitan French critic who reviewed Chamoiseau's first

autobiography. Médeuf's review is nothing short of eulogious, summarizing *Antan d'enfance* in poetic terms. He points out that the book is "densely autobiographical" and that the rendering of daily life in the book helps readers (inclusive plural *nous*/us) savor it. He also emphasizes the suggestive power of the book, noting the difference between what is said ("le dit") and what is not said ("le non-dit"). Médeuf concludes by linking the autobiography to a tale. In duplicating a Parisian-based newspaper's review, *Antilla* and Martinicans seem to yield to the metropolitan press's opinions about their artistic productions.

Raphaël Confiant wrote an article entitled "Patrick Chamoiseau ou la réconciliation avec notre entour" on Chamoiseau's autobiography. Confiant declares that Chamoiseau's talent ("le génie") in his autobiography and other books is his ability to allow Martinicans to appreciate their cultural world: "Le génie de P. Chamoiseau dans ses textes romanesques comme dans ce récit de la Haute Enfance qu'est 'Antan d'enfance' est de nous permettre d'aimer notre entour" (40). Confiant also contends that Chamoiseau renews the Martinican gaze upon themselves and their cultural identity. To Confiant, Chamoiseau's writing contributes in establishing the autonomy of Martinican literature vis-à-vis its French source. This is very interesting and contradictory at the same time: the aspects that Confiant perceives as supporting autonomy in the works of Chamoiseau (and in his own works) are seen by other Martinicans (such as René Menil) as aspects that cater to exoticism for a foreign readership. In the same article Confiant contends that there is not in fact a contradiction because, by using Creole with French in his writing, Chamoiseau does not want to impress Parisian critics but rather contributes to helping Martinicans appreciate themselves and their immediate environment: "Car le frottement qu'il gère entre le français sa langue d'écriture et le créole, sa langue d'imaginaire, sert, non pas à faire joli, mais bien à arpenter au plus près, au plus exact ce réel qu'il nous faudra bien apprendre à aimer un jour."[22] Of course, Confiant is obviously biased as a codefender of La Créolité, but what is important here is that his assessment of Chamoiseau's autobiography attests to certain criticisms that Chamoiseau had received prior to the publication of *Antan d'enfance* or after. Confiant's article is derived from his intervention as the president of Banzil Kréyol-Matinik, an association devoted to the promotion of Creole language and culture. The article was in fact Confiant's introduction of *Antan d'enfance* during the 8th International Week for Creole organized by Bannzil Kréyol on Tuesday, October 23, 1990, in Rivière-Pilote, Martinique.

In *Antilla*, there is an introduction stating that *Antan d'enfance* was having a great success with both the Martinican audience and the French critics. The article then reproduces verbatim the article "L'enfant Chamoiseau" by Hector Bianciotti in *Le Monde*'s November 2, 1990, edition as well as Milan Kundera's "Les Cent dix-sept sortilèges de Patrick Chamoiseau" in *Le Nouvel Observateur*. It is interesting to note that the Martinican newspaper magazine establishes a difference between the Martinican "audience" and the French "critics." This attests to the paucity of literary or aesthetic criticism in Martinique: the French critics are given more importance, since their reviews are reproduced word-for-word without any commentary or criticism from the Martinican journalists. Martinican journalists privilege Biancotti's and Kundera's viewpoints, both of which were highly positive.[23]

In the article "Une conscience d'adulte dans un regard d'enfant," Georges Desportes reviews *Antan d'enfance* in *Antilla* (no. 412, December 7–13, 1990, pp. 39–40). Although there is no indication about the identity of the reviewer, some traces in the writing suggest he is Martinican, especially his use of the inclusive *nous*/we and *nous*/us as well as the possessive adjectives *notre*/*nos*/our: "L'art de Chamoiseau est de vous faire vivre dans l'intimité de nous-mêmes, de notre ville, du peuple, de notre langage, sans complexe; avec chaleur et sympathie. On se retrouve à pleines pages dans nos laideurs secrètes comme dans nos beautés et nos amours les plus saugrenues et les plus folles" (40).

I found Desportes's article to be the most critical Martinican piece because he balances his appreciation for the autobiography with criticism of some aspects of Chamoiseau's work. Desportes praises Chamoiseau for capturing the past through a thematic orientation of his autobiography, thereby avoiding the pitfall of the pretense to render the past absolutely. He also contends that Chamoiseau's use of the three subjects (*je*/*tu*/*il*) is a sign of modesty from the author who started writing his autobiography early on (Desportes wrongly uses the term "mémoires," which in French is seen as a subcategory of the autobiographical genre; "memoires" focus on external historical events, while autobiography is more concerned with the personal events of a life.) Additionally, Desportes sees the use of the three subjects as Chamoiseau's strategy to avoid a too personal autobiography and to distance himself from such an intimate subject. Desportes theorizes that, by using the third-person singular pronoun (the nameless boy, *le négrillon*), Chamoiseau presents this character as a symbol of the collective Martinicans. But then, Desportes makes a very revealing statement that such a symbol will be perceived, not by the native Martinicans, but only by the white foreigners and all the "Others": "Le négrillon n'a pas de prénom ni de nom, il s'identifie par sa couleur et son anonymat substantive. Et par là même, il se présente comme symbole singulier du collectif local, tel qu'il serait perçu, non pas par les autochtones, mais par le blanc étrangers [sic], et tous les Autres" (40). The interesting point in Desportes's review is that, as a Martinican, he observes that the autobiography was written for a foreign French metropolitan audience, a fact he alludes to by citing "le blanc étrangers" (the white foreigners). This is very important since it contradicts Chamoiseau's ambition (and the intention of Créolité) to exist for a Martinican audience. Desportes's article also reproaches Chamoiseau for forcing Creole into existing French words; he gives the example of Chamoiseau using "macawon" for "macaron," "malcadi" for "mal caduc" and "sikdôj" for "sucre d'orge." Desportes ends his article by challenging the author to contradict him (Desportes), and he encourages readers to read the autobiography: "Ces restrictions étant faites, je laisse le lecteur à son appétit de lecture, et à l'auteur la charge de me contredire" (40).

Another critical reaction by one of Martinique's literary and political figures sheds some light not only on La Créolité but also on Chamoiseau's first autobiography. René Menil's reaction was published in *Le Figaro* of February 5, 1993, and was reprinted by *Antilla* (no. 526, March 5, 1993, p. 33), on the occasion of Chamoiseau's winning of the Goncourt Prize. The French journalist (whose name is not mentioned in *Antilla*) asserts that the Creolité movement wanted to break away from the "elitist" Négritude in order to conquer a "popular" public. René Menil was at the forefront of the cultural movement that preceded Négritude, as he was one of the leaders of the student manifesto, *L'Etudiant noir*, published in 1932. The journalist then lets René Menil contend:

> *Chamoiseau et ses amis . . . se disent au centre de la vie; ils pensent que tout aboutit à eux et que tout ce qu'ils font est différent. En réalité ce qu'ils appellent la Créolité a été construit au cours d'une evolution des mentalités. On peut citer une vingtaine d'écrivains qui ont apporté leur contribution à cette aventure que le prix Goncourt a fortement médiatisé [sic]. Mais si Chamoiseau s'était exprimé en Français cela n'aurait pas nui au livre. Je ne vois pas l'intérêt esthétique ni l'intérêt de la vérité qu'on veut faire passer en ajoutant des mots créoles. On peut se de-*

mander si ce n'est pas un peu d'exotisme à usage externe. (33; italics in original)

From this critical assessment of Chamoiseau's winning of the Goncourt Prize and of the new Créolité movement, Menil makes an important point in questioning the use of Creole language as an aesthetic tool and indicates that it is used to create an exotic sense for a readership outside of Martinique. Menil goes on to question the independence and dignity of the Creolité movement for bragging about external prizes: "*Si vous êtes maîtres de vous-même, il faut manifester cette souveraineté et non pas se féliciter d'avoir été reconnu par un jury parisien*" (italics in the original). Menil's criticism is also echoed in another Martinican writer's reaction to the Créolité movement when I study the reception of Raphaël Confiant's *Ravines du devant-jour.*

CONCLUSION: THE AUDIENCE PARADOX

Chamoiseau's first childhood autobiography *Antan d'enfance* bears the marks of the militant *Eloge de la Créolité*, and the autobiographer uses the performance of the Self both theatrically and linguistically to express the power of Creole orality. *Antan d'enfance* is a balance of the intrusion of the oral into a written text and an attempt to theorize childhood. According to Mariane Loust in her article "L'enfance toujours recommencée" (*Le Monde* February 22, 2005, in the rubric "Culture"), the "Haute Enfance" collection was created based on data from a market study and corresponds to the desire of the publisher to equate readers' desires with authors' skills. Loust's opinion came from her review of *À Bout d'enfance* by Chamoiseau, and she concludes that "Haute Enfance" publishes books that are "on demand" and that do not reflect the highest productions of the writers. Although the critique is applied to the third volume of Chamoiseau's autobiography, Loust's reaction is very revealing of the paradox of Chamoiseau and his Créolité movement in their claim to cater to a Martinican audience. Although the market study under question does not reveal it, it is certainly geared more toward a French readership than a Martinican one.

The acclaimed reception of Chamoiseau's autobiography in France, which was merely echoed in Martinican newspapers and magazines, reveals the contradiction that the defenders of La Créolité have to face to write original productions theoretically aimed at their local audience but which end up primarily serving the French audience. René Menil and Georges Desportes's reactions to La Créolité and *Antan d'enfance* attest to a minimal critical assessment of both the movement and of the autobiography. The paradoxical reception of Chamoiseau deepens because, despite Desportes's presentation of *Antan d'enfance* as written for a French metropolitan audience, Chamoiseau received the Prix Carbet, organized by the association Carbet, which aims at making artistic productions in Martinique autonomous.[24]

Raphaël Confiant

*Defense and Illustration of Créolité
and Its Complacent Reception*

Raphaël Confiant is one of the authors, along with Jean Bernabé and Patrick Chamoiseau, of *Eloge de la Créolité* (1989), a manifesto for a new literature in the French Caribbean—a literature that, through its use of Creole, is rooted in the realities of the islands.

Confiant's narrative in *Ravines du devant-jour* juxtaposes standard French, Creole, and local Martinican French. He takes liberties with the French language in order to point to the realities of Martinique, and he employs the Creole language even when a French equivalent is available. Confiant takes this compromise with the French language to another level in his autobiography. My contention is that, after the publication of the manifesto *Eloge de la Créolité* (1989), Confiant uses his autobiography to defend and illustrate the theoretical arguments of Créolité. Since Créolité is in essence a matter of identity, what better space than an autobiography to express one's personal confrontation with questions of identity? I believe that the autobiographer uses and adapts the Western genre of autobiography for a "defense and illustration" of the Creole language and identity.[1] Confiant, during an interview with René de Ceccaty published in *Le Monde*, defines the traumatic relationship that the Martinicans have with the issue of language:

> We, Creole people, in general, have a traumatic relationship with the French language. We are descendants of people who were deprived of their original languages (African) and who were summoned to invent a new language in the hell of slavery. We never accepted Creole as being

ours, the more so since the Master scorned it much, regarded it as "gib-
berish." . . . From the 1930s, when the colonialist ideology was called
into question, when Aimé Césaire developed the idea of *Négritude*,
when one started to dispute the intellectual supremacy of the Western
man, fatally our relationship with the French language was shaken.
We found our veneration of French suspect. We wondered whether the
Creole language did not deserve another look. I was very early on a
militant of the Creole language and culture. The difficulty came from
Creole's orality. Creole was used literarily only in a playful way. The
oldest text in Creole goes back to 1754 (3). As it was forbidden for the
slaves to learn how to read and write, the Masters were, paradoxically,
the first to have written in Creole. Our generation decided to break this
folkloric relationship with the Creole, to cease making it a soft patois, a
language of chirping hummingbirds. (1–2)[2]

The term *illustration* has two meanings: to show or exemplify, and to
make something grand, illustrious. The above defense of Creole is certainly illustrated (exemplified) in *Ravines du devant jour*, where the author quotes Creole sentences abundantly, providing the reader with a
French translation and a glossary at the end. The second meaning of illustration is also operant, since Raphaël Confiant elevates Creole from a
debased language to its place next to the "noble" French language. The
narrator's preference for Creole over French is consistent with this purpose of giving back to Creole its *Lettres de noblesse*. Throughout the book,
Raphaël shows that he is opposed to the adults' insistence that Creole is
the language of sugarcane cutters and not fit for people outside of the
working classes. Confiant uses irony to deconstruct the anti-Creole theories proclaimed by the schoolmistress and his aunt, "tante Emerante," as
young Confiant perceives these theories to be ridiculous. It is therefore
not surprising that, at the end of his autobiography, Confiant sadly re-
grets that the passage of time and life away from the countryside have
killed the Creole language in him: "Le créole, qu'ils nomment avec condescendance 'patois,' va s'enfouir au plus secret de toi, jusqu'à en paraî-
tre effacé à jamais, te causant, sans que tu en aies claire conscience, mille
et une meurtrissures d'âme" (The Creole language, which they conde-
scendingly refer to as "patois," will hide in the most secret part of you,
even appearing forever forgotten, causing you, without your being clearly
aware of it, a thousand and one torments in your soul) (251). The term
Créole refers both to a person and a language in the Caribbean. Confiant
is himself an illustration of the term *Créole:* he is a Creole person—not of
single-race heritage but rather a mixture of different races.

In this chapter, I will also show that the reception of Confiant's autobiography in France was generally positive, owing to the popularity of the Créolité movement, and its reception in Martinique followed in the same footsteps, echoing the positive reviews by French critics and media. Only one critical reaction by a fellow Martinican writer and journalist, Guy Cabort-Masson, reveals the contradiction of the Créolité movement, which claims to write for a Martinican audience but which actually receives literary recognition from metropolitan France, an audience the movement originally intended to distance itself from. The reception of Confiant's autobiography in Martinique contradicts the stated agenda of Créolité—to give the Martinican reader priority. Ultimately, this chapter deals with the cultural rhetoric around Martinican national literature through analysis of the paradoxical transnational reception of an autobiography by one of the champions of Créolité.

Raphaël Confiant was born in Martinique in 1951. Early in his life and career, he wrote exclusively in Creole. These early works, published in Creole, were restricted to only three hundred print copies and therefore had a limited readership. Among his publications in Creole are *Jik dèyè do bondyé* (1978), *Jou Baré* (1981), *Bitako-a* (1985), *Kôd Yanm* (1986), and *Marisosé* (1987). Confiant thought that writing in Creole—a language that developed on sugarcane plantations during the slavery period, the native language that is the closest to people from Martinique—would enable him to truly reach out to his audience of fellow Martinicans.[3] For the defenders of Créolité, this linguistic choice is not a rejection of Négritude, which valorized African history and culture, since Creolists believe that this movement was necessary at its time. They consider the whole evolution from Négritude to La Créolité to be dialectical: viewed from a historical perspective, Glissant's movement *Antillanité* (which stresses embracing the multiplicity of ethnic and cultural elements in the West Indies rather than looking universally toward Africa) serves as an antithesis to Négritude, and in turn La Créolité serves as the synthesis of these two movements. Therefore Créolité's founders, Raphaël Confiant, Patrick Chamoiseau, and Jean Bernabé, are careful not to denigrate Aimé Césaire, their fellow countryman and cofounder of Négritude; instead, they see his efforts as necessary but limited since Césaire was looking to Africa as a mythical source of origins and thus was not rooted in the realities of the Caribbean. "To a totally racist world, self-mutilated by its own colonial surgeries, Aimé Césaire restored mother Africa, matrix Africa, the black civilization. . . . Aimé Césaire had exclusively the formidable privilege of symbolically reopening and closing again the circle in which are clasped two incumbent monsters: Europeanness and Africanness, two forms of exteriority which proceed from two opposed logics" (*In Praise of Creolness*, 79–80).[4] This statement rejects both Africa and Europe as sites of identity construction for Caribbean people, although they uphold Césaire's place in history. Even so, in a pamphlet that Confiant wrote on his own, *Aimé Césaire, une traversée paradoxale du siècle* (1996), Confiant makes a harsh criticism of Césaire's legacy, reproaching him for writing in standard French instead of Creole and blaming him for diverting Martinicans from their own reality by pointing to Africa as their motherland. Confiant even states that Césaire's entire literary production is a repression of Césaire's own Créolité, the same essence that characterizes every Martinican who was raised speaking the Creole language. Rejecting the "Europeanity" and "Africanity" of Négritude, Créolité pleads for an inward-focused vision of the Caribbean grounded in the French Caribbean's realities: "la vision intérieure," reached by writing in Creole.

After writing exclusively in Creole in the 1970s and 1980s, Confiant was persuaded to write in French by his fellow countryman Patrick Chamoiseau, coauthor of *Eloge de la Créolité*. The necessity of reaching a larger audience and marketing his works motivated Confiant to write in French. A prolific writer, he published numerous full-length novels in French with French publishing houses. These works include *Le Nègre et l'Amiral* (1988), *Eau de café* (1991), *Commandeur du sucre* (1994), *L'Allée des soupirs* (1994), *La Vierge du grand retour* (1996), *Le Meurtre du Samedi-Gloria* (1997), *L'Archet du Colonel* (1998), *Régisseur de rhum* (1998), *Le Cahier de romances* (2000), *Brin d'amour* (2001), *Morne-Pichevin* (2002), *Nuée ardente* (2002), *Le Barbare enchanté* (2003), *La Lessive du diable* (2003), *La Panse du chacal* (2004), *Adèle et la pacotilleuse* (2005), and *Case à Chine* (2007). In addition to his impressive production of novels, Raphaël Confiant also wrote texts in a shorter form for the Parisian publishing house Editions des Mille et une nuits: *Bassin des ouragans* (1994); *La Savane des pétrifications* (1995); *La Baignoire de Joséphine* (1997); and *La Dernière java de Mama Josépha* (1999). It is important to point out that Mille et une nuits publishes inexpensive books costing only ten French Francs (approximately US$1.50). All these short novels by Confiant take place in Martinique, and in three of these the narrator-protagonist, Abel, can be seen as an alter ego (or a double) of the author.

Confiant's short novels as well as his autobiography, *Ravines du devant-jour*, are not entirely written in standard French. The autobiography, published in 1993 and awarded the Casa de las Americas award, arrives directly after Confiant's period of writing solely in Creole and after trying his hand at two novels written in French. *Ravines du devant-jour* tells the story of a young Martinican boy, from the time he is five years old to age nine. The boy is distinguished from his fellows by his red hair and lighter skin, characteristics that earn him the Creole nickname "Chabin." Raphaël is a mixture of black, white, and Chinese heritage, and he tells the story of his upbringing in the rural community of Macedoine (in Le Lorrain) where he lives with his paternal grandfather "Papa Loulou" and his numerous aunts. The later chapters show a change of scene as the young Confiant moves to the capital city Fort-de-France to live with his nuclear family. This autobiography is remarkable not only for its usage of the second-person singular pronoun *tu* (you) for the subject, which establishes a distance between the narrator and the character, but also for its humor, its variety in the tone of the numerous anecdoctes, as well as its wordplay that incorporates the different languages of the autobiographer's childhood. Space and time are the main organizers of Confiant's autobiography, as is hinted in the title, *Ravines du devant-jour*: "Ravines" refers to the children's space, a place of enjoyment and experience, while "le devant-jour," a Creole word for the dawn, describes the children's favorite time for outings. The narrator contends that, when he reaches the age of nine, his newfound awareness of time brings his childhood to an end: it is at this critical point that the days of the week bring organized school and religious activities and, consequently, the end of the freedom of his Creole childhood.

The autobiography is based on oppositions: the Creole language versus the French language, the countryside versus the town, and the children's world versus the adults' world. This system of opposites brings a certain balance to the text, as the autobiographer's childhood progresses from the countryside of Macedoine to the city of Fort-de-France, while emphasizing the opposition between Creole and French languages in the two locations. In both the countryside and the town, the opposition between children and adults is made evident in episodes such as the one below, which illustrates the reactions of the adults to the autobiographer's curiosity and relentless questions. The narrator describes how his grandmother, Man Yise, and the maid, Léonise, alternately respond to his inquisitiveness:

When you ask Man Yise why no one ever sees Man Cia's baby, she gives
you a slap as usual. Léonise, for her part, throws a proverb at you: "All
food is good to eat, Chabin, but not all words are good to say." Then
from your great height of six years, you realized that you just broke
this procedural rule, which states that the businesses of older people
are their businesses and that the businesses of the kids remain theirs as
well.[5]

Confiant's *Ravines du devant-jour* was never translated, so my translation is just an attempt. I will leave some passages untranslated because,
as the founders of La Créolité have stated, there is an opacity in the Creole language that should be preserved. Confiant learns that there is an
adult world that is forbidden to him, and that he should watch what he
says and not meddle into adults' matters. This opposition between children and adults continues when the children find a place called "Ravine
Coubaril," a pleasant refuge for the children far away from the adult
world. The same opposition is shown in the memorable chapter "l'Anté-
Christ," where the children, following their leader Sonson, challenge
the adults who are trying to teach them Catholic doctrine.

From the very beginning of his autobiography, Confiant gives the
impression that Creole is the "natural" language for Martinicans, while
French is a foreign language in his community. Creole is the language
that is closest to his family's immediate concerns and realities, which
are dominated by rural activities at his grandparents' place in Macedoine. Confiant shows how the language issue was already familiar to
him at a young age: when he attends school, he and his classmates are
forbidden to use Creole. The schoolmistress tried to convince the light-
skinned narrator that Creole is a language for Negroes—good only for
sugarcane plantations. This prohibition of Creole only provokes the
narrator's aversion to French, which he refers to as "Français-France":

You hate the France-French that [the schoolmistress] wants to force
you to speak and, at the same time, you detest the more diluted French
in use in your family. You do not want to express yourself in any language other than Creole and the schoolmistress declares war on you.
She has a foolproof trap: the first student she catches speaking Creole in the enclosure of our school, is forced to wear around his neck a
rough collar, on the end of which hangs a sort of molar (of a "manicou," the students affirm, meaning, in our Creole language, the opos-
sum of the tropics). (79)[6]

This passage reveals a hierarchy of language, where Creole occupies the lowest rank: "Français-France" is regarded as the most superior, followed by the French spoken in the narrator's family, and then, in last place, Creole. Still, the narrator does not agree with such a hierarchy and will illustrate his disagreement through subversive irony: the young Raphaël, unobserved, catches the schoolteacher speaking Creole while she is having sexual intercourse with his uncle, Parrain Salvie: "This evening, the schoolmistress celebrated her promotion by having herself fucked upright behind a door by uncle Parrain Salvie. Very curiously, she seemed to have forgotten the sacred French language since she howled: 'Ba *mwen dòt! Dòt! Dòt!*' (Give it to me again, my darling! Again! Again!)" (83).[7] The young Raphaël notes her false pretense: the supposedly genteel and cultured teacher, at the height of pleasure, is herself using the forbidden Creole language. In the eyes of the young boy, the theory of the superiority of French over Creole is ridiculously contradicted when in a moment of ecstasy the schoolmistress uses the taboo language that she had been forbidding her students to use.

Prior to the sexual scene, the schoolteacher had already undermined her own credibility as a decorous authority on language when, interacting with the students, she makes her first mistake and winds up betraying the logic of her argument that Creole is a language for only Negroes on plantations. She betrays this argument's logic by actually being able to understand the forbidden Creole language that no "lady of France" should know: "Our schoolmistress is a lady of France, although she is as black as a mortal sin, because she powders her cheeks with pink and wears high heels. We had never suspected that she could understand our Creole until the day when she slapped a student who insulted his neighbor with a resounding '*Bonda manman'w!*' (your mother's bottom!)" (81–82).[8] This scene reveals the schoolteacher's understanding of Creole, and the author contends that from this day on she has lost prestige in the eyes of the students. They never bothered to learn French words that they did not already know, since the equivalents already existed in Creole. Through irony, Confiant shows the reader that Creole is native and natural to the people of Martinique, and that French is the impostor. Confiant ridicules the so-called superiority of French in order to praise the spontaneity of Creole; in doing so, he also derides the adult world and its hypocrisies.

One distinctive feature of Confiant's autobiography, as evidenced by the scene in which the schoolmistress shouts her pleasure in Creole, is that the young Raphaël is a "voyeur," and through his eyes we see decisive moments about the position of the Creole language in relation to

French. His visual act may be seen as a subversion of the hierarchy that posits French as a language superior to Creole, since it is through vision that he catches the contradiction.

The opposition of Creole and French continues through the chapter "Anges dépeignés," which narrates the failure of the white plantation owner De Cassagnac's daughter's wedding. Continuing his subversive strategy, Confiant introduces irony through a conversation the boy overhears: the husband-to-be and his brother speak not in French, as the child expects, but in a patois from France, which sounds to Confiant's ears similar to Creole but different all the same. By quoting the dialogue in relation to its crooked and secret contents, Confiant makes this patois sound funny. The substance of the conversation is that the two brothers had just played a trick on De Cassagnac by stealing his jewelry, and they were about to leave without the groom bothering to marry the plantation owner's daughter. This interchange serves to reinforce the young Confiant's belief that Creole is better than French. He eavesdrops on the conversation from the top of a tree under which the two brothers talk, allowing the boy to hear a different dialect of French. It is ironic that the term "patois," which has been used to denigrate Creole, also refers to their regional dialect of French.

In another decisive moment in the autobiography, Raphaël accompanies his aunt, tante Emérante, on a trip to the town of Grande-Anse where language is an important signifier of status, and he shows the irony in his aunt's recommendation not to speak Creole. During their stay in the town, the sea level suddenly rises one night and threatens to destroy the sleeping town.

> Judging that from now on we are in honorable company, Aunt Emérante prohibits you to use the idiom of sugarcane cutters [Creole] and instead she reads to you from *Intimités* [a Harlequin-like romance in magazine form with photos] every evening, so that you may improve your French vocabulary. . . . She cannot repress a small cat-like shout when she realizes the alarming mass of the sea which is driven in the blackness of the night, as if ready to leap on the town to swallow it. This town is quiet. People are sleeping stiff-and-hard, and even the dogs do not bark. "*Yo pa pou konnèt, fout!*" (And they do not care!) she says in a monologue, both amazed and admiring at the same time, uttering, without realizing it, the Creole language she was ashamed of. (165)[9]

Again, the autobiographer expresses the idea that despite all the repressions they endure, Creole is the first learned language of Caribbean people, which they revert to in emotional situations, showing their natural bond with the language.

The author's conviction that Creole is the language that most appeals to the natural senses of his people is exemplified again when the young Confiant leaves the countryside to spend some time with his paternal family in town. As he arrives, Confiant lets the reader know of his discomfort in speaking Creole in front of his urban immediate family; he is even afraid to speak French for fear he might mispronounce it. Leaving the family sphere that is centered on European values and the French language, young Confiant likes to watch the common people of Martinique in their daily occupations; he even ventures out to the most dangerous neighborhoods of Fort-de-France to hear a different dialect of Creole: "In Terres-Sainvilles, one only hears the hardest Creole, made of unpronounceable words for the mulattos of the downtown area and of interminable swearwords which have the gift to charm you. This is because, in the city too, your close relations did not succeed in persuading you not to hang out with the rejects of humanity" (197).[10] While Confiant's nuclear family is well-to-do, his cousins are among the "mulâtres" to which he refers. Therefore, the autobiography portrays the character of young Raphaël as a reflection of the adult, Raphaël Confiant, champion of Creole identity. It is very significant that Confiant realizes his progressive loss of Creole only when he moves to town to live with his nuclear family. Confiant clearly shows a preference for his grandparents and the countryside over his nuclear family because of the Creole language spoken there; this preference parallels his fondness for Creole over French. In addition, Confiant does not describe his nuclear family, especially his father and mother, as powerfully as he describes his grandparents, Papa Loulou and Man Yise.

Ravines du devant-jour is the story of the repression of the autobiographer's native language, yet Confiant suggests that the realities that are true for the child are not necessarily true for the adult. Confiant emphasizes the difference between himself as a child and as an adult by several means, including the use of the second-person singular pronoun, *tu*, to convey the narration of his autobiography. This usage allows the Confiant to go back to his childhood to "defend and illustrate" Creole, a language that had been repressed in him on multiple levels during his childhood. At the beginning of the final chapter, Confiant expresses regret that his "errance Creole" (Creole wandering) had to end; it was a time of liberty and natural expression: "Childhood for you was finished after your nine years. Finished, the soft Creole wandering among the grandmothers, the godmother, the aunts and their friends, all people of great attitude and burning love! Finished, the crazy root-edness in the language of the Negros which, happily, is not written and with which, therefore, one does not have to exhaust oneself to respect any Spelling Rule!" (243).[11] One perceives in these two sentences Confiant's vision. It is a vision exemplified by his autobiography and his other works: French is the language of oppression and it limits expression, whereas Creole is a native language that allows freedom of creation and expression. This reading of Confiant's autobiography as a return to a happy period of life, the time when Creole was a natural part of him, is consistent with the current environment that the author has constructed for himself, where today he writes his novels. Laurent Sabbah describes Confiant's realm as follows:

> Raphaël Confiant is a Martinican. He lives in a West-Indian hut. The objects of Western modernity are summarized by a fax, a telephone and a television set. Among his wife and children, his typewriter, his books and his goats, it is there that his novels are born. To create, to invent, to remember, he needs his island, its landscapes, its inhabit-ants and its memory. For Confiant, success does not have anything ostentatious, to the point of being almost aggravating! His glance is not turned towards Europe or America, it scans Martinique, his Marti-nique. His framework of life is voluntarily modest. A way, perhaps to show that its richness is elsewhere, one built elsewhere on a language, Creole.[12]

There is a harmony between the autobiographer's working environment and his rejection of bourgeois life as it appears in the autobiography. At the end of the autobiography, the author describes how he progressively lost Creole within himself and how he longed for the rural life he en-joyed with his grandparents in the countryside. The adult writer seems to recreate the conditions of his rural childhood environment as a stim-ulus for creativity, since, as Laurent Sabbah states, the author refuses modernity by preferring the simpler and more rural lifestyle.

Confiant says that his paternal grandmother is half Chinese, and be-cause of the lightness of his skin, he deduces that he has some white blood, as well as some black blood: "Tu sens confusément que le chabin est un être à part. Nègre et pas nègre, blanc et pas blanc à la fois" (You confusedly feel that the "chabin" is a separate being. Black and not black, white and not white at the same time) (42). The narrator's real-ization exactly mirrors the thesis by the authors of *Eloge de la Creolité*, in their attempt to define Creole language and culture: "We are at once

Europe, Africa, and enriched by Asian contributions, we are also Levantine, Indians, as well as pre-Columbian Americans in some respect. Creolness is *'the world diffracted but recomposed,'* a maelstrom of signifieds in a single signifier: a Totality. And we think that it is not time to give a definition of it" (*In Praise of Creolness*, 88; emphasis in the translation).[13] This diversity and complexity illustrates the theory of Créolité, and the following lines from the manifesto actually could be used to describe Confiant's own diverse ethnicity: "The son or daughter of a German and a Haitian, born and living in Peking, will be torn between several languages, several histories, caught in the torrential ambiguity of a mosaic identity. To present creative depth, one must perceive that identity in all its complexity. *He or she will be in the situation of a Creole*" (*In Praise of Creolness*, 112; emphasis in the translation).[14] Still, this illustration of the Creole language can be questioned because Confiant himself has acknowledged Creole's limitation for descriptions. In René de Ceccaty's interview with the author for *Le Monde*, the interviewer asked Confiant if he felt limited in changing from writing exclusively in Creole to writing in French, to which Confiant replied:

> On the contrary! I discover a greater freedom. Creole is a rural language, accustomed to indicate immediate realities. Its conceptual level is very limited. When one is trained to write a novel in an oral and rural language, one faces many difficulties, because a concept must be expressed through periphrases. Freedom, for the Creole writers, paradoxically, is French, because French is a fully formed language with which one can play. When I write in Creole, I cannot play because I am obliged to build a tool. . . . I repeat that writing in French is a pleasure whereas writing in Creole is a toil. I am much more at ease in French description. A peasant does not describe a tree, for example. He lives in complete intimacy with nature. Creole does not have a descriptive level: it lacks adjectives which are necessary to describe a landscape. (4)[15]

Is there a contradiction between Confiant's endeavor to promote the Creole language both theoretically and practically and this confession of its limitations? I think that Confiant is honest, and as a skilled writer, he knows the strengths and weaknesses of both languages. It is no wonder that the occurrences of Creole in *Ravines du devant-jour* are mostly within monologues or dialogues; it appears that Creole is the best option to represent the social reality of Martinique in conversations among local people. This, of course, gives the narrative a local flavor that cannot be rendered in French. In contrast, French is a supple language for descriptions, and it is obvious that most descriptive passages in his autobiography are either in standard French or in local Martinican French. Confiant is well-informed about Creole because he published two dictionaries of the Creole language: *Dictionnaire des titim et sirandanes: Devinettes et jeux de mots du monde Creole* (1998) and *Dictionnaire des néologismes créoles* (2000). Keeping these facts in mind, it could be said that Confiant, in *Ravines du devant-jour*, pleads for a promotion of the Creole language and compromises with the French language, narratively speaking, in order to better represent the world of his childhood. It appears that the authors of *Eloge de la Créolité* want to enrich their writing's artistic qualities by including a combination of Creole and French, thereby expressing the realities of the French Caribbean.

In discussing the stylistic elements of Confiant's text, Pierre Lepape, a French reviewer for *Le Monde*, claims that Confiant uses "Français-banane" in his autobiography: "It is this third language, the *Français-banane*—or more exactly a frenchified version, Westernized by the literary act itself—that Raphaël Confiant in his childhood memories most frequently uses" (3).[16] I believe this to be a misinterpretation of Confiant's stylistic strategy, a method that in fact aims at revalorizing the Creole language while mocking or playing with French. The authors of *Eloge de la Créolité*, including Confiant, were aware of the danger of using degenerate French; they make a point of disassociating themselves with such a usage:

> The French so called "Français-banane," which is to standard French what vulgar Latin is to classical Latin, constitutes undoubtedly what is most stereotypical in interlanguage, and that by which it irresistibly conveys ridicule. . . . As for us, our defense of Creolness will never be that of an idle and parasitic crouching. Now, a whole series of verbal productions can easily, if not carefully watched, turn successfully into epiphytic plants which, moreover, are prone to divert the river-language from its Creole mouth. (*In Praise of Creolness*, 109–10)[17]

Confiant's autobiography is a mixture of standard French, Creole, a regional dialect of French, and so-called français-banane from Martinique. Interestingly enough, it is this regional dialect of French that could be called "patois," and not Creole, that is often given this negative denomination. Confiant himself makes fun of the "français-banane" by reproducing ironically the way it is used by a "nègre-marron," a rival of his uncle Parrain Salvie: "En outre, il (le nègre-marron) abreuve toute personne rencontrée de salutations charmeuses en français-banane.

Du genre: 'Ah! Qu'elle est jolie au jour d'aujourd'hui, oui, la 'tite demoiselle. Elle est comme si dirait la Sainte Vierge Marie, mère de Dieu et moi-même, je trilbiche devant sa belleté, je tombe par terre, oui'" (115; I left this passage untranslated). Is this the type of French that Confiant uses in his autobiography? Obviously, even though the autobiographer's style is to use Creole to represent the Martinican world, he does not fall into using such a type of French, which sounds uneducated. It is true that at times, along with standard French, Confiant uses a different French, but the latter cannot be characterized as "français-banane." Obviously, words such as "accoreur," "belleté," and "décesser" are not standard French, but they derive from Creole and may be intended for the Creole speakers.[18] This could be considered ironic, as the autobiographer prefers to use expressions that are typical of the Martinican French even while a standard French equivalent is available. I think that rather than using "français-banane" (found only in the mouths of people he wants to ridicule), Confiant is using a form of regionalism, a French that is typical to Martinique, and the autobiographer does this by juxtaposing standard French, Martinican French, and Creole, as exemplified by the passage where Man Yise had a premonition of the death of her husband, Papa Loulou:

> Femme de hauts présages, Man Yise ne sourit plus depuis un bon paquet de jours. Elle ne l'interbolise plus, son homme, lorsqu'il oublie de se propreter les pieds en revenant de son jardin. Elle l'appelle "Loulou" et non "Misyé-a" (Monsieur). Elle veille à ce que son tabac soit toujours à portée de main. Quand il fait la sieste, elle nous ordonne d'aller jouer le plus loin possible et ceux qui dérespectent cette injonction reçoivent force coups de balai-coco sur le dos. Papa Loulou n'a rien soupçonné. Il continue à se lever au devant-jour, à seller Avion, son cheval marron si fougueux que le béké de Valminier a voulu l'acheter à maintes reprises contre etcétéra d'argent, et à disparaître dans la campagne Dieu sait où. D'ordinaire, Man Yise ronchonne : "Hon! Nonm-taa, dwé ni an zitata nan kòy. Sa I ka valkandé toupatou fè ki a? (Hon! Ce bougre-là doit avoir un esprit dans le corps sinon pourquoi il cavalcaderait partout de cette façon?) . . . " (21)

Expressions such as "interbolise," "un bon paquet de jours," "se propreter les pieds" "dérespectent," "devant-jour," "béké," and "etcétéra d'argent" are particularities of French as used in Martinique; the Creole quotation is in Martinican dialect or a lexical creation by Confiant as well; all the rest is standard French. It can be said that this mixture of different languages gives Confiant's autobiography a tone that is true to Martinique as he represents the language usages in his society. Moreover, Confiant can be credited for rejuvenating the French language with his wordplay and through the creation of his own neologisms such as "sérieuseté" and "maudition," paralleling the character in his story, his young friend Sonson who was known for his creativity with Creole; René de Ceccatty speaks of "français créolisé" in that regard.

Already in *Eloge de la Créolité*, the authors defend themselves against regionalism; similarly, Chamoiseau encouraged Confiant, who had confined himself to writing only in Creole, to reach out to a broader audience by writing in French. In *Ravines du devant-jour*, the autobiography's multilingualism indicates an appeal to multiple audiences. In *Le Monde*, the French reviewer Pierre Lepape expresses the view that Confiant's autobiography invites the audience (in this case a French audience) only as spectators from a distance:

> Suddenly, here we are ourselves transformed into voyeurs, into amateurs of picturesque, into gatherers of exotic, into collectors of singular expressions, savory dialects and deliciously incongruous speech. We are here tourists in a book which, even so, we feel at every moment delivers more than a bunch of postcards. We admire and we are at the same time ashamed of our pleasure; invited to the table, fed with succulent meals, but nicely excluded from the family of hosts, their allusions, their jokes, of all this life that continues under the ornaments of the festival. (3)[19]

This French reviewer's reaction to the autobiography is very instructive. It states that Confiant wrote primarily for a Martinican audience. At another level, this indicates that Confiant remains true to himself by writing literature for his own people, offering a vision of the world typical of his own people. With all the regional Martinican French and abundant Creole quotations, it is clear that Confiant wanted to address primarily a Martinican audience. However, in the beginning of his autobiography, there is also a reference to a non-Martinican audience when Confiant feels it necessary to explain an expression in French that is typical of Martinique: "Our housing personnel had the habit of uttering with an enigmatic air: 'Papa Loulou est chimérique.' In *our dialect*, this word means abrupt flashes which suddenly cloud the glance of the person who is in the midst of speaking to you about completely pointless things" (19; emphasis mine).[20] Confiant's relationship with the audience here seems to be the opposite of that of Amadou Hampâté Bâ in *Amkoullel*, as the Caribbean autobiographer appears to give precedence to the Martinican-Creole speaking audience over a French audience.

In *Le Pacte autobiographique*, Philippe Lejeune gives a structural definition of autobiography by framing it as a channel of communication between the writer and the reader; the autobiographer has a pact with the reader to ascertain the authenticity of the narrative. Lejeune's definition, which gives a dominant role to the reader, was further developed in *Lecteur et lecture dans l'autobiographie française* by Jaccomard, who insists that identifying the different readers for whom the autobiography was intended could bring autobiography studies to a new level. Jaccomard revives the notion of "horizon of expectation" ("horizon d'attentes" in French) from Hans-Robert Jauss's Reception theory. This horizon of expectation can be determined partly through what structuralists call "paratext," that is, all written information having to do with the text. The search for the traces of a potential readership in the text takes into account the relativity of the author's viewpoint, and the analysis of the potential readership reveals the author's position in relation to the story the readers are asked to believe.[21] In the first chapter, I have examined the horizon of expectation possessed by readers of Bâ's autobiography by using traces in the text and around the text, noting the author's various declarations to his privileged French audience. I also included the reaction of a distinguished African reader, Yambo Ouologuem. I can apply the same procedure to Confiant, because the reaction of *Le Monde*'s reviewer, Pierre Lepape, quoted above, shows that this Frenchman's horizon of expectation was not satisfied as he was expecting standard French in Confiant's autobiography. This helps me infer that Confiant wrote his autobiography with the horizon of expectation of Martinican people foremost in his mind. It does not exclude the possibility that he also wanted to reach a French audience, but this comes second in his order of priorities. His abundant use of Creole expressions and dialogue indicates the priority of a Martinican audience, while the in-text translation of Creole phrases into French and the glossary at the end of the book show that Confiant had a French readership in mind secondarily.

One distinctive feature of Confiant's autobiography is his exclusive use of the second-person singular *tu* to narrate his childhood story. Even though other autobiographers have employed the second-person singular before, its usage is rare, and in Confiant's writing it suggests a different meaning. *Ravines du devant-jour* narrates a return to childhood in order for the mature Confiant to relive his connection with the Creole language, a connection that was severed at the age of nine, when his autobiography ends. The *tu* in Confiant's self-narrative refers to the young Confiant upon whom the critical gaze of the adult is cast. It could therefore be said that the use of the second-person singular *tu* (you), although unconventional, is truer to the definition of autobiography than the first-person singular, *je* (I). Since autobiography consists of a person in the present reflecting on the person they were in the past, the use of *tu* effectively establishes a corresponding distance between two temporally distinct subjects: in this case, the younger and the older Confiant. This distancing between the two different personalities of the same person may be ironic, but it rings true and gives a more objective dimension to the text.

What is remarkable about Confiant's autobiography is the variety of emotional intensity displayed in his anecdotes: tragedy, drama, and comedy all have their place in young Confiant's world.[22] The autobiography opens with a family tragedy, when a warning from the bird of ill omen ("L'oiseau-cohé") precedes the grandfather Papa-Loulou's death ("la prophétie des nuits" [13–27]). In the drama repertoire, there is Leonise's recovery from her long sickness, aided by the skills of Indian healers in the chapter called "Bondieu couli" (94–107). Another dramatic episode is the Western-style duel between Téramène (who was engaged to Raphaël's Aunt Clémence) and a relative, a fight that is started because Téramène's family was said to have dispossessed the Confiant family of a piece of land long before. The scene is dramatic as the two fighters use an old style of combat, and the feared outcome is happily avoided as both of them survive. Not to be neglected is the author's own drama with the Creole language that is systematically repressed in favor of French. Among the most comical stories is one in the chapter "L'Anté-Christ" (84–93), in which the kids play tricks on the adults who are trying to teach them religion. This story could be better called a dramatic comedy because it is surrounded by an atmosphere of death: Sonson, the kids' hero, endeavors to invoke the devil by using a voodoo spell, and he refuses to shower for nine days in order to challenge the priest l'Abbé Stégel. The dramatic but comic standoff between the young man and the clergyman is one of the most memorable scenes of the autobiography. The chapter "Epousailles" (149–58) also falls into the comic and dramatic categories: it describes the trick that Papa Loulou's plays on his daughters' two suitors, substituting his older daughters for the younger ones whom the suitors had intended to marry.

The autobiography also contains a historical element; in the midst of describing innocent childhood, Confiant mentions key historical events in Martinique. "Le temps de l'Amiral Robert" comes as a significant leitmotiv for the autobiographer as it closely precedes his birth. Other historical events that are present in the narrative are the Martinicans' uprising (recounted in the chapter "Communisse, cathéchise et grève") and the distant Algerian war, the violence of which is reflected in Fort-de France at the end of the book when the autobiographer moves in with his nuclear family. These scattered historical accounts add a serious dimension to the innocent tone of the autobiography because of the atmosphere of tragedy and death that surrounds them.

Through the story of his childhood, Confiant portrays himself as an example of Créolité in practice, illustrating the theory presented in *Eloge de la Créolité*. The exemplification is linguistic when the Creole language is side by side with French and is given priority in many instances, especially in the dialogues and regional expressions of key characters from Martinique. Confiant illustrates Creole by giving it grandeur, using it with pride, through his own lexical creativity as he "creolizes" French vocabulary and grammar. Thus the autobiographer reaches what the founders of La Créolité referred to as a "vision intérieure" (internal vision), achieved by using Creole. The autobiography stays personal by revealing that Confiant replays the drama of his childhood: being severed from Creole usage at the age of nine. This return to childhood through autobiography could be considered a revenge on life as well as a defense of Créolité. What is most dramatic at the end of Confiant's autobiography is that, starting at the age of nine, the young Confiant begins his self-contradiction by becoming an ally of the enemy language: he is the best student in his French class. This paradox may explain the author's dilemma with the two languages when he decided to devote himself to writing in his adult life. The exotic dimension of the autobiography for the different groups of readers reinforces its paradox: in 1993 *Ravines du devant-jour* was awarded the Prix du livre "Jet Tours" (a branch of Air France) and was selected by a committee composed of specialists in tourism! There is obviously an exotic side to Confiant's work for a French audience fond of localisms and amused by the autobiographer's play with the French language, and this may be a contradiction as well as a concern that puts the very concept of Créolité at risk.

THE RECEPTION OF CONFIANT'S WORK IN FRANCE

The reception of Confiant's autobiography in France has been positive. His work certainly benefited, in terms of popularity, from its association with the novelty of the literary movement La Créolité. Critics also appreciated the humor in Confiant's autobiography, as well as his linguistic creativity with what has been referred to as the "français créolisé." Pierre Lepape's review of *Ravines du devant-jour* in *Le Monde* (June 18, 1993) is a case in point of the opinion of French journalists and critics toward the new movement of La Créolité. His review of Confiant's autobiography is largely positive, but he also reveals France's ambiguous attitude toward the new movement. In an effort to popularize La Créolité in France, Pierre Lepape urges France to act quickly in support of La Créolité before France is outdistanced by the United States where, he claims, every book from the Caribbean written by a "mixed-racial" author is acclaimed by Americans. Lepape wants France to retain its leadership and influence on literature in Martinique: "Il conviendrait même d'accélérer le mouvement si nous ne voulons pas une fois de plus nous laisser souffler la place par les Etats-Unis. Là-bas actuellement on se jette avec voracité sur tout ce qui s'écrit d'indien, de caribbéen, d'antillais, de 'mélangé' à tel point que des écrivains blancs et blonds se plaignent de discrimination." Lepape's appeal to a more "patriotic" and favorable reception of La Créolité by French authorities is also a call for an extensive readership of its authors in France. Lepape's reading also reveals the "outsider" status of French metropolitan readers of Confiant's *Ravines du devant-jour*, noting that they are made to feel like guests at the dining table where they don't understand the inside jokes like tourists in a foreign linguistic and cultural zone. This uneasy and paradoxical position of the French metropolitan reader, according to Lepape, is a necessary evil because it is indispensable to a regional literature. On that note, Lepape identifies a perfect metropolitan audience for the literature promoted in Confiant's autobiography: French readers who are fond of regional expressions and regionalism. For Lepape, exoticism is a necessary evil when it comes to the reception of Martinican literature in metropolitan France because of the geographical remoteness of the island.

Other reviews by French newspapers are evidence of the positive reception of Confiant's *Ravines du devant-jour* in France; however, I will explore further the content of the French reviews in my discussion of the reception of *Ravines du devant-jour* in Martinique, since most French articles were reproduced in local Martinican newspapers.

RECEPTION IN MARTINIQUE: ECHOS OF FRANCE?

France-Antilles is the daily newspaper in Martinique, while *Antilla, Antilla Magazine, Karibèl,* and *Karibèl Magazine* are weekly publications. They all sporadically include a literary review section alongside the news and political columns. Another periodical, *Le Naïf,* does not offer literary reviews and is thus irrelevant for an analysis of the reception of Confiant's autobiography. It should be noted that Confiant worked as a journalist at both *Antilla* and *Karibèl,* which may result in some positive bias in their reviews of his literary productions. As a whole, the general reception of *Ravines du devant-jour* in Martinique has been positive as it appears through the periodicals. The reception in Martinique shows also some complacency and a lack of critical evaluation of Confiant's autobiography since most of the reviews praise the work and offer little criticism.

A review by Adams Kwateh in the biweekly *France-Antilles Magazine* reveals that Confiant wrote his autobiography at the request of the director of a publishing house (Gallimard). The review, titled "L'Odorat de l'enfance," points out the autobiography's focus on a specific historical period and notes that Confiant seems to address one person using the pronoun *tu* and another group by the use of other pronouns. Kwateh's review tends to focus on the stylistic and thematic elements of Confiant's life story. He neither praises nor criticizes the work; rather, he just summarizes episodes of the autobiography and declares that Confiant strove to conquer the "real." In the same issue of *France-Antilles Magazine,* Marius Gottin interviews Confiant. The introductory comment to the interview mistakenly portrays *Ravines du devant-jour* as a *roman* (novel). In the interview, Confiant speaks about the experience of writing his autobiography and contends that one does not remember one's childhood but rather one reconstructs it. Gottin reproaches Confiant for letting the adult speak in his autobiography rather than the younger Confiant, and Confiant answers that the difficulty has to do with the change of language: when he was a child he spoke Creole, but he is now obliged to describe his childhood not in Creole but in written French. Confiant labels the process of writing his Creole childhood in French as a "translation." He emphasizes that this is also a proof that Creole literature is much closer to Martinican identity than is literature written in French. Of course, with this explanation, one perceives the paradox of Confiant: he is forced to write in French to express a Creole experience. We are well aware that in translating an experience into another language, one loses something, and this is the substance of Confiant's paradox: Creole would have expressed completely what he intended to say, but he has to resort to French because of the limitation of written Creole. In saying this, Confiant is consistent with what he had declared in his interview with René de Ceccaty (quoted earlier in this chapter).

In *Karibèl*, Georges-Henri Léotin reviews Confiant's autobiography in an article entitled "Pour fêter une enfance" (no. 26, July 1993). The reviewer declares that *Ravines du devant-jour* is not a remembrance of the past, but rather a reconstruction of a childhood. The reviewer portrays the act of reconstruction as a bouquet of flowers, noting that other flowers that are missing are parts of the psychologically repressed Self. Léotin notes also that the autobiography has the same setting as some of Confiant's previous novels such as *Eau de café* (1991) and *Le Nègre et l'Amiral* (1988), both of which take place in the 1950s in the countryside of Confiant's native Grande Anse (in Le Lorrain). Yet Léotin warns that the autobiography is not a mere replica of *Eau de café* because *Ravines du devant-jour* is more classical and more reserved than the lyrical earlier novel. He notes that there is a serene tone in the autobiography, which is closer to Saint-John Perse's *Eloges* than Césaire's *Le Cahier*. In making that last statement, Léotin is implying that Confiant's autobiography is truer to Martinican Creole identity than Césaire's epic poem is. Léotin's review, however, reads Confiant's autobiography in contrast to the novel, focusing on the style, but neglecting the difference of genre.

In a September 1993 issue of *Antilla*, there is a report on Confiant receiving the prize Casa de Las Américas for *Ravines du devant-jour* (no. 550, September 10, 1993). Like Léotin, the reviewer, Georges Desportes, reads the autobiography as a déjà vu, claiming that it reminds him of Confiant's novel *Eau de café*. He reproaches Confiant for using a language that is unfit for the children of his generation but appropriate for an adult; he sees this language problem as a challenge that Confiant could not overcome. Writing for a Martinican audience, Desportes praises Confiant's style, which revives childhood memories shared by all Martinicans. Nowhere does Desportes categorize *Ravines du devant-jour* as an autobiography. Still, he notes that the usage of the pronoun *tu* establishes a distance between the younger and the older Confiant, and Desportes states that Confiant's childhood is true to life as it is a childhood as lived by all Martinicans, who are made to rediscover their childhood through Confiant's story. Desportes's positive review of Confiant also supports the commonplace belief that postcolonial autobiographies tend to privilege the community rather than the individual, since for Desportes the autobiography of one person (Confiant) is that of the whole (the Martinicans). The assimilation of a personal autobiography to a collective memory is also an authentication of Confiant's autobiography as truly Martinican.

Besides the local reviews, the Martinican reception is dominated by French critics and journalists whose positive articles are reproduced in both *Antilla* and *Karibèl* as evidence of the enthusiastic reception of *Ravines du devant-jour* in metropolitan France. For example, a review by Gérard Meudal in *Libération* was reprinted in *Antilla*, entitled "Un Enfant Confiant: Ni Nègre ni Blanc, ni métis ni mulâtre: *Ravines du devant-jour* ou l'enfance de Raphaël Confiant, gamin à la fois haï et redouté" (no. 547, July 30, 1993). Meudal reads Confiant's autobiography as evidence of Confiant's awareness of his difference from the other Martinicans: neither black nor white and with a Chinese heritage. He shows how Confiant had to come to terms with his identity as a "Chabin" and how he acted accordingly. Meudal considers Confiant a rebel, going so far as to compare him with Gavroche (the epitome of the Parisian street boy in Victor Hugo's *Les Misérables*). Catechism and French school, which restricted his freedom, become the enemies of Confiant's childhood. Meudal's review, while not totally positive, does not criticize or praise; it is a neutral review of Confiant's autobiography that focuses on the themes and the characters instead of the literary aspect.

François Salvaing wrote a review titled "Une enfance martiniquaise" in *L'Humanité Dimanche*, which was reproduced in *Antilla* with the introductory title "L'Humanité et le dernier Confiant: Le succès de l'auteur du *Nègre et l'Amiral* auprès de la critique française se confirme. A suivre" (no. 545, July 16, 1993). The *Antilla* title announces that Confiant's success among the French critics is being confirmed by their reviews of his autobiography. François Salvaing states that it was a difficult task that Confiant undertook in writing his childhood memories. He notes that Confiant avoided sugarcoating his childhood and made it realistic by alternating sad and happy moments. He also remarks that Confiant attained distance by using the second-person singular to tell the story. In addition, Salvaing points out the anthropological dimension of Confiant's autobiography in informing the French reader about the real Martinique and some of its culture (such as the wake of a deceased person, the carnival, and so on). Salvaing claims that Confiant is not the central character of the autobiography, but rather that language is. He points out the delight of a French reader in learning certain expressions that are peculiar to Martinique. Salvaing ends his review by comparing Confiant to the storyteller Maître Honorien in Patrick Chamoiseau's *Texaco*. Salvain's review is more concerned with the stylistic features of Confiant's autobiography. Salvain is positive in his appreciation of the work, yet in trying to relate the work to a French audience, he emphasizes its cultural and linguistic aspects, which somewhat "exoticizes" Confiant's autobiography.

Antilla reproduces an excerpt of a review in *Le Point* titled "Le Passé murmuré de Raphaël Confiant" (no. 544, July 9, 1993, p. 5). *Antilla*'s introduction to the review reads, "La critique française continue de donner un large écho au dernier livre de R. Confiant. Témoin, cet extrait du *Point* qui situe cette production dans le renouveau de la littérature antillaise." *Antilla* emphasizes the positive reception of Confiant's autobiography by the French critics and in the French press as evidenced by this article from *Le Point*. The reviewer points out the melancholy of Confiant's prose as the most important aspect of his childhood memories. The reviewer is J. P. A. in *Le Point* (no. 1083, June 19, 1993).

Antilla reproduces Pierre Lepape's review of Confiant's autobiography in *Le Monde*, but does not name Lepape as the author of the review (no. 542, July 2, 1993). The introductory note in *Antilla* points out the elegiac reception of Confiant in France as evidenced by *Le Monde*'s review: "Le nouvel ouvrage de Confiant fait l'objet d'un accueil enthousiaste de la part des critiques français comme en témoigne cet article élogieux du journal Le Monde." *Le Monde*'s critic makes the paradoxical statement that Caribbean writers have always written for a metropolitan French audience: "'Depuis les temps de l'antan jusqu'au jour d'aujourd'hui' les écrivains de Martinique, de Guadeloupe et de Tahiti s'adressent, qu'ils le veuillent ou non, aux Français d'en-France. Leurs romans, leurs poèmes, s'inscrivent, exotiques, singuliers, dans les marges de notre patrimoine littéraire national, pas dans celui des populations antillaises." The reviewer points out that *Ravines du devant-jour* shows how untenable the situation of Martinican writers is. Lepape says ironically that Caribbean writers should share their exotic writings with a complacent French readership. He notes that this situation is also unbearable for the metropolitan French audience as well. Lepape also asserts that Confiant does not denounce anything in his autobiography—a claim that, as I have demonstrated, is not entirely accurate because Confiant's autobiography is a subversion of French language and its ideological position vis-à-vis Creole. The reviewer declares that by using *tu* Confiant addresses the (French) reader, but says the reader is quickly evicted from this position. The French reader is put in the position of a "voyeur" and a tourist. Lepape asserts that, in rejecting the *Français-France* and Creole, Confiant uses a third language, *Français-banane,* in his autobiography. He states that metropolitan French readers' misunderstanding due to the language is the price to pay for the success of Confiant's autobiography, and he indicates that French readers who like regional expressions will delight in reading Confiant who is, paradoxically, an antiregionalist. Lepape also shows that there is sadness in the book, namely, the drama of a culture in search of words that pertain to it and that can be shared with the rest of the world. This review is the most thorough and the most critical piece written about Confiant's autobiography; the reviewer warns the French reader of the possibility of not completely understanding the nuances in *Ravines du devant-jour.*

In *Antilla* (no. 526), Guy Epaminondas wrote an article in which he reported that the editor of the collection "Haute Enfance," where Confiant's autobiography was scheduled to be published, felt bewildered at the announcement that Confiant had been selected to receive the prize Casa de Las Américas for his manuscript *Ravines du devant-jour.* Epaminondas's astonishment came from the fact that the manuscript was yet unpublished. Confiant replied in the next issue of *Antilla* (March 12, 1993), saying that, unlike in Europe, the prize Casa de las Américas could be given to an unpublished manuscript, and he justified the fact by saying that Cuba lacked paper due to the U.S. embargo, which delayed the printing of his manuscript into a book. Confiant defends himself from the allegation that the prize was given to him as a favor from the Cuban government. Confiant rebuts it by stating that he has always been opposed to communism and that his opposition puts him out of favor with the Cuban regime. Confiant also said that he refused the US$3,000 that accompanied the prize.

In retrospect, Guy Cabort-Masson's critical reaction to the Créolité movement and to its literary productions merits some attention, even though it was written a year before Confiant's autobiography was published. Cabort-Masson's reaction nevertheless sheds some light on the popular acclaim of any work by the Creolists in France that may deny their works its authenticity and its "national" Martinican originality when the recognition comes from abroad and the foreign occupier. Guy Cabort-Masson (1937–2002) was a public figure in Martinique. An anticolonialist and a Martinican nationalist, he deserted the French army where he was an officer to join Frantz Fanon and the Algerians during the Algerian War for Independence. After the war, he returned to Martinique where he worked with Aimé Césaire and contributed to mass education. Cabort-Masson was also an essayist and wrote many essays on Martinican cultural and political situation including *Les Puissances d'argent en Martinique: l'État français, la caste békée et les autres* (1984) and *Martinique, comportements et mentalité* (1998, winner of Prix Frantz Fanon). He was also a novelist who published *La Mangrove mulâtre* (1986), *La Passion Raziéla* (1987), and *Qui a tué le Béké de Trinité?* (1989). He collaborated as a journalist in two Martinican periodicals: *Antilla* and *Le Naïf*. Finally, Cabort-Masson published an autobiography *Pourrir, ou Martyr un peu* (1986).

Guy Cabort-Masson's reaction to La Créolité and its productions appeared in *Karibèl* (no. 17, May 1992, p. 23). Cabort-Masson's article was reproduced in *Karibèl* under the in-house title "L'attaque (gratuite)" (22–23). In his original article, titled "La Dérive culturelle/Les puissances d'argent à la Martinique," Cabort-Masson attacks Creolité writers for submitting to the French media and to the "money powers" in Martinique, as he refers to it. He contends that the "good taste" and cultural acceptance of Martinique is dictated from Paris through the articles of *Le Figaro* and *Le Point*. He says that this paradoxical situation deprives Martinican readers of the opportunity to form their own opinions about Martinican literary productions because French critics have provided the opinions for them. He also attacks Martinican intellectuals for their uncritical stand as accomplices to such a system of cultural domination. This leads them to parrot the praise of Martinican productions by the Parisian editorial machine and to merely replicate what had already been written by metropolitan French critics. Cabort-Masson says that the new generation of Martinican writers is more prone to media pressures than keeping its dignity when it receives praises from Parisian critics, unlike older writers such as Césaire and Glissant. Cabort-Masson condemns the entire movement of La Créolité for using an exotic-sexist-linguistic trend to make their mark in Francophone productions, thus forfeiting their dignity. He criticizes the hypocrisies of the Créolists who write against white hegemony but are quick to brandish an article from a Parisian critic praising their work; Cabort-Masson contends that one of the weaknesses of La Créolité is that it panders to market considerations.

In the same issue of *Karibèl*, Jean Bernabé offered a retaliation entitled "La riposte (circonstanciée)/Cabort a soif d'une reconnaissance toujours refusée." Bernabé, one of the leaders of La Créolité, answers by attacking Cabort-Masson on the subject of his childhood as they are both from St-Joseph in northwestern Martinique. He portrays Cabort-Masson as someone whose expectations have failed and who is bitter; the attack is more personal and more biographical. Bernabé claims that Cabort-Masson is frustrated to have been outdistanced by his younger Martinican counterparts in three domains: nationalism, Creole, and literature. Another rebuttal by Confiant in the form of an open letter follows. He also accuses Cabort-Masson of writing in bad faith, claiming that Cabort-Masson (with whom he collaborated at *Antilla*) once sought help from him when he wanted to publish his novel *Grazièla* in France. Cabbort-Masson's novel, despite Confiant's recommendation, was rejected. Confiant goes on to show that the accusation of mercantilism applies better to Cabort-Masson himself than Confiant because the former had himself published a book by an obscure publishing press and sold it in Martinique at a higher price. Confiant ends his open letter by threatening to publish three indicting documents that show how he helped the older writer if Cabort-Masson does not stop his attack on the Créolité movement (*Karibèl* no. 17, May 1992, pp. 26–27). We see engaged cultural rhetoric around Créolité: Cabort-Masson considers Créolité as servitude and a false revolt courting the French readers' recognition, whereas the Creolists attack him for jealousy and bitterness at having failed where they have succeeded.

CONCLUSION: THE MARTINICAN READER AS STRANGER

The positive reception of Confiant's autobiography in Martinique was a "newspaper success" strategically orchestrated by the leaders of La Créolité, who were all working in major Martinican newspapers (*Antilla* and *Karibèl*) in order to control public opinion of their books. There is definitely a bias in the reception of Confiant's *Ravines du devant-jour* in both *Antilla* and *Karibèl*. The other newspapers that could have brought a dissenting voice, the daily *France-Antilles* or the biweekly *France-Antilles Magazine,* followed in the trend of "uncritiquing" the writings by authors of La Créolité. Although I do not entirely agree with Cabort-Masson, I believe he is right in claiming that the Créolité movement was in search of a paradoxical kind of recognition from metropolitan France. The numerous articles by French critics that are reproduced in both *Antilla* and *Karibèl* show that Martinican Creolist writers—including Confiant—wanted recognition from French journalists and critics. Perhaps the Creolists assumed that there were not enough credible critics in Martinique to review Martinicans' productions accurately. However, it is also true that the Créolité movement was more in search of sensational recognition than fair criticism from Martinicans, especially a few years after the movement's creation. By echoing the positive reception of *Ravines du devant-jour* in France, both newspapers run by Raphaël Confiant and his group also control Martinican public opinion about their productions. The reception of Confiant's autobiography exemplifies the paradoxical situation of La Créolité and the political and cultural rhetoric about "national" literature in a postcolonial situation. At best, this situation reveals that Martinique is, in actuality, in a colonial relationship to France, from which it begs for recognition, whereas its manifesto *Eloge de la Créolité* aimed at writing for a Martinican audience so that their works would be recognized locally. Therefore, the missing link in the reception of Confiant's autobiography is the reaction of the actual Martinican reader. No actual reaction of the lay Martinican reader was reproduced in local newspapers apart from biased Martinican journalists' reviews. The study of the reception of Confiant's *Ravines du devant-jour* reveals the failure of the Créolité movement to fulfill its claim to cater to a Martinican audience in its search for an authentic Martinican literature rooted in the language and realities of the island. Ultimately, the Martinican reader is a stranger in the house of the reception of Confiant's autobiography.

Maryse Condé

Autobiographical Space and
Lukewarm Reception

Maryse Condé is a prolific writer, known for her fictional works, but known also for being at odds with critics, one of whom has called her "the recalcitrant" daughter of Africa.[1] Yet Maryse Condé is much more: in addition to being a Guadeloupean, she has attained international fame and is known as a globetrotter, a cosmopolitan writer who has made the questioning of identity a fundamental part of her fictional creations. In this chapter I explore the "autobiographical space" of Maryse Condé in three of her texts—*Heremakhonon* (1976), *La Vie scélérate* (1987), and *Le Coeur à rire et à pleurer* (1999)—focusing on the limits between fiction and self-representation. I also show that Condé's autobiography was neglected in France and in Guadeloupe, and only became popular once it was adapted for the stage. In addition, I analyze the American reception of the translated version of the autobiography, which was intended for an academic rather than popular audience.

Maryse Condé's first novel, *Heremakhonon*, raised much criticism for its depiction of certain Caribbean realities and for its controversial central character, Véronica, whom many critics have read as Condé's alter ego. After some denials and corrections by the author, it appears that her relatively recent work, *Le Coeur à rire et à pleurer*—her only acknowledged autobiography—sheds some light on the similarities between Véronica and Condé. The autobiographical space of Condé, or the rewriting of her Self through personal characters, can also be expanded to include one of the characters of *La Vie scélérate*: Thécla, in whom some critics have also detected a resemblance to the author. By analyzing these earlier fictional characters in light of the more recent information from Condé's acknowledged life story, it can be said that the two novels contribute to Condé's autobiographical space—despite the author's protests to the contrary.

Heremakhonon is the story of a young Caribbean woman, Véronica Mercier, who travels to postcolonial Africa to find her peace of mind by connecting with her African ancestry. Once there, she experiences political and personal chaos, and eventually she decides to go back to Paris, where she had been living before her departure for Africa. Véronica is very determined in her search for her identity, to the point of neglecting the sociopolitical reality of her immediate environment. She throws herself into the arms of Ibrahima Sory, the African prince, who she believes will reconcile her with her identity. She navigates between the present and the past, between Africa and her childhood in the Caribbean. She is torn between two realities, each of which she rejects, neither of which she can call "home."

In 1999, Condé received the Prix Marguerite Yourcenar, awarded to a French-speaking writer living in the United States, for *Le Coeur à rire et à pleurer*. This autobiography chronicles the coming of age of a young Guadeloupean girl who was the last child of elderly parents. With the intuition that her birth was unexpected and the impression that her parents were using a façade to keep a certain social status, the young Maryse grows up questioning her family, the multiracial world surrounding her in Guadeloupe, and also her family's frequent stays in Paris, sometimes with a critical tone. Her brother, Sandrino, provides her with answers on taboo subjects, and as Maryse reaches her late adolescent years, she rebels against her mother's authority. Nevertheless, toward the end of the autobiography, as she gains independence in Paris, distance makes her realize that she misses her mother, whom she will never see again.

The autobiography opens with a portrait of Condé's family, follows with her birth, and ends with the autobiographer in her later adolescent years in Paris, where she continues her higher education. The manner in which the autobiographer describes her parents and relates to them is noteworthy. From the beginning, in the first chapter, Condé's parents are labeled by her brother Sandrino as a pair of "alienated souls" ("Papa et maman sont une paire d'aliénés" [14]). The word "alienated" seems to structure the autobiography, since from the first chapter this sense of alienation puzzles the young Condé, and as the narrative unfolds, she herself describes to the reader how her parents are alienating themselves by putting on airs and separating themselves from the "common" Creole-speaking Guadeloupeans. The quest for identity, a theme throughout the autobiography, will lead Condé to try to be different from her parents, to escape from their alienation. Confined to a bourgeois world where Creole is prohibited and French is the standard, Condé will later wish for a less restrictive life, even wishing that she had a "normal family":

> Because of my parents' paranoia, my childhood was lived in a constant state of anxiety. I would have given anything to be the daughter of ordinary, anonymous folks. I got the impression that the members of my family were exposed to a volcano whose burning lava threatened to engulf them at any moment. I hid these feelings as best as I could behind a mask of make-belief and turbulence, but they nevertheless kept gnawing at me. (54)[2]

Paradoxically, when Condé was asked about her childhood in *Entretiens avec Maryse Condé* (1993), an interview with Françoise Pfaff that was conducted years prior to the publication of the autobiography, she declared that her early years were not all that interesting. *Le Coeur à rire et à pleurer*, however, confirms the opposite: it reveals interesting information about Condé's internal struggle for identity and also about the relationship between Condé and her mother. It appears that Condé wrote her acknowledged autobiography in part to make amends with her mother, Jeanne Quidal-Boucolon, with whom she had a complex relationship.

Condé also wrote *Le Coeur à rire et à pleurer* as a means to make amends with the literary world, with which she was at odds ever since her first novel, *Heremakhonon*, was criticized for its political incorrectness in the context of the 1970s, especially in the leftist circles in France and in Africa. The work was not well received in literary circles for its portrayal of a "negative" protagonist, Véronica, and for its critical representation of and relationship with postcolonial Africa. It is thus understandable that Condé tried to dissociate herself from the negative protagonist Véronica during subsequent interviews.[3]

In *Le Coeur à rire et à pleurer*, Condé devotes her autobiography to her childhood, a period that was instrumental to the formation of her personality. Her parents' alienation was already evident in *Heremakhonon*, as Véronica, an alter ego of Condé, is very critical of her parents, who thought that they were better than any black or mulatto in

Guadeloupe because of their education and bourgeois status: "And yet I was ashamed. Ashamed of this desire that my whole education claimed to demolish. We have nothing to envy [the mulattos], I was repeatedly told. Nothing? Then why imitate them up to a certain point?" (123–24). Critics have rightfully claimed a resemblance between Véronica and Condé, which is obvious at times, especially insofar as the family portraits and narratives that Véronica recalls as part of her childhood in Guadeloupe are confirmed two decades later in *Le Coeur à rire et à pleurer*. In her autobiography, Condé portrays her family as members of the black bourgeoisie who render her childhood and subsequent quest for identity very difficult—a leitmotiv that had already structured *Heremakhonon*. The fact that *Le Coeur à rire et à pleurer* was dedicated to her mother shows that Condé wanted to honor her memory, in spite of the fact that their relationship was often conflictive, as the autobiography reveals.

Despite the simplicity of her self-narrative, Condé's writing demonstrates that she is aware of the field of autobiography both at the theoretical and practical levels. In fact, Condé's style is marked by rhetorical sophistication. To answer the question "How do I tell the story of my life?" she uses a familiar literary genre—the tale—only to subvert it by playing on the ambiguity of the word "contes" and by privileging its less serious meaning. The autobiographer is therefore confronted with the theoretical question of the opposition between fiction and reality. The autobiographer makes portraits and tells stories of family members and people that influenced her life, while revealing the uneasiness of growing up in a black bourgeois family in the Caribbean community where language, race, and identity are serious and interrelated issues.

In *Le Pacte autobiographique*, Lejeune notes that prolific writers such as François Mauriac and André Gide promoted their novels rather than their autobiographical works, but according to Lejeune, this is only in appearance because, in actuality, such writers want the reader to see their novels as a continuation of their life stories or of certain social realities, thereby giving the impression that the novel is truer than autobiography in the description of social facts. Lejeune coined the term "l'espace autobiographique" to refer to this phenomenon. He refers to it in *Le Pacte autobiographique* on two occasions: "En effet: au moment même où *en apparence* Gide et Mauriac rabaissent le genre autobiographique et glorifient le roman, ils font *en réalité* bien autre chose qu'un parallèle scolaire plus ou moins contestable: ils désignent l'espace

autobiographique dans lequel ils désirent qu'on lise l'ensemble de leur
œuvre" (41; Lejeune's emphasis).

And again:

> D'un côté, toute sa vie (Gide) et son oeuvre semblent tendues vers la
> construction et la production d'une *image* de soi. Il ne s'agit pas là de
> ce qu'on appelle banalement une "inspiration autobiographique," mais
> d'une stratégie visant à constituer la personnalité à travers les jeux les
> plus divers de l'écriture. Sans doute faudrait-il forger un mot nou-
> veau pour distinguer cette attitude générale en face de l'écriture, de ce
> qu'il est convenu d'appeler *stricto sensu* "autobiographie," c'est-à-dire
> le récit rétrospectif de la génèse de la personnalité assumé par l'auteur
> lui-même. Quand ce jeu de textes comprend aussi un récit autobiogra-
> phique *stricto sensu*, j'ai choisi de le désigner par l'expression "espace
> autobiographique." (165; Lejeune's emphasis)

Critics have pointed out the resemblance of certain heroines in Condé's
fictions to the author herself—similarities that Condé sometimes denies. In the specific case of the controversial *Heremakhonon*, Condé acknowledges that there are some autobiographical aspects of the novel,
but she refuses to label the work as "autobiographical" or to allow that
the main character, Véronica, be equated with herself. This is essentially what Condé tells Françoise Pfaff in *Conversations with Maryse
Condé*:

MC: People have said, "deep down she is alienated, she must have
     sold out to the reactionaries" and so forth. *Heremakhonon*
     was not fictionalized autobiography at all. It was a novel of
     protest.

FP: But it does include some autobiographical elements.

MC: The whole section on childhood and the family milieu is true
     to life. These are things you don't invent. Also autobiographi-
     cal is the portrayal of West Indian society in terms of the
     important Blacks, the ones who see themselves as a high-
     class Black bourgeoisie but who are, on the whole, terribly
     alienated. . . . This whole section is truly autobiographical,
     whereas the rest of the novel contains little autobiographical
     material—the strike, Birame III's disappearance, the charac-
     ter named Saliou whom I knew and who died in jail. I never
     met Ibrahima Sory, the minister; truly a pity. . . . I first wrote
     Heremakhonon entirely in the third person. But when I read it
     over, something didn't click. I had not succeeded in giving it

the impact I wanted it to have. It was both a forged confession and false evidence. So I rewrote it entirely in the first person. I think this proves Véronica is not me. (Or is it the other way around?) But it would also be wrong to assert that she is not me at all. (40–41)

These ambiguous statements were made in 1993, six years before the publication of her acknowledged autobiography, which sheds new light on the autobiographical nature of Condé's first novel.

Many incidents described in *Heremakhonon* (1976) are present in *Le Coeur à rire et à pleurer* (1999), sometimes using the same words that were used in the novel, especially the sections of *Heremakhonon* that refer to life in the Caribbean. Such is the section where Véronica recalls how, as a child, they used to make fun of a distant relative who displayed peasant manners while eating. This relative, named Séraphin, is distinctly identified in the chapter of the autobiography entitled "Gros plan":

> The only relation my mother kept in regular touch with was one of her cousins from Marie-Galante. Twenty years her junior he went by the heavenly name of Séraphin. He was a hefty, taciturn, and awkward boy who reeked his rustic origins. When he spoke, his French sounded like Creole and he got his genders and possessive adjectives wrong. . . . This dutiful boy was the laughing stock of my brothers and sisters. During Sunday lunch whenever my mother offered him a second helping he would never fail to reply with a polite shake of the head: "Thank you, Cousin Jeanne, I've eaten my fill!" (*Tales from the Heart*, 95)[4]

Heremakhonon contains a passage that is remarkably similar: "We had a cousin, though. Cousin Séraphin. Sometimes he used to come for Sunday lunch with his wife, cousin Charlotte. At the end of the meal he used to say: 'Thank you, cousin Marthe. I've eaten my fill'"[5] (13). In addition, Condé uses the same techniques of characterization in describing her own parents in *Le Coeur à rire et à pleurer* as members of the black bourgeois who put on airs in order to pretend that they are superior to the commoners, as she did in describing Véronica's parents in *Heremakhonon*.

The internal monologue that characterizes *Heremakhonon* shows the portrait of a person dear to the protagonist: Mabo Julie. The name is the same in both books, and an entire chapter is devoted to the character of the faithful and affectionate nanny in the autobiography. Mabo Julie is described as a surrogate mother to the autobiographer as well as to Véronica; in both cases, Mabo Julie understands the young girl better than her natural mother does. A comparison of the role of Mabo Julie in the two books is startling. In the Caribbean reminiscences that crisscross *Heremakhonon*, Mabo Julie appears as an island of happiness in a sea of sadness and turmoil:

> Our house was one of the prettiest in town. It had a balcony, high windows, and bougainvillea on the balcony. My nurse was called Mabo Julie; she used to wear starched petticoats under her dress. She loved me. She would always stand up for me and gave me great slices of angel cake in the kitchen. And cups of chodo. Unfortunately, she died when I was sixteen. That same year I was initiated to love and death. (34)[6]

In chapter six of *Le Coeur à rire et à pleurer*, entitled "Mabo Julie," Condé talks fondly about the love that she received from Mabo Julie and gives a heartbreaking account of her horrible death.

> *Mabo* Julie was the maid who had cradled me in her arms and walked me round the Place de la Victoire to be admired by those who had eyes to admire my silk, tulle, and lace blouses. She had helped me learn to walk, picked me up and comforted me whenever I fell. . . . As for me, I loved her like my own mother who, I knew, was jealous. (*Tales from the Heart*, 46; emphasis in the translation)[7]

Clearly, the autobiography reveals that *Heremakhonon* reflects the author's own experience in Guinea and Guadeloupe, a fact that conflicts with Condé's attempts to dissociate herself from the protagonist Véronica. In all her works there are many resemblances between the author and her characters, who share with her nomadism, the quest for identity, and an ironic perspective on life.

Blurring of boundaries between fiction and reality can also be seen when comparing Condé's descriptions of her own parents and her characterizations of Véronica's parents. Both the autobiography and *Heremakhonon* use a depiction of a similar event, a holiday trip, to demonstrate the bourgeois striving for social status. In *Heremakhonon*, Condé describes Véronica's parents' failed attempts at social climbing among the mulatto community in Saint Claude:

> They were looking for an excuse to parade at Saint-Claude, the mulatto stronghold where the blacks used to walk on tiptoe, the Bakra having fled higher up. So we had our holiday at Saint Claude. We rented a villa from some hard-up mulattoes who had bakery and patisserie at Trois

Rivières where they now lived. And believe me it was total anonymity. Eighty miles from La Pointe where his name carried so much weight, the Mandingo marabout was a complete unknown. . . . We were not intruders at Saint Claude. We simply did not exist. (122)[8]

In her autobiography, Condé describes a nearly identical holiday, where her parents' hopes of increased social status were dashed:

According to the rigid social geography at that time the region of Trois Rivières, Gourbeyre and Basse-Terre belonged to the mulattos. Saint Claude and Matouba were the realm of the white Creoles who vied for it with the Indians. My parents' place, however, was on Grande Terre. . . . However much my parents drove around in their Citroën C4, however often my mother wrapped her neck ostentatiously in her golden choker and my father swaggered around with his Legion of Honor ribbon that had such an effect in La Pointe, nobody paid us any attention. (*Tales from the Heart*, 117)[9]

Condé's other novel, *La Vie scélérate*, also has some autobiographical aspects that can be corroborated through comparison with Condé's life narrative. In particular, the novel's character Thécla, the rebellious daughter of a black bourgeois family whose life is dominated by inconsistency and who travels among various continents, shares many similarities with Condé. In an interview with Condé entitled "Child Abuse or Conflict of Interest?: Maryse Condé's Autobiographical Writings," Hal Wylie also notes the correlation between Condé and some of her characters. When Wylie expresses his suspicions "that the character Thécla in the novel *Vie scélérate* . . . was an autobiographical projection on unexpressed aspects of her inner self," Condé replied:

[Thécla] is a very autobiographical character, belonging to the same generation as I do, wanting to write a highly political novel and incapable of doing that, at the same time being divided between her ambitions, ideas and life, and ending up marrying a white man, as I did, and not being able to come to terms with that. . . . I wanted to pass a judgment on her. There's a sort of negativity in her that's not in the others. I wanted to judge her and judge myself at the same time . . . or maybe I was Thécla at the time and I became someone else. . . . She remained Thécla and I changed. (292–93)

Wylie concludes by stating that the character of Thécla was written at a pivotal moment in Condé's life, and he assumes that Thécla may have facilitated the autobiographer's transition from Africa and Europe back to the Americas. As a matter of fact, like Condé, Thécla appears as an independent woman who lives her life among various continents. As in the case of Gide and Mauriac, Condé's novels are another way of projecting the Self, a way of expressing through "fictional" characters her own successes, ideas, and disillusions. Even though, as Condé states, Thécla is not totally her and she is not totally Thécla (much as she said that Véronica is not her and she is not Véronica), she seems to agree with Gide's and Mauriac's vision that the novel is sometimes truer than autobiography (life), since under the disguise of fiction, an author can have more freedom to express certain ideas and visions. The same idea is also shared by James Arnold in his article "The Novelist as Critic," in which he portrays *La Vie scélérate* as the novel in which Maryse Condé moved closer to her Caribbean home. Arnold contends that the novel, which Condé herself has described as a fictionalized saga of her own family, is different from her previous novels concerned with the exploration of race and cultural identity (715). This seems to be typical, as autobiography is about the story of the development of a personality and each author creates a personal myth of her/his character.

In *Je est un autre*, Philippe Lejeune sees the interview (written, oral, or televised) as a continuation of a written autobiography. Yet, in the case of Condé, *Le Coeur à rire et à pleurer* arrived after the interview with Pfaff in which she made some autobiographical statements; subsequent interviews also featured autobiographical content. In a filmed interview from 2003 entitled *Maryse Condé Speaks from the Heart*, Condé confides to the interviewer Susann Wilcox that *La Vie scélérate* is only apparently a novel about family and return to origins—it is also a reflection on writing; the novel is simple, yet complex. Condé is against the categorization of literature, claiming that borders are restrictive. For her, literature is a search for the writer's own voice. In that respect, it could be added that Maryse Condé, in search of her own voice, has battled against any restriction of her creative abilities even if it implied borrowing from her own childhood memories and her experience in Guinea to write her first novel. Condé's autobiographical space is continued in her interview with Susan Wilcox, where she opened her heart to the interviewer and talked about her mother, her childhood, and the act of writing. Having achieved international fame and having battled against critics who wanted to restrict her work to autobiography, implying that they suspect a limitation of creativity and imagination in her works, Condé has proved that it is possible to blend genres and express her creativity. As she confides to Wilcox, she believes that any categorization of genres is restrictive for the artist. Even prior to the interview with Wilcox, in the "Avant-propos" (foreword) of *En Attendant le Bonheur* (a retitled and slightly reworked edition of *Heremakhonon* published by Robert Laffont in 1997), Condé declared against the critics of *Heremakhonon*: "D'aucuns voient, dans une réflexion lucide et désenchantée, une tentative de glorification. D'autres, dans un récit familial, un roman à clef. Ils croient se reconnaître ainsi que certains de leurs proches et crient à la trahison. Quand cela serait, reprocher à un écrivain de trahir le reel est un non-sens. Car pour lui il n'y a de réel que l'imaginaire" (15). The foreword is dated 1988 but appeared in the Robert Laffont edition of 1997. *Le Coeur à rire et à pleurer* is also the story of an identity quest, an escape from the alienation of her parents. Because this quest is replicated in some of Condé's fictional works, there is an overlap between the author's life and her literary productions: in other words, her autobiographical space. Condé's use of many protagonists to write herself and her shifts between denial and recognition of autobiography are traits of the nomadic writer in search of creative freedom.

CONDÉ'S RECEPTION IN FRANCE: BETWEEN THE OFFICIAL AND THE POPULAR

In 1999, Condé received the Prix Marguerite Yourcenar, an honor given by French authorities to a work written by a Francophone author living in the United States; and while this suggests that *Le Coeur à rire et à pleurer* was well regarded by French officials, it says very little about the reception of Condé's autobiography in France. The prize was announced in *Le Monde* in its section "Monde des livres" on November 5, 1999. Strangely enough, *Le Monde* did not produce a review of Condé's autobiography. However, upon publication, *Le Coeur à rire et à pleurer* was reviewed in another newspaper, *Le Temps*.[10] The reviewer (who is not identified) wrote a positive review of Condé's autobiography by portraying it as a way for the autobiographer to return to her childhood in order to make sense of the adult she has become. In its December 30, 1998, edition, *Le Figaro* listed Condé's autobiography among those impending publications that would be scrutinized by critics. Yet the French press did not produce any serious critical review of Condé's *Le Coeur à rire et à pleurer*. While *Le Coeur à rire et à pleurer* did not receive in-depth coverage from France's major newspapers, Condé's autobiography did garner media attention when it was adapted for the stage.

ON STAGE: MAKING THE AUTOBIOGRAPHY POPULAR

The adaptation of a prose work for the stage may indicate that the work is already popular or suggest that the adaptation is designed to increase the work's popularity, and the stage versions of Maryse Condé's autobiography seem to fall into this latter category. As with Hampâté Bâ's memoir, which was reworked for the stage, the dramatic performance of an autobiographical work contributes to its popularity. According to an article from the June 2, 1999, edition of *Le Figaro*, a theatrical reading of Condé's *Le Coeur à rire et à pleurer* was performed in France. In the paper's theatrical section, it was announced that Martine Pascal and Martine Maximin would perform a dramatic reading of *Le Coeur à rire et à pleurer* on June 22, 1999, just a few months after its publication. This information was also reported on the Web site Fluctuat.net, which confirms that a dramatic reading of *Le Coeur à rire et à pleurer* by Martine Pascal and Martine Maximin took place at the Théâtre Artistic Athevains on June 22, 1999.[11] According to an article posted on the Web site Gens de la Caraïbe, Condé's autobiography was to be put on stage again at the Musée Dapper and Le Théâtre du Grand Large by Alain Courivaud, with a reading by Martine Maximin and music by Antoine Bory. The performance was scheduled to run from May 3 to May 24, 2004. The reviewer (GDC) writes, "Les souvenirs de jeunesse se racontent avec émotion, mais aussi avec humour et dérision: la découverte de soi dans une difficile rencontre des Antilles et de la Métropole" (Childhood memories are told not only with emotion but also with humor and sarcasm: self-discovery in a difficult confrontation between the Caribbean and the Metropolis). The dramatic reading focuses on the emotional and humorous parts of Condé's autobiography, emphasizing her struggles to comprehend the clash between the Caribbean and metropolitan France as she experienced it on French soil. Almost the same information was repeated in *L'Humanité*, which announced that Alain Courivaud adapted *Le Coeur à rire et à pleurer* for the stage and that the play was performed at the Théâtre du Grand Large on May 22 and 24, 2004. The reviewer points out that Condé's discovery of the conflictive relationship between metropolitan France and her Caribbean colonies is seen through the eyes of the young Condé, who is also puzzled by the paradox of the Caribbean bourgeoisie who attempt to force their way into French culture (*L'Humanité* of May 22, 2004, p. 42; under the rubric "Culture"). Maryse Condé herself uses her autobiography to reassess historical events as they relate to the Caribbean: thus in

L'Humanité of May 10, 2006, Condé quotes part of her autobiography as an example to explain how the issue of slavery has been deeply silenced in the contemporary Caribbean isles. She declares she is happy to have taken part in the Committee for the Commemoration of Slavery. She refers to the part of her autobiography where she came to be aware of race issues and exploitation. In this chapter, entitled "Leçon d'histoire," Condé recounts how as a child, during a walk with her parents, a passing white girl took advantage of her. To the young Condé, who was unaware of the history of her people, this is an opportunity to understand why two little girls would reenact race and power relationships as if master and slave. After being mistreated by the white girl, when Condé asks her why she is dealing with her in such manner, the genuine response from the girl is: "Je dois te donner des coups parce que tu es une Négresse" (42). The lesson that Condé learns from this painful experience is that racial intolerance is a learned behavior: prejudice is taught.

The relatively lukewarm reception of Condé's autobiography in France could be explained by the fact that, although she has a literary presence in France, Condé does not live there. Moreover, her autobiography may have been considered too personal, and her discussion of serious family drama and race matters may have been deemed too serious for a wider audience. In contrast, the two leaders of Créolité, Confiant and Chamoiseau, presented their respective childhoods in a more playful and humorous fashion, therefore making their autobiographies more enjoyable to read. Of course, the popularity of the Créolité movement helped Chamoiseau and Confiant. Maryse Condé, who had never associated herself with the movement, wrote a deeply personal autobiography in order both to settle accounts with herself and the literary world and to pay tribute to her mother. Indeed, the English title of the autobiography, *Tales from the Heart*, does not quite capture the meaning of the French "Le Coeur à rire et à pleurer," which could be also translated as "my heart torn between laughter and tears." In recounting her bitter childhood in a complex family, Condé does make amends with herself, but the story is devoid of the humor that might have helped to make it appealing to a French audience. Perhaps the dramatic performances of the autobiography were a way to mitigate the serious tone of Condé's autobiography and to make it more palatable to the public.

RECEPTION IN THE UNITED STATES BY WAY OF
TRANSLATION: AIMING AT THE SCHOLARS

Because of Maryse Condé's stature as a university professor in the United States and as an established Francophone writer whose many novels
were already translated into English, a study of the American reception
of her translated autobiography is appropriate. Maryse Condé's husband, Richard Philcox, translated her autobiography as *Tales from the
Heart: True Stories from My Childhood* in 2001 (reedited in 2004). Prior
to this translation, a review in *The Boston Globe* (November 28, 1999) by
Robert Taylor had announced that Condé had received the Prix Marguerite Yourcenar for *Le Coeur à rire et à pleurer*. With the arrival of the
English translation, Condé's autobiography then was made available to
the American audience. A review of the English version of the autobiography was printed in *The Washington Post* on October 24, 2001; it
was a positive review, highlighting Condé's detailed portraits of familial relationships. Yet, as is usual in the English-speaking world, the reviewer, Michael Upchurch, wrongly categorizes Condé's *Tales from the
Heart* as a memoir rather than an autobiography. Also, in its September
9, 2001, edition, *The Washington Post* listed *Tales from the Heart* as part
of "equally celebrated lives." Dolores and Roger Flaherty published a review of Condé's autobiography in the February 1, 2004, edition of *Chicago Sun-Times*. That review is essentially a summary of *Tales from the
Heart*, and the reviewers mistakenly claim that "Condé [is] largely unknown in this country because she writes in France," omitting the fact
that nearly all of her novels were translated by her husband and made
available to an American readership. What one could infer here from
the reviewers' comment is that while Condé is not a popular author in
America, she is nevertheless acclaimed in the scholarly world where her
books are read and included in course syllabi. Translation has played a
big part in Condé's positive reception in America, although that audience is more scholarly than popular. The 2004 reedition of *Tales from
the Heart* is another sign that the book was selling well and had a positive reception in the United States.

Yet, as her weekly journal for the French newspaper *Libération* in
November 2000 reveals, Condé is not entirely comfortable with translations of her own work. In this journal, Condé's opinion of the English versions of her books, translated by her husband Richard Philcox,
reveals her discomfort, her sense that the translated book no longer
reflects her.

> Richard is also my translator: he is afflicted by my indifference. I have
> no longer any interest in my books translated into English. At the time
> of their publication, Richard is alone to watch for the New York Times
> and the Village Voice. I do not doubt his talents and neither do I ap-
> ply to him the proverb "Traduttore, traditore." Simply, I do not find
> MYSELF in those translations. Words, it is well known, are used not
> only to create signification. They also play, they make love. They com-
> pose music. I am not sensitive to the music of a translated text, created
> with foreign sounds, therefore different, independent of my choice. (6;
> Condé's emphasis)[12]

Condé's lukewarm reaction to the translations of her books shows that she does not take pride in them, but sees them as a necessary evil to promote herself and her work.

Le Coeur à rire et à pleurer allows an intertextual reading of Maryse Condé "in reverse" through her literary achievements that go hand in hand with the projection of herself. The reading of Maryse Condé's *Le Coeur à rire et à pleurer* as part of Condé's autobiographical space is the repositioning and recontextualization of the renowned literary figure in the nexus of autobiographical productions. The only acknowledged autobiography by the Guadeloupean author helps to understand the writer's discomfort in accepting the labeling of her first book *Heremak- honon* as an autobiographical fiction. Following the denials and half confessions one finds that, in designating an "autobiographical space" where her readers without doubt will recognize her through some char- acters, Condé also designed for herself a "creative space," the right for creativity away from any academic labeling. This search for creative free- dom is continued, though surreptitiously, in her self-exclusion from the Créolité movement. Condé is also a Francophone writer who has given many interviews where she talks about her personal life. One could say that Condé projects herself through not only her fictional works and her only avowed autobiography, but also through her numerous inter- views. Condé distinguishes herself from most Francophone writers by the fact that she has seen the whole spectrum of literary production and criticism, as, until recently, she was a university professor and a writer, both full-time. That position of theorist and practitioner permits her to be not only critical of her own work but also to engage in dialogue with critics who attack her works. What is more, she also is able to point her critics and interviewers in certain directions regarding how to read her books. She projects an image of herself as both a writer and scholar in the documentary with Susan Wilcox, to whom she reveals that *La Vie scélérate*, apparently a novel about family and return to origins, is yet more complex: it is in fact Condé's theoretical statement about writing. Maryse Condé is playing on the literary world in search of a free way of expressing her artistic talents, and this is evidenced by the contradictory statements—such as "I think this proves Véronica is not me. (Or is it the other way around?)"[13]—that she makes in interviews. The author of many dramas, Condé is also playing her role in the literary world, an actress who gives the interviewers what they are expecting or who steers them into another direction, or better yet, who confuses them. That multifaceted personality has earned Condé much criticism, but ultimately, she is the main actress and mistress of her game in the literary world because she plays various texts that reflect her person: physical, emotional, and literary. The autobiographical space of Maryse Condé is the play of texts that relate to her personal life of happiness and sadness, her cosmopolitanism and yet her strong attachment to her native Guadeloupe; this autobiographical space also makes room for personal interviews where the author projects a version of herself. *Le Coeur à rire et à pleurer* did not receive a popular acclaim in terms of written reviews, but this was supplemented by dramatic performance to make it more popular. Unlike Bâ's *Amkoullel, l'enfant peul*, whose staging came after a popular success of the book, the staging of Condé's autobiography is meant to remedy its unpopularity. The reason for the lack of popular acclaim of the autobiography, despite Condé's stature, I believe, lies in the focus of the autobiography on more painful memories than happier ones. The sad tone of the autobiography contributed to a lukewarm reception, in spite of the Prix Marguerite Yourcenar it received from French officials. If the English translation of the autobiography makes it accessible to a public of scholars, Condé distances herself from such an enterprise, since, she claims, the translated work no longer reflects her style.

Francophone African and Caribbean Autobiographies and Their Mixed Reception

My book concentrates on autobiographies written by authors from two geographically different areas, Africa and its diaspora, with French as the common linguistic connection. This study shows that Francophone autobiographers' adoption of a canonical genre does not necessarily result in complete imitation and can allow for a spectrum of creativity and modification. My analysis of these texts serves as a theoretical and practical reflection on the differences and similarities among Francophone African and Caribbean literary productions in the postcolonial era. The relationship between autobiographical writing and the various audiences implied by each narrative problematizes the issues of authenticity for autobiographies by postcolonial subjects, since they mainly have a Western audience in mind and publish their works through the publishing houses of the (former) colonizer.

In my comparative analysis of African and Caribbean autobiographies, I have encountered recurrences of certain common themes: identity construction, colonization, race relationships, postcolonial positioning, orality, struggle with the autobiographical tradition, and the paradoxical nature of the works' receptions by readers.

For the two geographically distinct groups of authors, the use of autobiography as the site of identity creation is a shared characteristic. Bâ, Barry, and Mudimbé all deal with who they were and who they are now, and the same applies to Chamoiseau, Condé and Confiant. A concern for both groups of authors is the desire to create an identity that includes the collective; this specific commonality confirms the idea that autobiographies by blacks are more community-centered, as previously asserted by Mohamadou Kane, János Riesz, and James Olney. The definition of identity in both groups of autobiographies includes the community, even in the more personal autobiographies by Mudimbé and Condé, and this is done through the common notion of race. Bâ defines himself and his community against the danger of "depersonalization," while Barry questions her Self, divided between two continents, finally declaring that she prefers the African community. For Confiant and Chamoiseau, identity is obviously foregrounded on the theory of Créolité, which establishes a common identity through the Creole language and culture, thus including the community. Still, some divergences can be observed in these autobiographers' shared intention of identity construction: for African autobiographers, identity is structured around a binary opposition (black/white), whereas for the Caribbean autobiographers, the attention is given to various skin tones, even within the same race.

Another point where Francophone African and Caribbean autobiographies converge is the recourse to oral tradition. All of them, with the exception of Mudimbé, refer to elements of oral tradition such as storytelling (Bâ, Chamoiseau, Confiant, Barry) and the tale (Barry and Condé). In that line, a divergence appears in the narrative techniques used by both groups. Caribbean autobiographers are more inventive and more contentious in the way they write autobiography than their African counterparts. As I pointed out in my chapter on Confiant, his linguistic creolization of French and the underlining irony that sustains his writing show some originality, or an attempt to write differently; the same applies to Chamoiseau, who introduces three grammatically differentiated subjects that are all versions of his own identity. These innovations show an awareness of the art of writing autobiography with the purpose of proposing something different, something original. Condé also appears to bring some new elements to the genre by showing that she is aware that writing autobiography is not about telling the exact truth, but rather about telling stories, which she calls ironically "*contes vrais*" (true tales).

The analysis of the reception of Caribbean autobiographies reveals both variety and contradictions. For La Créolité's two founders, Confiant and Chamoiseau, the receptions of both their autobiographies were positive, yet those positive receptions proved to be controversial to their literary movement. In becoming more popular in France than in Martinique, these autobiographies contradicted the initial goal of La Créolité: to cater to a Martinican audience first. Their popularity in France was due to the *nouveauté* of their literary movement and also to the exoticism of their works for the foreign reader. The lack of Martinican critical reactions could be explained in part by the scarce number of critics in Martinique. More importantly, it is due to the fact that both Chamoiseau and Confiant managed to have control of Martinican public opinion because they collaborated in major Martinican newspapers and magazines, which were obviously biased and which unashamedly replicated the laudatory reviews by the metropolitan French critics. It could be said that the autobiographies' "popularity" in Martinique was a press success rather than a genuine Martinican success. Since both childhood autobiographies appeared immediately after the publication of the literary manifesto *Eloge de la Créolité*, they serve as a test of (and ultimately as a contradiction to) the theories expressed in the manifesto. Créolité, as embodied in the texts of *Antan d'enfance* and *Ravines du devant-jour*, fails in its mission to cater to a Martinican audience. By contrast, Condé's autobiography did not enjoy the same positive reception that her Martinican counterparts received, but her autobiography was popularized through stage adaptations. The English translation of her book was targeted for a scholarly rather than popular audience in the United States.

La Créolité faced some local criticism, as evidenced by the reactions of René Menil and Guy Cabort-Masson, yet it could be said that by 1993, when Confiant published *Ravines du devant-jour*, the Creolists had culled all critical opposition because they controlled the press. Already in 1991, Confiant gave an interview in which he reproached his fellow Martinican writers for their hypocrisy in the face of the success of the Créolité movement: "Moi, ce qui m'écoeure, c'est la mauvaise foi de cette lumpen-intelligentsia qui crève d'envie d'être éditée à Paris mais qui n'en a pas les moyens intellectuels" (*Karibèl*, no. 4, November 1991, p. 24). Confiant attacks Martinican intellectuals for wanting to have their own work published in France, but lacking, according to Confiant, the intellectual abilities to do so. In his quote Confiant deliberately attacks leftist Martinican intellectuals whom he labels "*lumpen-intelligentsia*," a critique certainly directed at Cabort-Masson. The audience problem of course has existed for some time, but Confiant does not solve the dilemma: How can a literature that advocates the primacy of the Martinican audience end up catering to a French audience and boasting about its success in the foreign arena?

Confiant, in another interview with René de Ceccaty, explains his reason for writing in French:

> The abnormal is what I did: to publish five books in Creole and to remain for twelve long years in this refusal. It was only a public refusal, of course, because, while publishing my Creole books and while defending my very "nationalistic" positions, I was also writing at home in French! In Martinique, my Creole novels sold three hundred copies, whereas my novels in French sold four thousand copies. I could not be indifferent to that.[1]

In this interview Confiant confesses that he was very sensitive to the fact that while his novels in French sold more than four thousand copies, his novels in Creole only sold three hundred copies.

My study has aimed at analyzing Francophone autobiographers and their readers transnationally: in their country of origin and in France. France is a major interlocutor in Francophone productions, and the differences that old versus new colonial ties engender are reflected in France's differing reactions to the various Francophone autobiographies. Although Martinique is an overseas *département* of France in the Caribbean, both Chamoiseau and Confiant deeply believe they are still living under colonial domination. Chamoiseau himself wrote a book, *Ecrire en pays dominé* (1997), in which he retraced the history of the racial, social, economic, cultural, and psychological domination of Martinique by France. My study shows that French readers have a preference for Caribbean writers over their African counterparts, and this is explained first by the popularity of the Créolité movement and by the fact that metropolitan French readers have the ambiguous feeling that the Creolists are French writers, albeit racially different ones who are speaking about another culture in a far-away land. This situation casts Chamoiseau and Confiant's works as "exotic" in the eyes of the metropolitan reader. The French reviewer Pierre Lepape's reaction is very revealing of the ambiguous position of the French reader, who feels he has been invited to the dining table but is left out by the inside jokes. The patriotic stand that Lepape takes, entreating the French authorities to "protect" the new movement for fear it might be more attractive to an American readership, is an indication that France wanted to have a certain control over the literary production of Martinique. The paradox is deep here considering the original goals of the Creolists as stated in *Eloge de la Créolité*. In the context of Lepape's comments, the very autobiographies intended for a Martinique audience become simply another means for France to exert its control over Martinique's literary production.

Caribbean writers bring more innovative elements to the autobiographical genre than their African counterparts, and this may be explained by the different political situations that inform the two geographical entities. As a rule, Francophone African countries became independent from France after 1960, while Guadeloupe and Martinique are still under the administrative jurisdiction of their former colonizer as overseas *départements* of France. Chamoiseau and Confiant have actively demanded that Martinique become autonomous and independent, criticizing the artificial nature of the island that has become a *"colonie de consommation"* (consumer colony) living on subsidies from France. The political claims for independence are articulated in *Eloge de la Créolité*, which seeks a new identity for the Caribbeans. In the Caribbean autobiographies, especially those of Confiant and Chamoiseau, there is a more overt endeavor to shake up the status quo both at the literary and political levels. Therefore, the autobiographies of both writers can be read as the continuation of *Eloge de la Créolité*. Nevertheless, this is only at the aesthetic level because the study of the reception of their autobiographies shows that Chamoiseau and Confiant contradict their initial endeavor and do in fact maintain the status quo by neglecting the Martinican audience and by focusing instead on the metropolitan French audience as a way to obtaining fame and popular success.

In postcolonial criticism, when a formerly colonized—or, in the case of the French Caribbean, presently colonized—person writes, there is a tendency to view the author as "writing back" to the colonizer. The situation becomes more complex when the writer is a woman, and postcolonial works by women authors are often labeled as "feminist." My reading of Barry and Condé shows that one should refrain from labeling these women writers who write in a contestatory tone as "feminist." Neither of the two writers has ever acknowledged the Western label, and they even expressed discomfort in referring to it. It is very revealing that an African woman critic, Irène D'Almeida, questions the validity of applying this label to Barry. I propose that Kesso Barry, who resembles Alice Walker's paradigm of a "womanist," could also be read as a "misovire"—a term coined by the Cameroonian woman writer Werewere Liking—in the African context; she should not be seen as a feminist, but rather as a woman who is frustrated with the quality of African men around her, eager to find a better one. Kesso and Condé, despite writing in a style that cast them as "recalcitrant daughters of Africa," are not "feminist" in the Western meaning, but rather are critical of their community, which they do not reject categorically.

For all the autobiographies in this study, I have examined the other side of the writing process: namely, the reception of these publications. For all of the autobiographers, the recurrent question has arisen: For whom do they write? Mohamadou Kane and János Riesz have already addressed this issue and have emphasized that, due to the limitation of the readership in Francophone Africa, most African writers write mainly for a European audience. I concur with Riesz, whose generalizations apply also to the autobiographical genre, but I want to problematize the implication of his conclusions. In concluding that autobiography is a tool to understand African cultures, Riesz is not aware that he is imposing on African autobiographies the same function that French colonizers applied to the narratives of their African students during the colonial era: let them write about themselves and their "African soul" for the understanding of the colonizer. This colonial function is revived by Riesz in the postcolonial era and reveals the audience dilemma that African authors experience in writing autobiography. As I demonstrated in my discussion of each African autobiography, the publishing house is generally in France, and even if this may be for marketing facilities, the implications are larger, since the publishing houses have a certain form of control over the material, which will be presented primarily to a French metropolitan audience. The study of the reception of the works by Chamoiseau and Confiant reveals that the same could be said of these active defenders of La Créolité, who wrote their autobiographies "on demand" after they were approached by Gallimard for a new collection of childhood autobiographies, "Haute Enfance."

Most African autobiographies were not reviewed locally, in part because they were written in exile and in part because they had been published abroad, which made the books less accessible in Africa. Among the readers, French reviewers of African autobiographies tend to be eulogious, as they were in reviewing Bâ, and to avoid criticism altogether. Sometimes, the reviewers may also misread or misjudge the popularity of an author, which was true of the French reviewer who claimed that Mudimbé was unknown in France. Most French reviewers of Caribbean autobiographies were more eulogious than critical. The only critical piece was written by Pierre Lepape. The French reviewers tended to focus on the linguistic novelty of the Créolité movement while neglecting Chamoiseau and Confiant's contribution to modern autobiography. One would have expected that the reviewers would have at least pointed out that Chamoiseau and Confiant had written postmodern autobiographies that used multiple subjects and that cast a critical eye on the act of writing autobiography. By ignoring the subversive aspects of the authors' use of genre, the Western critics reinforced Gusdorf's claim that non-Western autobiographies can only imitate the West.[2] In my analysis, French reviewers definitely demonstrated a bias toward the autobiographies by the practitioners of La Créolité over African autobiographies, and they completely neglected the Guadeloupean Maryse Condé, who is not part of that literary movement. It is even revealing that while Gallimard published two Caribbean writers, Chamoiseau and Confiant, for its collection "Haute Enfance," it did not bother to publish any African autobiographer for that collection. This is a true indication of the Caribbean autobiographers' favored status over their African counterparts.

What these distinct and divergent receptions show is that both African and Caribbean autobiographies are deeply entangled in the paradox of "the audience from the heart" and "the audience from reason" (Mohamadou Kane). When African autobiographers write about the past, which includes the colonial experience, and when they have their work published in France despite the existence of publishing houses in Africa, they do two things: they betray their own community as the first and privileged audience, and they reduce the authenticity of their work by writing with a European audience in mind, thus self-censoring their work and submitting it to editorial censorship.

Both African and Carribean autobiographies are victims of miscategorization by French intermediaries who filter the image of the works for readers. The French reception of *Amkoullel* reveals that French reviewers and authorities see Bâ's memoir as a "novel" and categorize it as such in their listings. In an interview with Kesso Barry, Herzberger-Fofana calls Barry's autobiography a "romanticized biography." In the Martinican reception of works by both Chamoiseau and Confiant, not only do the reviewers not distinguish between the autobiographies and previous fictional works by the authors, but they also miscategorize the autobiographies as "novels" or "narratives." I argue that the reviewers and critics lacked the mastery of theoretical categorization of autobiography in the 1980s and 1990s when those autobiographies were published. This may reveal that critics were not prepared for the reception of autobiographies from Africa and the Caribbean.

The autobiographers themselves have exerted some "resistance to autobiography." Mudimbé's reluctance to call *Les Corps glorieux* an autobiography, Condé's belated recognition of the genre, and Confiant and Chamoiseau's play on multiple subjectivities are prime examples that Francophone writers resist the autobiographical genre. Bâ's *Amkoullel* is the epitome of that resistance at cultural and aesthetic levels, as I showed in Chapter 1 when he had to struggle with a Western version of the Self and had to abide by French editorial rules. Bâ actually produced more biographies of others than memoirs of his own life. Kesso Barry also resisted the act of writing autobiography, claiming that the art of speaking about oneself is a "White man's disease," which she had caught when she decided to write her autobiography. With this comment, Barry signaled her preference for the communal Africa over the self-centered West. As Bart Moore-Gilbert rightly puts it in *Postcolonial Life-Writing: Culture, Politics and Self-Representation*, "Moreover, the material conditions of the production and circulation of postcolonial life-writing bind it to the West in ways which inevitably influence its mode of Self-representation. Indeed, most of the texts I examine were first published in the West, many postcolonial life-writers have been located there for substantial lengths of time and the majority of their readers are, in all probability, westerners" (Introduction, xxv-xxvi). Moore-Gilbert summarizes what I have undertaken in this book: to reveal the complexity of writing autobiography by analyzing it in the context of the readers addressed in the text and outside the text, using my hypothesis that postcolonial autobiographers should write primarily for their communal audience. My study shows that although it is true that most African and Caribbean autobiographers do write for a community, most of them do not prioritize their community of origin (Bâ, Condé, Mudimbé, Barry), or they use their community as a rhetorical device or an excuse to promote themselves to Western readers (the Creolists, Confiant and Chamoiseau).

In my study of the selected autobiographies, I noticed that African autobiographers use the rhetoric of exemplariness more so than their Caribbean counterparts. In the rhetoric of exemplariness, each author sees herself/himself as exceptional. Bâ casts himself as an escapee from the hell of colonization and offers himself as the example of an African who triumphed over colonialism by keeping his own culture and faith. Kesso Barry sees herself as an extraordinary woman, but makes her autobiography more complex and illogical by trying to set herself as an example for her own daughter Sandra, who is biracial and was born in France, not in Africa. Her autobiography is also entangled in a series of contradictions and is geared toward various addressees, diverting from the rhetoric of exemplariness (setting herself as an example for her daughter), which she had used in the beginning of her text. Mudimbé sees himself also as an exceptional African and regards himself as a metaphor for modern Africa. Yet my reading reveals that the rhetoric of exemplariness in Mudimbé's autobiography is geared exclusively toward a minority: Francophone African scholars who want to succeed in the North American university. The rhetoric of exemplariness is intentionally absent from all three Caribbean autobiographies. Condé did not write to set herself as an exemplary Guadeloupean woman, but rather as an exception to the model. As for Confiant and Chamoiseau, their identities are obviously foregrounded on the theory of Créolité, which establishes a common identity through the Creole language and culture; however, their childhood autobiographies do not depict them as examples. Yet, in the reception of Confiant's autobiography, the Martinican critic Georges Desportes gives *Ravines du devant-jour* a cachet of exemplariness and authenticity, stating that its story is true to all Martinicans. Therefore, although there is not an intentionality of examplariness in those autobiographies, there is a recognition of common traits by some Martinican readers. In Confiant, what could be considered rhetoric of exemplariness is not geared toward the Martinican community but rather toward the smaller community of La Créolité, since, as I demonstrated, his autobiography could be read as a defense and illustration of the tenets of Créolité.

Considering my personal reading and reception of the selected autobiographies, my horizon of expectation as an African reader approaching African and Caribbean autobiographies was disappointed, mainly because of the autobiographers' dismissal of their communal audiences. I definitely share Yambo Ouologuem's discontent with *Amkoullel* for its emphasis on the European rather than the African readership. I was equally disappointed by the audience inconsistencies of Kesso Barry's autobiography, which give it a wandering quality. Mudimbé's intellectual autobiography did meet my horizon of expectations as it is geared more specifically toward an African readership of scholars, albeit this community is a smaller and restricted one. Confiant and Chamoiseau's autobiographies are the most disappointing in their use of the "postcolonial exotic" paradigm to cast themselves as marginals who strive for popularity, thereby compromising the authenticity of their autobiographies and their service to their community. Condé is the only autobiographer who had an honest and personal goal: to make amends with the community of critics. Her autobiography appears therefore as an implicit intellectual autobiography because it can be read against and confirms her first (autobiographical) novel.

My study of Reception Theory reveals and accentuates the postcolonial paradox in the relationship between Francophone autobiographers and their readers. This paradox can be detected in the works themselves, through their resistance to the genre, in their clashes of ideology and of aesthetics, and in their use of the "postcolonial exotic" paradigm, especially in the autobiographies of Confiant and Chamoiseau. In the Introduction, I set out to reconcile postcolonial studies with Francophone studies; in the Conclusion, I now approach what Françoise Lionnet calls a transcolonial study, that is, a geographical comparative approach to texts, as quoted by Valerie Loichot: "The word *transcolonial* allows us to exit the chronological thinking introduced by the prefix *post* in *postcolonial* and also to bypass the nation as primary reference in the word *transnational*. Lionnet, like Mbembe, insists on the need to propose a geographical instead of a historical comparative approach to texts" (*Orphan Narratives*, 196<->97; Loichot's emphasis). The transnational study of the reception of Francophone African and Caribbean autobiographies as they refer to their past or present colonizer has brought my work closer to Lionnet's sense of a *transcolonial* approach, or what Valérie Loichot refers to as *transgeographic* or *transcultural* (*Orphan Narratives*, 200). Lionnet and Loichot's understanding of transcolonial is useful in reconciling the difficulties of studying two entities that exist in different historical phases of (post)colonization.

In closing, I would like to suggest that the Francophone autobiographies have received what could be termed a "mixed reception" since all of the autobiographies in this corpus reveal a complex reception at home and in France. The complexity of this mixed reception is rooted in the postcolonial situation of the autobiographers: Coming from a communal society, how does the autobiographer write about her/himself, and to whom does he/she write? The receiving end, be it indigenous to the autobiographer or French metropolitan, challenges the self-projection of the autobiographer. The indigenous reader may want to recognize his shared values in the autobiography (Yambo Ouologuem), whereas French readers may overlook the stylistic innovations of those foreign autobiographers in preference for the exotic dimension of their works.

Because this study has focused on a single autobiographical work by each author under consideration, there is still much work to be done. Chamoiseau's and Confiant's series of autobiographies is a goldmine for the critical researcher. Chamoiseau wrote a triptych, a series of three autobiographies devoted to his childhood, and it will be worth studying Chamoiseau's construction of the Self in those autobiographies. After *Ravines du devant-jour*, Confiant wrote another autobiographical work, *Le Cahier de romance* (2000), which, unlike *Ravines du devant-jour*, focuses on a housemaid, Rosalia. He also wrote a series of three fictional works, where the protagonist, Abel, could be read as his alter ego. A study could focus on Confiant's autobiographical space, the nexus between *Antan d'enfance* and the three novels: *Bassin des Ouragans* (1994), *La Savane des pétrifications* (1995), and *La Baignoire de Joséphine* (1997). Ultimately, the political dimension in Francophone autobiographies is undeniable and must be studied as well as the influence of politics in their reception, as I showed in the study of Bâ's *Amkoullel*, which was influenced by multiparty elections and by the Algerian civil war. A study of the politics of autobiography may include politics as an intratextual theme or an external force that influences the autobiography, and additionally it may consider the politics surrounding the diverse strategies used by the autobiographers to position themselves in the publishing market, the negotiation of popular success at home and/ or abroad.

NOTES

INTRODUCTION

1. See, for example, Glissant, *Le Discours antillais;* and Chamoiseau, *Écrire en pays dominé.*

2. Prince, "Introduction to the Study of the Narratee," 13.

3. Lejeune, *Le Pacte autobiographique.*

4. Wimsatt and Beardsley, "Intentional Fallacy," 748–56.

5. Jaccomard, *Lecteur et lecture dans l'autobiographie française contemporaine.*

6. Lüsebrink, "Du Journal de voyage au témoignage," 83–100.

7. Olney, "Value of Autobiography for Comparative Studies"; Watts, *Packaging Post/Coloniality*; and the Library of Congress Catalog all use the term *autoethnography* liberally.

8. M. Kane, "L'écrivain africain et son public." This 1966 article by the Senegalese critic obviously needs to be recontextualized. Kane referred to the dilemma of first-generation Francophone (colonial) African writers as well as to the new generation postindependence Francophone African writers. Forty years later the nature of Francophone African literature has changed and, more importantly, so has the nature of autobiography itself.

9. Jauss, "Identity of the Poetic Text," 7–28.

10. See Fanon, *Peau noire, masques blancs*, 33–42.

11. Huggan, *Postcolonial Exotic.*

12. Watts, *Packaging Post/Coloniality.*

13. Maryse Condé expresses her discontent with the Créolité movement in her article "Chercher nos vérités." In this article, Condé scolds Chamoiseau and Confiant for hypocritically using Créolité to court the literary circles in Paris for the promotion of their works.

14. Geesey, "Why African Autobiography?"

15. Autobiography is particularly important as a reflection of an identity crisis. Psychiatrist and sociologist Franz Fanon chose the autobiography of Mayotte Capécia, *Je suis Martiniquaise* (1948), and the autobiographical novel

of René Maran, *Un Homme pareil aux autres* (1947), as revelations of the identity trauma in the Martinican psyche in his seminal book *Peau noire, masques blancs.*

CHAPTER 1: HAMPÂTÉ BÂ

1. Aggarwal, "Pour une recherche de l'autonomie auctoriale"; Chap. 5 in *Amadou Hampâté Bâ et l'africanisme*, 198–244.

2. Plusieurs amis lecteurs du manuscrit se sont étonnés que la mémoire d'un homme de plus de quatre-vingt ans puisse restituer tant de choses, et surtout avec une telle minutie dans le détail. C'est que la mémoire des gens de ma génération, et plus généralement des gens de tradition orale qui ne pouvaient s'appuyer sur l'écrit, est d'une fidélité et d'une précision presque prodigieuses. Dès l'enfance, nous étions entrainés à observer, à regarder, à écouter, si bien que tout événement s'inscrivait dans notre mémoire comme dans une cire vierge. Tout y était: le décor, les personnages, les paroles, jusqu'à leurs costumes dans les moindres détails. Quand je décris le costume du premier commandant de cercle que j'ai vu de près dans mon enfance, par exemple, je n'ai pas besoin de me "souvenir," je le vois dans une sorte d'écran intérieur, et je n'ai plus qu'à décrire ce que je vois (13).
[All translations in this chapter are my own.]

3. Je n'ai gardé aucun souvenir des péripéties de notre voyage de retour. Etait-ce une période de sommeil de mon esprit, un accès d'amnésie infantile? Je ne sais. En revanche, je me souviens parfaitement de notre arrivée à Dokoumbo, à sept kilomètres environ de Bandiagara (225).

4. Si l'on relit maintenant le texte d'Amadou Hampâté Bâ à la lumière de ces configurations caractéristiques des genres oraux, il apparaît que les expériences de voyage qui sont vécues et relatées au XXè siècle sont en fait représentées selon le "modèle initiatique" de la tradition orale. . . . Ainsi, les événements entourant le premier voyage d'Amkoullel se prêtent aisément à une présentation sur le mode du conte. En effet, comme les orphelins des contes, comme Soundjata, Amadou Hampâté Bâ et son père adoptif, Tidjani, se trouvent sur le chemin de "l'exil" suite à une injustice qui fait basculer l'équilibre familial et communautaire (22–23).
Christiane N'Diaye sees in Bâ's difficulties in writing a first-person narrative in the European tradition the proof that autobiography is not just a genre "borrowed" by Africans, but rather "adapted" by them to their context, by integrating oral elements in it.

5. Son costume était d'une blancheur remarquable, mais au lieu de flotter et de laisser l'air circuler librement autour du corps comme les vêtements africains, il épousait strictement les formes du Blanc, comme si c'était pour lui une carapace de protection. . . . Quant à la carapace des membres inférieurs, c'était bien la plus étrange: elle descendait jusqu'aux chevilles le long des deux

jambes qu'elle enserrait étroitement. Les pieds, eux, étaient cachés dans des chaussures noires, fermées, qui reluisaient comme de l'ébène bien huilé. De toute évidence, ces chaussures ne ressemblaient en rien à celles des Noirs, habitants normaux de la terre ferme (186–88).

6. I will show later through numerous textual indications that Bâ was in fact addressing a European audience primarily.

7. Le roi, précédé de son seul chambellan, passa devant son fils sans même lui jeter un regard. Personne ne s'en étonna, le fait de ne pas manifester ses sentiments envers ses enfants faisant partie des coutumes africaines *que les Européens comprennent d'ailleurs assez mal.* Chez nous, c'est aux oncles et aux tantes qu'il appartient de manifester extérieurement leur affection pour leurs neveux et nièces qu'ils considèrent comme leurs propres enfants (482).

8. A la longue, ses proches amis et moi l'incitâmes à passer aux actes, d'autant que, depuis des années, il nous régalait déjà de la plupart des anecdoctes savoureuses qui figurent aujourd'hui dans ses Mémoires. Il reprit donc papier et stylo et commença à écrire. C'était, je crois, vers 1975 ou 1976. Comme il était à la veille de repartir en Afrique, il emporta son manuscrit pour le continuer sur place, et quelques mois plus tard, de retour à Paris, il me remit le début de ce qu'il avait fait. Selon notre habitude, je le lui relus à haute voix. Plutôt que d'un récit de vie personnelle, il s'agissait d'une sorte de collection d'anecdoctes, sans réel fil conducteur et sans que lui-même s'implique vraiment dans le récit. Le plus souvent, il passait sous silence ses propres sentiments ou réactions devant les événements. En fait, il s'était livré par écrit à un travail de "conteur traditionaliste africain" pour qui se raconter soi-même est plutôt indécent et qui s'efface devant la chose transmise, réserve à laquelle venait s'ajouter la traditionnelle pudeur peule. Chaque anecdote, prise en soi, était un petit bijou, mais tel quel l'ensemble était difficilement publiable. J'appelai des amis à la rescousse. Au cours d'une conversation, on évoqua la nécessité pour le lecteur moderne (occidental ou africain), de s'identifier à un personnage central dont il puisse épouser les émotions et réactions, ce qui était d'ailleurs le cas dans *l'Etrange destin de Wangrin.* Dans le présent récit, ce personnage central, ce ne pouvait être que lui-même. . . . A la fin, il dit: "J'ai compris." Et ce qui est admirable est que cet homme de plus de soixante-quinze ans se remit au travail et recommença tout depuis le début! En quelques années d'écriture (qu'il interrompit vers 1979 ou 1980, lorsqu'il consacra presque tout son temps à l'alphabétisation des Peuls), cela donna ces merveilleux Mémoires dont la suite reste à publier. Dans cette nouvelle version, l'enfant Amkoullel, puis le jeune homme Amadou Bâ, ont pris vie sous nos yeux, mais l'auteur est tout de même resté fidèle à sa pudeur peule: les confidences s'arrêtent à la porte de son intimité (Heckmann, "Genèse et authenticité des ouvrages." Afterword in Bâ's *Oui, mon Commandant!* 389–94).

9. Bâ's struggle from oral to written narrative is also an illustration of the

debt the postcolonial autobiographer has to pay in order to conform his text to Western norms.

10. Sous l'apparente ingénuité de l'"authentique," les récits de vie—biographies, autobiographies, témoignages oraux—servent des finalités qu'une pragmatique met à jour et interprète. Examen de conscience, confession, investigation psychique, consécration d'un renom, argument politique, mode de promotion sociale, ou, au contraire, acte d'accusation, voire d'auto-accusation, les récits de vie, toujours, s'inscrivent dans le fonctionnement d'une institution: une église ou secte, instance du pouvoir politique ou judiciaire, médecine, institution culturelle, médias. Est-ce l'institution qui suscite le témoignage, et en organise le discours? La rhétorique des récits de vie n'est-elle pas, au sens fort, une stratégie qui conforte la bonne conscience de l'institution?" (7).

11. Le manuscrit d'Amadou Hampâté Bâ contenait de nombreux développements sur certains aspects de la culture ou de la sociologie africaines. En raison de l'importance de l'ouvrage, il a été décidé, en accord avec l'auteur, de privilégier le récit et de supprimer une grande partie de ces développements. Le lecteur pourra les retrouver dans des ouvrages de l'auteur plus spécialisés (N.d.E) (Bâ, *Amkoullel*, Editor's Note, 16).

12. C'était l'époque où le Blanc, qu'il ait tort ou raison, avait toujours raison, du moins en règle générale. Et pourtant je vais avoir l'occasion, peu après, de constater que même au fond d'une brute il peut y avoir une étincelle de bonté, et qu'il ne faut jamais désespérer de l'homme (412–13).

13. Quand je pense à ce que certains Tall ont fait subir à ma famille, je me rappelle le comportement si noble d'un Tall comme Alpha Maki, et je me dis qu'il faut fermer les yeux sur les travers des hommes et ne prendre d'eux que ce qui est bon. Ce qui est bon en nous est commun; quant aux travers, nous avons tous les nôtres, et moi aussi j'ai les miens (318).

14. Il était environ dix-sept heures quand, un soir, la pirogue accosta devant Sansanding. Je sortis du rouf où je me reposais. Le spectacle qui s'offrait alors à ma vue me fit douter de mes laptots: "Sommes-nous bien à Sansanding? —Oui, répondirent-ils. —Sansanding, la ville du roi Mademba? —Sans aucun doute, c'est bien Sansanding." Je ne pouvais en croire mes yeux. Toute la rive était dégradée. Le palais en ruines semblait avoir été avalé par le sol. La belle place de sable fin, que l'on ne devait jadis nettoyer qu'à la main, n'était plus qu'un terrain à l'abandon où se tenait un misérable petit marché de village aux hangars boiteux, non entretenus, souvent à moitié renversés par le vent du nord (484).

15. Ce jour-là, en cet instant, j'ai divorcé d'avec le monde et pris la ferme résolution de me conformer tout le reste de ma vie, au conseil de mon maître: servir, servir toujours, mais ne jamais chercher ni les honneurs, ni le pouvoir, ni le commandement (490).

This episode appears as an intruder in the narrative of Bâ's autobiography devoted to his childhood; the account is about what the narrator witnessed twenty-eight years after he was age seventeen. Still, the autobiographer seems to have in mind a point to make since this parallel of the two stages of his life has led him to draw a conclusion that will mark the rest of his life.

16. M. Assomption était particulièrement fier de Bouyagui Fadiga, qu'il appelait "un pur produit de la culture française." Et c'était bien là, effectivement, ce qu'avec les meilleures intentions du monde on voulait faire de nous: nous vider de nous-mêmes pour nous emplir des manières d'être, d'agir et de penser du colonisateur. On ne peut dire que, dans notre cas, cette politique ait toujours échoué. A une certaine époque, la dépersonnalisation du "sujet français" dûment scolarisé et instruit était telle, en effet, qu'il ne demandait plus qu'une chose: devenir la copie conforme du colonisateur au point d'adopter son costume, sa cuisine, souvent sa religion et parfois même ses tics (499).

17. Je ne sais comment me vint automatiquement aux lèvres une formule que j'avais entendue bien des fois dans la bouche des officiers à Kati et que je prononçai d'un air sérieux, la soulignant d'un geste énergique: "Eh bien, si tout le monde est prêt, en avant marche!" Le plus grave est que, tout à coup, je me sentis bêtement fier de moi-même. Coiffé de mon casque colonial, oubliant pour un instant mon statut *d'écrivain temporaire à titre essentiellement précaire et révocable*, je me prenais pour un chef (518; emphasis mine).

18. Ce livre joliment réussi sur le plan technique avec une belle iconographie signée Philippe Dupuich n'a pas d'autre objectif que de pousser ceux qui ne connaissent pas encore le Sage de Bandiagara à se rattraper en allant consulter au moins une partie de sa grande œuvre.

19. Sur le papier, il lui fallait employer une langue terrible pour retranscrire et retrouver cette sorte de vibration propre aux mille et un dialectes africains. Car lorsque l'on passe de l'oral à l'écrit, on doit tout changer, sans pour autant que le sens en soit altéré. Tout se fige sur le papier. Il faut être un immense artiste pour que cette fixation ne soit pas un appauvrissement, mais un rebond.

20. En France, nombreux sont les lecteurs du grand écrivain malien: ils ont découvert avec *Amkoullel, l'enfant peul* et *Oui, mon Commandant*, deux livres de mémoires, l'envers du décor de la colonisation française, vu par un enfant de l'Afrique de l'Ouest, devenu, adulte, un grand maître de la mémoire orale du continent noir (8).

21. This book was first published in Africa by the Nouvelles Editions Africaines in 1976. Its republication by the French publisher Stock is a sign that French people wanted to discover Bâ anew by reading what he had published before *Amkoullel.*

22. On doit donc à Hampâté Bâ les plus belles pages d'un musulman sur Jésus, qui, dit-il, est "l'Esprit de Dieu." Il rappelle aux catholiques mais aussi aux musulmans l'essence même d'une fraternité religieuse souvent oubliée. Dans l'Islam, écrit Hampâté Bâ, "Jésus, Moïse et Mohammed sont considérés comme les plus élevés dans la hiérarchie de la communion avec l'unité de Dieu. C'est dire, souligne-t-il, sur quel plan l'Islam situe Jésus-Christ. Il est d'ailleurs canoniquement interdit à tout musulman de proférer à l'adresse de

Jésus des paroles qu'il ne siérait pas d'adresser à Mohammed. Tout manquement à Jésus doit être puni au même titre qu'un blasphème contre Mohammed lui-même. Il ne fait pas de doute, en Islam, que celui qui blasphème contre Jésus est promis à l'enfer" (8).

23. There appears to be a mistake in the translation: it should read "Koullel's younger brother," rather than "Amkoullel's younger brother," as in the memoir, Bâ himself states that "Am" as in "Am-Koullel" was given him as a comparative and shorter version of his uncle Koullel.

24. "Aide sociale," July 25, 2007. *Amkoullel* is catalogued with books aimed at helping raise teenagers, teenagers with depression, troubled adolescents, and so on.

25. "Théâtre Sans Frontières," July 25, 2007.

26. Aperçus de la vie culturelle et artistique en Franche-Comté, Online newspaper *Aperçus*, February 2004.

27. "Thierno Bokar," Theatreonline, October 12, 2004.

28. "Nouveau Programme de français en classe de 2° A," Web site for Academie d'Amiens, January 2000.

29. "En classe de Seconde," Éducnet, August 3, 2007.

30. "Lectures en classes de seconde et première," Web site for Académie de Nancy-Metz, Inspection Pédagogique Régionale des Lettres, September 2001.

31. "La lecture au lycée dans les documents d'accompagnement," Web site Academie d'Amiens, August 20, 2007.

32."Conseils de lecture," Web site for Collège Jean Moulin Le Pecq, August 20, 2007.

33. "Les romans et récits pour la classe de sixième," Web site for Savoirs CDI, April 1, 2004.

34. Il s'agissait de trouver des romans et récits écrits par des auteurs d'Afrique Noire Francophone, afin de proposer aux élèves des lectures différentes, avec comme objectifs: la découverte d'auteurs en grande partie inconnus, la découverte de la francophonie (la langue peut présenter des différences notables avec celle à laquelle nos élèves sont habitués), la découverte à travers ces romans de réalités humaines loin des caricatures habituelles ("Nouvelles et romans d'Afrique francophone," Les dossiers de Weblettres, April 26, 2005).

35. L'espace culturel francophone n'apparaît explicitement que dans les programmes de seconde, dans la partie "histoire littéraire et culturelle." En première, il est remplacé par l'espace culturel européen. Ce parallèle montre bien la position d'extériorité où on le situe; son entrée est liée à ce qu'on appelle plus couramment l'ouverture culturelle et le dialogue des cultures (Chaulet-Achour, Web site for Ministère de l'Education nationale, October 2000, 6).

36. Entre misérabilisme empreint de fatalité souvent condescendante et optimisme béat sur les beautés de la "misère au soleil," les médias véhiculent une image fort partiale et partielle du Sud dans les esprits des jeunes Français du début du XXIe siècle. Leur dernière année doit contribuer à leur

donner quelques clés pour saisir la diversité, la complexité et les formidables dynamismes et forces de changement actuellement à l'œuvre dans les pays du Sud (Dietrich, "Nouveaux programmes de Terminale," Web site for Académie de Grenoble, August 20, 2007, 1).

37. The course entitled "Autobiographies, Autoscopies" is listed on the Web site for Université de la Sorbonne Nouvelle, Paris III for September 2005.

38. "Bibliographie nationale française Livres," Bibliographie nationale française, September 2007.

39. L'enfant noir, comme le présentent Camara Laye et Hampâté Bâ, est sur le point d'être révolu. Il faut s'enfoncer profondément dans l'Afrique pour trouver l'enfant noir de Camara Laye (Borgomano, "A l'écoute de Ahmadou Kourouma," *Mots Pluriels*, September 2002, 2).

CHAPTER 2: VALENTIN MUDIMBÉ

1. Si le premier genre me permet d'assumer mon présent, en raison de mon enfance, il est volontairement et systématiquement, partiel pour que cet ouvrage puisse être qualifié d'autobiographique au sens strict du terme. Si le second genre semble relever de l'essai, il est, quant à lui, par trop subjectif, restreint, et même occasionnellement, doctrinaire pour prétendre être un essai de bon aloi (II).

[All translations in this chapter are my own.]

2. Mudimbé, *Parables and Fables*.

3. Josias Semujanga in "De l'autobiographie intellectuelle" (in *Récit de vie de l'Afrique et des Antilles*, 53–99) shares the same view when he defines *Les Corps glorieux* as an "intellectual autobiography," in which the author recounts the history of his social and intellectual life, after having been consecrated as a writer through his previous publications.

4. Lejeune, "L'ordre du récit dans *Les Mots* de Sartre," in *Le Pacte autobiographique*, 197–243.

5. The English translation leaves out the irony contained in the French literal translation: "Clothes do not make the monk." The irony resides in Mudimbé being mistaken for a monk even though he no longer wears monk's clothes.

6. Dès ce moment, explicitement, je me suis mis à me percevoir, de plus en plus, comme signe, comme question pour d'autres. Georges Balandier, de passage à Duke où il reçut un doctorat honoris causa devait me le confirmer au moment où je le quittai. M'embrassant, il me dit: "n'oubliez pas que vous êtes un ambassadeur." De qui? Pour quelle mission? De nouveau ce sentiment de me percevoir détaché, sujet et objet, et soumis à des attentes d'autrui: un pur pour-autrui, réifié. L'analyser? (127).

7. Mon projet d'agir, comme enseignant, dans le contexte politique zaïrois, ne pouvait rien modeler de décisif. Je ne pouvais attendre aucune explosion à partir de mes enseignements de philologie à Lovanium ou Lubumbashi. Aujourd'hui, je me dis: la clé est là, en mon enfance une fois de plus. Ma peinture

voulait saisir le souffle de la vie en sa nudité; ma poésie, comme mes essais, se moquaient des humeurs et dérives d'inspirations bourgeoises, mais mon travail universitaire, malgré la décomposition politique de mon pays, voulait témoigner d'une éducation et de sa compétence. Il relevait d'une mission religieuse: sauver (162).

8. Mais sa clé secrète fut d'adapter, instinctivement, une discipline séculaire, acquise durant son adolescence au style de compétitivité et de productivité de l'université américaine. Une journée bénédictine est divisée en trois: huit heures de prière, huit heures de travail et huit heures de repos. Une laïcisation de *l'Ora et labora* lui avait, depuis de nombreuses années, permis de revoir le contenu des trois composantes de la grille sans en altérer la signification. Il pouvait, de ce fait, compter chaque jour, sur huit heures de travail intellectuel personnel, huit heures de travail administratif et d'enseignement, huit heures de loisir et de repos (128).

9. Il est noir, bien sûr, et africain, en plus. Qu'il pût lire l'ancien grec sans dictionnaire, maîtriser le latin, en plus d'une dizaine de langues modernes, travaillât plus de dix heures par jour, ne pouvait convaincre. Il lui fallut prendre en charge de nouvelles inimitiés: il était à cent pour cent, membre du monde académique américain (129).

10. Josias Semujanga rightly analyzes autobiography as a discourse that follows a semiotic plot in which the autobiographer is the hero whose quest is to understand her/his life and receive self-praise, which sanctions the quest. Mudimbé's autobiography follows this pattern in which the hero has to master writing as a skill that will enable him to make sense of himself and the world around him: "De façon générale, le schéma narratif du récit autobiographique est le suivant. A la mise en route initiale, il y a un sujet sans écriture. C'est souvent une période pénible, du moins est-elle présentée de cette façon par le narrateur. A cette situation initiale de manque correspond un désir, une volonté d'apprendre et de maîtriser l'écriture. Cette phase virtuelle de l'écriture correspond au parcours initiatique du sujet qui, par l'apprentissage des signes culturels de son milieu, acquerra la maîtrise de l'écriture générale, d'abord, par des textes variés et d'écriture spécifique, ensuite, par un texte autobiographique. Généralement, ce moment coïncide avec la période de l'enfance, moment jugé propice à l'acquisition d'un ensemble de connaissances et de valeurs sur lesquels il compte pour réussir sa carrière d'écrivain. La troisième phase correspond effectivement à la performance du sujet écrivant. Il réalise une écriture variée allant de la fiction à l'essai théorique ou philosophique. En se réalisant comme sujet de quête comblé, il peut alors essayer de faire une rétrospection pour comprendre sa propre vie en usant des mêmes concepts qu'il a forgés pour comprendre le monde environnant. Enfin, vient l'autosanction pour donner un sens à sa vie et se justifier auprès de ses lecteurs. C'est le récit autobiographique proprement dit" (Semujanga, "De l'autobiographie intellectuelle," 58).

While this definition is attractive, it must not be generalized, as Semujanga is applying it to Mudimbé's autobiography, which falls into the subgenre called "autobiographie intellectuelle ou littéraire." As a matter of fact, if overgeneralized, this definition will exclude autobiographies as first publication by writers such as Kesso Barry or Ken Bugul from this category. The general line of autobiography as a quest for self-understanding and satisfaction through the mastery of writing could be retained, though, in the context of African and Caribbean writers, who by definition are "sujets sans écriture."

11. Je suis fait pour lui être arraché. Je comprends mal ses réticences. Elle souffre de ma froideur. Je condescends parfois à descendre de ma croix, l'écoute et lui parle, mais à distance. Je sais, déjà, comment me raidir en mon futur destin. Par exemple, afin d'éviter son contrôle, bien avant mes huit ans, nous communiquons en une manière de confrontation discrète, mais permanent. Si elle me parle luba, je lui réponds en swahili, indiquant ainsi mon intégration en un milieu culturel qu'elle connaît mal. Si elle m'adresse la parole en swahili, je lui réponds en luba ou, plus souvent encore en songye, marquant, en ce fait, ma descendance patrilinéaire et ma désapprobation pour sa pauvre connaissance du swahili. Mon jeu l'amuse, bien sûr. Elle n'en rit cependant pas. J'en éprouve un sentiment de puissance. Elle, par contre, paraît y trouver matière à affection. C'est comme une manière de caresse esquissée mais jamais achevée. Un lien très fort s'y dit et se nie tout à la fois. Aujourd'hui, je dirais que nous constituions un couple exemplaire. De fils à mère, on ne devrait pas parler d'amour mais le vivre en ce type de jeu sans menaces (30–31).

12. Mon enfance remonte: un cadre, un art, une vocation. J'en ai émergé et, depuis lors, tourne en un jardin, surpris. Les jeux étaient, visiblement, faits, dès le départ. Jusqu'en mes rébellions, j'haletais d'après des normes anciennes. Je mourrai fidèle à ce champ où [sic], plus exactement, avec les reflexes acquis de lui. Même les écarts témoignent, au total, de ce passé. Dieu contourné, la futilité des beautés du Dimanche oubliée et, avec elle, l'étendue des symboles chrétiens réduite aux illusions d'une foi, il me reste encore un fond de rêve, une culture catholique et ses vertus (158).

13. Ceci me ramène à l'usage colonial de la leçon gréco-romaine, précisément à l'ambiguïté de la colonisation: a-t-elle été si mauvaise, lorsqu'on la compare aux temps présents et aux caprices sanguinaires de nos princes? Dès le début de la conquête coloniale, les Africains ont vécu l'occupation comme péril. Elle a pu, çà et là, prendre des allures de salut. Ce fut le cas dans l'Afrique de l'Est et, en règle générale, en Afrique Centrale. Nombre de souverains locaux ont choisi d'être parties prenantes dans le nouvel ordre. Certains d'entre eux ont vite reculé lorsqu'ils ont compris l'ambition de l'occupant, comme ce fut le cas dans l'histoire de l'occupation du Buganda. D'autres, pour faire référence au livre de Yambo Ouologuem, ont joué les Salif. Un symbole détestable. Il est, hélas, aussi un modèle de l'ambivalence générale des soumissions et de leurs

hypocrisies. . . . Ainsi, Salif incarne notre signe de contradiction. Il accueille la conquête, se laisse corrompre et corrompt. La colonisation prend racine (177).

14. Et le Zaïre pourrait n'être qu'une métaphore. L'Etat y paraît être en relation d'isomorphie avec une machine linguistique. Avec le concours de la police chargée de tenir en alerte les citoyens et de maintenir une infrastructure en décomposition, nos régimes africains maintiennent, essentiellement, un ordre de discours. Celui-ci présente, en tout cas, des caractéristiques nettes. Il est, d'abord, un langage totalitaire et prétend s'offrir comme recommencement absolu. En réalité, analysé de près, on s'aperçoit qu'il mélange des registres divers et propose, en un rythme incantatoire, désirs et complexes de surcompensation déjà formulés ou, au moins, esquissés sous les premières républiques. De manière étonnante, ce langage couvre, en fait, la continuation des politiques coloniales et leurs usages (191–92).

15. Ainsi, le regard permanent sur moi ne suscite ni résistance, ni étonnement. Il me colonise, certes, mais qu'est-ce que cela peut dire? Cette surveillance, me semble-t-il, entre dans mes jeux secrets avec Dieu (15–16).

16. La colonisation comme raison du plus fort ne pouvait ainsi être, au mieux, qu'invitation à l'assimilation, à grandir. J'entends, donc: un réarrangement d'un espace physique, une domestication des humains selon un nouveau code de valeurs; colonisation au sens étymologique du mot (*colére*: cultiver), exactement comme nous pouvons décider de transformer un pan de forêt en un jardin érigé en transcendance, et que nous avons décidé de promouvoir la respectabilité d'un rôle (194).

17. Monsieur E. De Jonghe, dans *L'enseignement des Indigènes du Congo-Belge* (1931), se plaint du Noir devenu déraciné qui "se croit l'égal du blanc et même supérieur." Dois-je penser à mon père ou à moi-même aujourd'hui? (46–47).

18. Ai-je jamais cru en Dieu? Je n'en sais rien. Des années durant, la question me parut inutile. Je quittai la vie bénédictine par fatigue (75).

19. Il n'en demeure pas moins qu'il y a un problème important: un problème de crédibilité et de sincérité. Suis-je encore chrétien? Et, pourrais-je prétendre être, sans conflits, chrétien et nationaliste africain, et vivre en accord avec moi-même? (100).

20. Ce dimanche matin de septembre, comme probablement, beaucoup d'autres à venir, ma vie croise une question. Et, celle-ci s'impose, en arrêt, dans ma pensée: suis-je, vraiment, un lien entre le passé africain et la modernité de l'Europe chrétienne? (53–54).

21. Ce que je pense, malheureusement, est simplement désastreux. Oui, le christianisme me paraît, pour l'instant, la seule idéologie et le seul système qui, en Afrique non islamique, peut nous aider à maintenir l'intégrité spirituelle et morale des croyants et, en même temps, leur donner le courage et les raisons de persévérer avec une certaine dignité dans leurs rêves humains et, surtout, de surmonter les calamités et l'irrationalité que nous créent les politiques (98–99).

22. Oui, le christianisme signifie ainsi l'échec de mon passé, de ma tradition, et des croyances de mes ancêtres. Les vaincus adoptent la religion des vainqueurs presque toujours. Nous l'avons fait. J'en suis un exemple (100).

23. La route que j'ai prise a tout l'air d'un processus de dépossession: baptisé dans une religion "étrangère" à mon Afrique, tôt introduit dans un système scolaire et culturel dont les normes provenaient de l'Occident, j'ai appris, grâce à des maîtres admirables, à penser et à vivre les ressources extraordinaires d'un univers complexe et métissé. A partir de lui, je peux rêver d'élucider les contradictions majeures de mon appartenance à deux cultures, l'africaine et l'européenne; mais aussi, sans prétendre développer des théories, réfléchir sur les modèles et les structures susceptibles de concourir à une promotion humaine et spirituelle du peuple d'où je suis sorti (104).

24. Que la philosophie, au nom d'une authenticité mystificatrice ou sous prétexte d'une altérité culturelle africaine absolue, abandonne le lieu de notre modernité et de notre réification qu'indiquent dans notre histoire deux dates (celle du début de l'esclavage et de l'instauration de la colonisation) pour se réfugier dans les replis illusoires d'une tradition mythique, me paraît simplement scandaleux en termes d'urgence et de stratégies de survie. En somme, je le pense sincèrement, notre avenir ne réside, ni dans la célébration des gloses sur des antiquités nègres, ni dans le culte des épopées muséifiées, mais plutôt dans la conscience de ce que nous sommes aujourd'hui comme femmes et hommes. Nous pouvons et devons nous opposer à la raison néo-coloniale (179).

25. Stephan, "Ricoeur and Merleau-Ponty," 2.

26. Edie, *Merleau-Ponty's Philosophy of Language*, 73.

27. Je me remets à vous, mes anciens élèves et, à présent, amis, collègues, mes égaux. Il y a une foi à transmettre à la génération qui monte. Un esprit aussi. Je vous sais sevrés de naïvetés à propos des "traditions africaines." Je sais, aussi, que vous avez épuisé tous les secrets de la patience pour croire encore qu'il y a une limite aux coups de vos colères et à ceux de vos espoirs pour une meilleure Afrique. Vous avez raison d'espérer, malgré la bêtise générale qui nous entoure. Je sais, également, que vous avez parfois des doutes. Que des fois n'ai-je entendu ce propos effrayant: "La générosité ne paie pas . . . surtout en Afrique aujourd'hui." Pourquoi, bon Dieu, aimeriez-vous être payés pour votre foi? Demeurez ce que vous êtes: croyez en vous-même, en vos actions. Vous n'êtes pas seuls. Votre foi est, pour reprendre une métaphore venue d'un livre dont j'ai oublié tout, un anneau important et solide. Croyez-moi, vous êtes, nous sommes nombreux. Liés, entrelacés les uns dans les autres, nous finirons bien, un jour, par nous transformer en un câble capable de déplacer fleuves et montagnes, et de refaire l'Afrique du tout au tout (197–98).

28. Il nous faudrait une étude magistrale sur l'art et la société en Afrique Centrale qui puisse faire pendant aux excellents ouvrages sur l'art traditionnel. Pourquoi ne la feriez-vous pas, Hélouya, Jenny, Louise? J'écris ceci en l'au-

tomne de 1991. La saison est magnifique. Immensément, lumineusement belle. Et je pense à vous. Les belles dentelles des feuilles me disent un style. Je vous l'associe. Une nouvelle saison est là, la vôtre. Qu'en ferez-vous? (201).

29. En écrivant ces brefs *Carnets de Mère Marie-Gertrude*, V.Y. Mudimbé a en effet créé une nouvelle et forte figure africaine. Cet écrivain zaïrois, inconnu en France, né en 1941, enseignant actuellement à l'université américaine Duke, est apprécié dans le monde Anglophone dont il a utilisé la langue dans son quatorzième ouvrage, *The Invention of Africa* [Bloomington: University of Indiana Press, 1988] (Péroncel-Hugoz, "Romans").

CHAPTER 3: KESSO BARRY

1. Barry, *Kesso, Princesse peuhle*, 9.

2. Bâ, *Amkoullel, l'enfant peul*. Peul(e) or Peuhl(e) are the two orthographs designating the same people. For consistency, I maintained the same spelling with "h" as in Kesso. Throughout this study, I will refer to the autobiographer by the name "Kesso," which she gives as the title of her book, and as Irène d'Almeida did in her article on Kesso.

3. Si la vache peut être considérée comme un patrimoine identitaire commun, la conduite des troupeaux et la transformation du lait peuvent être considérés comme des patrimoines immatériaux spécifiques sur lesquels chaque groupe veille : un homme qui baratte le lait fera sourire tout le monde et une femme qui tisse la corde à veau se rend ridicule. Il y a ainsi des actes perçus comme spécifiquement féminins et d'autres comme spécifiquement masculins. La chaîne de transmission des connaissances valorisées est une clé de compréhension du patrimoine. Chez les pasteurs Peuhls, la chaîne patrimoniale se construit avec un maillon masculin, symbolisé par le bâton et les pâturages, et un maillon féminin symbolisé par la calebasse et le lait. Ce dernier relève plutôt d'un matrimoine (6–7).

[All translations in this chapter are my own.]

4. See Bourdieu, *La Domination masculine*.

5. The year 1948 is the date provided by Beverley Ormerod and Jean-Marie Volet in *Romancières africaines d'expression française*. Still, when one refers to the autobiography and historical facts, the autobiographer's date of birth seems to precede 1948. It is historically known that Guinea became independent in 1958, which would make Kesso a ten-year-old girl in 1958. Yet, Kesso herself contends in her first meeting with Sékou Touré that she was fourteen and that he was not yet the president: "Je suis partie un matin pour Conakry, seule. Dans l'avion, la première personne que je rencontrai fut Sékou Touré. Il n'était pas encore président, seulement maire de Conakry, mais il était l'homme de l'indépendance, le leader du RDA, que suivaient les yeux fermés tous les jeunes progressistes" (I left one morning for Conakry, alone. On the plane, the first person I met was Sékou Touré. He was not yet President,

only the Mayor of Conakry, but he was the man of Independence, the leader of the GDR, who was blindly followed by all the young Progressists) (139). Historically Sékou Touré became president of Guinea in 1958, and since the autobiographer declares that she met him when she was fourteen and he was not yet president, one can infer that she was born before 1948, approximately around 1943. This is confirmed by the autobiographer herself who mentions that she has never known her date of birth for sure: "J'ai quatorze ou quinze ans, je ne sais pas exactement (je n'ai jamais su mon âge, pas plus que ma date de naissance: c'était seulement 'l'année où Mme Diala était à Timbo'), et je suis à Dakar, à quelque semaines de cette date fatidique qui me sépare de mon retour au pays" (I am fourteen or fifteen years old, I do not know [I exactly never knew my age, not more than my birth date: It was only "the year when Mrs. Diala was in Timbo"], and I am now in Dakar, a few weeks away from this fateful date which separates me from my return to my country) (151).

6. Sandra, c'est à toi que je m'adresse. Il s'agit de ma vie et je pourrais commencer mon récit par: il était une fois dans le Fouta-Djalon une petite fille qui s'appelait Kesso. Elle était Peuhle, musulmane, et princesse de sang promise à un mariage royal. Je poursuivrais un récit où l'étrange et le merveilleux tisseraient une fresque multicolore pour te faire rêver. Mais ma vie n'est pas un conte, même si elle y ressembla le temps d'une enfance (9).

7. D'Almeida, "Kesso Barry's *Kesso*," 69.

8. Quand le matin, il sortait dans la cour et que les femmes, ses épouses, se mettaient à leur fenêtre ou devant leur porte pour essayer d'attirer son attention en espérant qu'il daignerait venir jusqu'à elles pour bavarder, je voyais ma mère, le corps tendu comme la corde d'un arc, tremblant de la tête aux pieds. Dans ces moments-là, je lisais dans son regard une telle imploration, j'y percevais une telle détresse, que j'en avais la rage au cœur. C'est certainement à cette époque que je me suis promis de ne jamais épouser un homme qui aurait plusieurs femmes (29).

9. A l'inverse de ma mère, elle avait toujours eu une forte personnalité et beaucoup de caractère que le grand âge n'avait pas émoussé. On disait que, toute jeune, elle s'était battue avec un fusil aux côtés de son mari, contre sa propre famille, à un moment où les deux clans se disputaient le pouvoir. J'ai souvent entendu les griots conter cette histoire, qui me plaisait particulièrement (31–32).

10. See Bourdieu, *La Domination masculine*, 41. "En fait, il n'est pas exagéré de comparer la masculinité à une noblesse" (86).

11. La force de l'ordre masculin se voit au fait qu'il se passe de justification : la vision androcentrique s'impose comme neutre et n'a pas besoin de s'énoncer dans des discours visant à la légitimer. L'ordre social fonctionne comme une immense machine symbolique tendant à ratifier la domination masculine sur laquelle il est fondé: . . . c'est la structure de l'espace, avec l'opposition entre le lieu d'assemblée ou le marché, réservés aux hommes, et la maison, réser-

vée aux femmes, ou, à l'intérieur de celle-ci, entre la partie masculine, avec le foyer, et la partie féminine avec l'étable, l'eau et les végétaux (22–23).

12. Je préférais m'amuser avec les garçons plutôt qu'avec les compagnes de mon âge, que je trouvais trop sages et déjà trop soumises. Il planait au-dessus des jeux interdits que je partageais avec les garçons l'idée de faute (73).

13. On lui rapportait que je passais mon temps à jouer au ballon avec les garçons, que je portais des shorts et seulement un maillot lorsque j'allais me baigner à la rivière, que je faisais du vélo et montrais mes jambes, on lui disait encore. . . Que ne lui disait-on pas? Tout cela était vrai, et je ne m'en cachais pas. Je passais le plus clair de mon temps avec les garçons de Mamou, j'aimais leurs jeux violents, que je préférais à ceux des filles de mon âge, et personne n'aurait pu m'empêcher de faire ce dont j'avais envie (55–56).

14. Nous étions nombreux pour ces chasses . . . et, au milieu de tous ces hommes, moi, la petite princesse incorrigible (91).

Je voulais être comme les garçons, faire comme eux, et rester digne (92).

Je préférais de beaucoup les jeux des garçons à ceux des filles (93).

15. À force d'être tourmenté, Alphadio, son tour venu, accepta de m'emmener avec lui; *"habille-toi en garçon, et viens avec moi"*, me dit-il un soir. *C'était un crime*, évidemment, mais je n'avais peur de rien, et Alphadio non plus. *Cette nuit-là, j'ai pénétré dans ce monde interdit aux femmes*, et j'ai assisté aux danses guerrières et aux luttes violentes de ces garçons à peine plus âgés que moi (93; emphasis mine).

16. Les notables étaient horrifiés; ils venaient voir mon père pour lui dire: "Almamy, comment pouvez-vous tolérer que cette femme vive parmi nous? Il est impossible d'imaginer ce qu'elle exige de nos filles. Elle les déshabille à moitié, on voit leurs jambes, et elle les fait jouer au ballon comme des hommes. Quand elles tombent, elles écartent les cuisses et . . . " (104).

17. Diallo, "Kesso: Princesse peuhle," 66.

18. La "misovire" ou plutôt le "misovirisme," si nous pouvons nous permettre ici d'en faire une idée, est né de la frustration de la femme africaine qui n'arrivait pas à trouver un homme répondant à ses aspirations au sein de l'Afrique moderne. Le "misovirisme" se distingue donc du féminisme radical et doit être appréhendé en termes dialectiques (Gallimore, "Écriture féministe?" 86–87).

19. Ma sœur était une vraie princesse peuhle, une jeune fille modèle, à l'image de ce que souhaitaient tous les parents. Respectueuse des traditions, elle se comportait en toutes occasions selon les vœux de ma mère. Les yeux toujours baissés lorsqu'on lui adressait la parole, elle ne parlait que quand on la questionnait et elle s'habillait décemment: jamais de robe qui laisse voir les genoux, ou de pantalon qui moule les formes; elle ne portait que le pagne et la chemise traditionnels (84).

20. Les jours de fête, lorsque nous mettions nos plus beaux habits, les hommes en boubou blanc ou bleu, les femmes avec leurs tuniques multico-

lores, et que le commandant de cercle et ses amis se présentaient dans leurs tenues ridicules, en short et en casque colonial, transpirant et soufflant comme des malheureux, nous n'avions aucune pitié pour ces hommes qui, à nos yeux, n'avaient aucune classe (129).

21. If at a first reading the autobiography seems to be divided in two complementary parts, happy childhood and fulfilled adulthood, this division proves to be problematic with further analysis. Even during the first part devoted to her happy and innocent childhood, Kesso left some traces of her uneasiness as an African woman living in Europe. Earlier in her autobiography she had made some interesting statements in the form of confession: "Aujourd'hui, je ressens la nécessité de me regarder, de parler de moi, de me remettre en question, pour mieux les comprendre, ce que furent mes choix: vivre à l'occidentale. J'ai trop joué le jeu des Blancs, j'ai, comme on dit, poussé ma balle trop loin dans leur camp, et me voilà vivant comme une soi-disant civilisée. Je raisonne, je m'inquiète à l'idée de ne plus savoir qui je suis" (Today, I feel the need to look at myself, to speak about me, to call myself into question, in order to better understand my choices: to live like a Western woman. I played the game of the White world too much, I have, as one says, thrown my ball too far into their court, and here I am living like a supposedly civilized woman. I reason, I worry that I no longer know who I am) (36). And later: "Je me dis souvent que, plus tard, je rentrerai en Afrique. Il ne fait pas bon à Paris être une vieille négresse, tandis que, chez moi, je serai respectée et aimée. J'étais une petite fille heureuse. Je me rends compte aujourd'hui, même si à l'époque je n'en avais pas conscience, que la vie était particulièrement facile et agréable pour moi à Mamou" (I often think that, later, I will return to Africa. It is not good to be an old black woman in Paris, while, at home, I will be respected and loved. I was a happy little girl. I realize it today, even if I was not aware then that life was particularly easy and pleasant for me in Mamou) (52–53). The deictic "aujourd'hui" repeated twice refers to the actual Kesso reflecting on her past life while longing for a return to Africa in order to live among the African family that values older people and kinship. She now is nostalgic about a happy childhood and knows she will not fit well in France as an old African woman, since, as she stated critically earlier, this is a country that gets rid of the older ones by putting them in an institution, while in Africa, the whole family takes good care of its elders. It is definitely an identity crisis that the autobiographer is undergoing, but the autobiography does not solve the crisis. Kesso Barry's autobiography seems to be typical of autobiographies by some African women who, at odds with their traditions, see in the Western way of life the only escape, but later realize that it was not the best choice. They are left in a state of "in-betweeness," undecided and torn apart between traditional and modern values, between Africa and Europe. The same situation is reflected in the Senegalese autobiographer Ken Bugul's *Le Baobab fou*, where, after rejecting African

traditions and a long stay in Europe, the autobiographer returns to African values while condemning the European ones.

22. Sékou Touré a pris en main, en 1958, un pays prospère, largement auto-suffisant, et même exportateur dans le domaine alimentaire, potentiellement riche par son sous-sol et ses infrastructures, ayant su mûrir une élite cultivée qui avait fait ses études en France, en Angleterre ou aux Etats-Unis, un pays qui aurait pu être un des phares de l'Afrique. Il a laissé à sa mort (dans son lit, le régime de terreur qu'il avait entretenu aurait fait échouer toute idée même de tentative d'assassinat) un pays ruiné, dévasté, anéanti, dont les éléments les plus capables avaient été assassinés ou avaient fui à l'étranger, sans l'ombre d'une organisation sociale ou politique, pourri jusque dans ses racines les plus profondes. Et pourtant, jusqu'à sa fin, cet homme a fait illusion, ses mensonges ont fonctionné, ses rodomontades ont été entendues. Par quelle mystérieuse magie? L'Histoire le dira peut-être un jour. Les Guinéens, eux, avaient compris depuis longtemps. Après sa mort, il n'a pas fallu plus de trois jours pour que la totalité des affiches portant son portrait ou des slogans de son cru disparais-sent totalement (181).

23. Votre livre est une oeuvre biographique romancée si bien qu'on a l'im-pression de lire un conte de fée entrecoupé d'événements assez tragiques par ex. je pense à l'événement qui est repris dans la presse et qui fait la fortune des médias populaires: l'excision. Vous-même relatez les circonstances dans les-quelles vous avez subi cette opération. N'est-ce plus qu'un souvenir lointain oublié dans les limbes de la mémoire? (393).

24. Cette opération m'a beaucoup marqué [sic], car elle m'a traumatisée. Avec le recul du temps, je suis venue à reconsidérer toute ma vie d'antan. J'ai beaucoup réfléchi là-dessus et ne vois pas l'utilité d'un tel acte qui selon moi n'a aucune raison d'être. J'ai écrit mon histoire afin d'attirer l'attention des pouvoirs qu'ils aident à faire disparaître une telle coutume que je considère comme une mutilation (393).

25. De Certeau, *L'Invention du quotidien*, 61.

CHAPTER 4: PATRICK CHAMOISEAU

1. Chocolat-première-communion
    l'écrire c'est saliver
    y penser c'est soufrir
    communier c'est chocolat. (93)
    La capsule
    aplatie
    effilée
    sonnait le fil et tranchait raide
    pouce fendu
    doigts bandés

saison-yoyo de combats bels. (134)

2. *Man Ninotte*:	On m'a dit que les tomates farcies sont péché-doigt-cou-pé cette année....
La marchande:	Si tu veux un kilo je peux te faire tel prix....
Man Ninotte:	Tu crois han?
La marchande:	Je crois, oui....
Man Ninotte:	Donne-moi cette espèce de dachine-là, chérie.... Je vais essayer quand même de la manger....
La marchande:	C'est tant....
Man Ninotte:	C'est pour les tomates?
La marchande:	Pour la dachine, oui.
Man Ninotte:	Eh bien, je ne vais pas manger de dachine non plus, ma chère....
La marchande:	Combien tu veux ta dachine?
Man Ninotte:	Je vais essayer plutôt de faire une salade de christophines. Où c'est que je peux trouver ça?
La marchande:	Prends la dachine, ma douce.
Man Ninotte:	An-an, j'ai plus besoin....
La marchande:	Fais-moi plaisir sur la dachine, petit sirop....
Man Ninotte:	Fais ton prix, ma doudou. (141–43)

3. Partageurs, ô

Vous savez cette enfance!

(il n'en reste rien mais nous en gardons tout). (17)

Dans notre mémoire commune, frères, il y a Matador. (66)

Commença une longue attente ô frères, la plus terrible je crois de nos communes enfances. (70)

Ô mes frères, vous savez, elle [la maison] meurt dans ses poussières. Elle s'étouffe de souvenirs. L'escalier a retréci. Le couloir est devenu étroit et un entrepôt l'a réduit de trois quarts.... Oh mes frères, je voudrais vous dire: la maison a fermé une à une ses fenêtres, se détachant ainsi, sans cirque ni saut, du monde se refermant à mesure sur sa garde d'une époque—notaire fragile de nos antan d'enfance. (186)

4. Mémoire ho, cette quête est pour toi (21).

Mémoire, passons un pacte le temps d'un crayonné, baisse palissades et apaise les farouches, suggère le secret des traces invoquées au bord de tes raziés. Moi, je n'emporte ni sac de rapt ni coutelas de conquête, rien qu'une ivresse et que joie bien docile au gré (coulée de temps) de ta coulée (22–23).

Mémoire sélective. Tu ne te souviens plus de sa disparition. Dans quels combles as-tu rangé sa mort? L'as-tu vu flottant ventre en l'air dans le bassin de la cour, ou gardes-tu trace de son corps recroquevillé sur une marche d'escalier? As-tu rappel de lui surgissant en plein jour, le cerveau naufragé sans boussole ahuri sous le balai des manmans? Il est sans doute possible qu'il ne mourut jamais, qu'il changea de maison au gré d'une aventure. Je ne le vois pas crevé, dérivant au fil crasseux d'un canal. Il s'est peut-être campé entre deux rêves, et il reste là, momifié dans une insomnie devenue éternelle. Mémoire, c'est là ma décision (62).

Mémoire, je vois ton jeu: tu prends racine et te structures dans l'imagination, et cette dernière ne fleurit qu'avec toi (71).

Il y a l'image du papa-cordonnier. Elle est incertaine. Qui parle mémoire? Quel rôdeur se souvient? (113).

Au négrillon, il récite La Fontaine, et le bougre en est avide ho mémoire, tu as donc des dégras dans les battements du coeur? (115).

Mémoire, tu t'emballes (177).

5. On ne quitte pas l'enfance, on la serre au fond de soi. On ne s'en détache pas, on la refoule. Ce n'est pas un processus d'amélioration qui achemine vers l'adulte, mais la lente sédimentation d'une croûte autour d'un état sensible qui posera toujours le principe de ce que l'on est. On ne quitte pas l'enfance, on se met à croire à la réalité, ce que l'on dit être le réel. La réalité est ferme, stable, tracée bien souvent à l'équerre—et confortable. Le réel (que l'enfance perçoit en ample proximité) est une déflagration complexe, inconfortable, de possibles et d'impossibles. Grandir, c'est ne plus avoir la force d'en assumer la perception. Ou alors c'est dresser entre cette perception et soi le bouclier d'une enveloppe mentale. Le poète—c'est pourquoi—ne grandit jamais ou si peu (94).

Où s'achève l'enfance? Quelle est cette dilution? Et pourquoi erres-tu dans cette poussière dont tu ne maîtrises pas l'envol? Mémoire qui pour toi se souvient? Qui a fixé tes lois et procédures? Qui tient l'inventaire de tes cavernes voleuses? (178).

6. Le négrillon mélancolique connaît alors le monde et questionne silencieusement sa vie (c'était, *je* crois, l'inexprimée inquiétude de l'enfance; mais il est aussi possible que ce furent de simples heures d'hébétude liées à l'idiotie dont le soupçonnaient certains autres négrillons, de ses bons vieux ennemis intimes) (51; emphasis mine).

7. Crosta, "Marronner le récit d'enfance," 2.

8. At a more complex level, Chamoiseau will continue his linguistic play in the writing of his semiessay/semiautobiography *Ecrire en pays dominé* in which he questions his status as a writer in a country that is still dependent on France, while refusing to confine himself to a certain exoticism. What is remarkable in this narrative is that next to the personal accounts of his life as an adolescent, a worker, and a writer, Chamoiseau tries to replay the history of the French Caribbean by entering the various Selves of the individual races that have shaped his country through the centuries, through the use of the first-person singular *je*. Chamoiseau therefore becomes one after the other, the native Caribbean Indian "Indien Caraïbe," a French colonizer, an African on the slave ship en route for the Caribbean, an East Indian, a Chinese, and a Syrian-Lebanese. One after another, he enters the vision of every individuality while

restoring a part of Caribbean history peculiar to each of them. In this case, the single person Chamoiseau becomes the sum of all the different personalities he entered, a concrete reminder of the theory of La Créolité as the mixture of various races, civilizations, and languages on a geographically restricted area.

9. Belle victoire, mais il dut apprendre à dormir en continuant à séventer. Il est possible qu'il n'y parvint, mais nul n'en témoigna jamais (49).

Une autre version de la genèse des poulaillers est possible (53).

La seule crainte de Man Ninotte en course derrière le sien était qu'on le lui vole mais, à l'écrire, j'ai soudain souvenance que rien à l'époque ne se volait (64).

Man Ninotte ne disposait jamais d'assez de place. Elle avait fini par étendre quelques lignes à linges sur le toit des cuisines, et l'homme d'aujourd'hui ne comprend toujours pas comment elle parvenait à y grimper (100).

10. Le négrillon ne connut pas cette époque où les manmans cuisinèrent côte à côte dans ces pièces, séparées par des cloisons de bois. . . . *Il imagine* la vapeur épicée troublant ces pièces où les manmans mettaient dehors leurs talents culinaires. Elles rivalisaient d'audaces afin de parfumer les saumures du poisson, faire lever d'odorantes fritures, mieux transmettre à l'univers qu'il y avait de leur côté, ce jour-là, non pas une misérable sauce de morue mais une tranche de viande-boeuf. *Il suppose* qu'en plus, elles chantaient, ou dialoguaient à travers les cloisons juste avant d'emporter leur canari dans l'escalier grinçant, vers une marmaille affamée par l'école, et vers les hommes affairés à leurs punchs en compagnie du soiffeur de midi, expert en cette visite exacte (52; emphasis mine).

11. Autour de ces misérables trophées, le négrillon organisa des cérémonies païennes. L'homme les serre aujourd'hui quelque part dans ses ombres (60).

Dessous le tueur se profila celui qui aujourd'hui est incapable du moindre mal à la plus détestable des mouches verdâtres (62).

12. Aucun des deux n'exerce plus. Ils vivent au relenti quelque part, entre des enfants et des petits-enfants qui ne se doutent peut-être pas des élevées de leur dévouement. Je les veux immortels désormais, aptes aux pérennités dont l'acoma cèle la maîtrise. C'est d'eux que l'homme d'aujourd'hui ramène son goût des mains ouvertes et tant d'inaptitude à dire non à ce qu'on lui demande. Il sait—en bienheureuse faiblesse—donner (112).

13. La médecine créole perdait ainsi ses voies de transmission. L'homme sait qu'il y a aujourd'hui des peuples brisés, auxquels il faut réapprendre d'élémentaires gestes de médecine et d'hygiène, qui sont en rupture avec leur propre génie, et qu'on tente de "développer" au rythme d'un autre génie. Un peuple défaille et meurt quand pour lui-même s'invalide sa tradition, qu'il la fige, la retient, la perçoit comme archaïque sans jamais l'adapter aux temps qui changent, sans jamais la penser, et avancer riche d'elle dans la modernité. Ainsi nous-même, par ici et par là (105).

14. *Je savais mesurer mes fièvres et l'aiguille de mes douleurs; mes boyaux,*

mon ventre, mon coeur, connaissaient l'herbe-guinée, les saveurs de l'à-tous-
maux et de l'herbe cha-cha. Mais pour vous, marmailles, corps neufs que je ne
connaissais pas, il fallait laisser faire l'homme docteur de la médecine (104).

15. Les conteurs de la ville étaient rares. En tout cas, le négrillon n'en avait jamais vu. Il rencontra le conte créole avec Jeanne-Yvette, une vraie conteuse, c'est-à-dire une mémoire impossible et d'une cruauté sans égale. Elle vous épouvantait à l'extrême avec deux mots, une suggestion, une chanson sans grand sens. Elle éclaboussait la mort avec du rire, cueillait ce rire d'un seul effroi. Elle nous menait aux rythmes des rafales de sa langue, nous faisant accroire n'importe quoi. Nous guettions Manman Dlo dans l'ombre de l'escalier. Nous prenions-courir à l'odeur d'un zombi qu'elle reniflait. Elle nous forçait à nous déshabiller au moment d'évoquer quelque diablesse détestant les vêtements. Elle apprit au négrillon l'étonnante richesse de l'oralité créole. Un univers de résistances débrouillardes, de méchancetés salvatrices, riche de plusieurs génies. Jeanne-Yvette nous venait de mémoires caraïbes, du grouillement de l'Afrique, des diversités d'Europe, du foisonnement de l'Inde, des tremblements d'Asie. . . , du vaste toucher des peuples dans le prisme des îles ouvertes, lieux-dits de la Créolité (125).

16. Les parleurs et blagueurs se dressaient droits dans un cirque jovial que l'on encourageait. En ce temps-là, aucun applaudissement, mais de précises modulations de gorge que la langue créole a aujourd'hui perdues (167).

17. Les Chinois laveurs de linge nasillaient des politesses mécaniques. Les nègres y surgissaient à moitié imbéciles, avec de gros yeux mobiles, un effroi permanent, Ils peuplaient le décor de serviteurs zélés, de barmen béats, de statues de jazz, de sauvages irrémédiablement grimaçants et dentelés. Leur apparition provoquait un éclat de rire généralisé de la salle qui devenait nerveuse. Le négrillon lui-même ne percevait entre lui et cette représentation aucune commune engeance. Indigène voulait dire nègre, sauvage aussi, méchant souvent. Nous étions Tarzan et jamais les demi-singes qu'il terrassait. Le processus des films fonctionnait à plein. Nous nous identifiions aux plus forts, toujours blancs, souvent blonds, avec des yeux sans cesse tombés du ciel, nous enfonçant sans le savoir dans une ruine intérieure. Le négrillon devra par la suite opérer la formidable révolution de se considérer nègre, et apprendre obstinément à l'être. Plus tard, il dut apprendre à être créole (171).

18. See Fanon, *Peau noire, masques blancs*.

19. Chamoiseau, interview by James Ferguson, "Return of the Creole," March 26, 2000, <http://www.patrickchamoiseau.cwc.net/interview.html>, 6.

20. In various interviews and publications, Chamoiseau in the line of the idea of Créolité, refers to himself and his fellow Martinican writers as "marqueurs de parole," who inherited the skill of the plantation storyteller, or "conteur creole." In the age of the written text, it is the duty of these "conteurs creoles" or "marqueurs de parole" to make obvious the cultural legacy of the oral literature inherited from the times of Slavery.

21. Chamoiseau and Confiant, *Lettres créoles*, 62–63.

22. Confiant, "Patrick Chamoiseau ou la réconciliation avec notre entour."

23. "L'enfant Chamoiseau" by Bianciotti and "Les Cent dix-sept sortilèges de Patrick Chamoiseau" by Kundera were both reprinted in *Antilla*, no. 411, November 30–December 6, 1990, 40–41.

24. "Patrick Chamoiseau Lauréat du Prix Carbet," 37.

CHAPTER 5: RAPHAËL CONFIANT

1. I borrow "defense et illustration" from Joachim du Bellay, the French poet of the Renaissance who is believed to have given French its *lettres de noblesse* by rejecting the Latin then in usage and in prestige in France. Du Bellay's manifesto *Défense et illustration de la langue française* (1549) was written to prove that French was as rich and noble a language as Latin, through some examples, and also by giving some recommendations on how to use French properly.

2. Les créoles, en général, ont un rapport traumatique avec la langue française. Nous sommes des descendants de personnes qui ont été privées de leurs langues originelles (africaines) et qui ont été sommées d'inventer une nouvelle langue dans l'enfer esclavagiste. Nous ne l'avons jamais acceptée comme étant la nôtre, d'autant que le maître la méprisait beaucoup, la considérait comme un "baragouin." . . . A partir des années 30, quand l'idéologie colonialiste a été remise en cause, quand Aimé Césaire a développé le thème de la Négritude, quand on a commencé à contester la suprématie intellectuelle de l'homme occidental, fatalement le rapport à la langue française en a été ébranlé. Nous avons trouvé suspecte notre vénération. Nous nous sommes demandé si la langue créole ne méritait pas un autre regard. J'ai été très tôt un militant de la langue et de la culture créoles. La difficulté venait de son oralité. Le créole n'était utilisé littérairement que de manière ludique. Le texte le plus ancien en créole date de 1754 (3). Comme il était interdit aux esclaves d'apprendre à lire et à écrire, les maîtres ont été, paradoxalement, les premiers à écrire en créole. Notre génération a décidé de rompre ce rapport folklorique avec le créole, cesser d'en faire un doux patois, un langage de colibris gazouillants (De Ceccatty, "Carrefour de littératures européennes," 1–2).

[All translations in this chapter are my own, unless otherwise noted.]

3. Durant de nombreuses années (douze ans), il produira des textes en créole. A travers cinq romans, il tente de se réapproprier une langue dénigrée par le colonisateur. Malgré une certaine condescendance et parfois même un certain mépris de ses compatriotes, il ne lâche pas prise, l'homme est pugnace. Du fétichisme et de la noblesse de la langue française, il n'en a que faire. Ses livres en créole publiés à compte d'auteur dépassent rarement les trois cents exemplaires, son compte en banque est alors dans le rouge mais il n'est pas question pour lui d'abandonner. Défendre le créole est devenu une mission. L'écrivain est exalté. Pourtant, son ami Patrick Chamoiseau saura le

convaincre d'écrire en français. Il accepte. Mais attention, la langue utilisée aujourd'hui par Confiant est triturée, désarticulée, reconstruite, en un mot, elle est créolisée. N'allez surtout pas lui parler de la pureté de la langue, il vous rirait au nez. Pour lui, en cette matière, le respect n'existe pas. Il faut abuser des mots et bousculer les phrases. Résultat: il publie des romans dans un français pas tout à fait 'académique.' Ils ont pour titre *Le Nègre et l'Amiral, Eau de café* et *Ravines du devant-jour*. On y trouve toute la 'diversalité' et toute la complexité du monde antillais. Avec ses acolytes, P. Chamoiseau et J. Bernabé, il écrit un manifeste, *L'Eloge de la Créolité*, avec le premier et il rédigera une anthologie *Lettres créoles: tracées antillaises et continentales de la littérature (1635–1975)* et c'est seul qu'il lancera un pamphlet, *Aimé Césaire, le paradoxe*. Les romans comme les essais de Raphaël Confiant sont toujours l'occasion de livrer combat contre les impérialismes *culturels et pour la reconnaissance de l'identité antillaise*" (Sabbah, "Raphaël Confiant," 94–95).

4. À un monde totalement raciste, automutilé par ses chirurgies coloniales, Aimé Césaire restitua l'Afrique mère, l'Afrique matrice, la civilisation nègre.... Aimé Césaire eut, entre tous, le redoutable privilège de, symboliquement, rouvrir et refermer avec la Négritude la boucle qui enserre deux monstres tutelaires: l'Européanité et l'Africanité, toutes extériorités procédant de deux logiques adverses (*Eloge de la Créolité*, 17–18).

5. Lorsque tu demandes à Man Yise pourquoi on ne voit jamais le bébé de Man Cia, elle te fiche une calotte comme d'habitude. Léonise, pour sa part, te lance une sentence: "Tout manger est bon à manger, Chabin, mais toute parole n'est pas bonne à dire." Alors du haut de tes six ans, tu enfreins cette loi de céans qui veut que les affaires des grandes personnes sont les affaires des grandes personnes et que les affaires de la marmaille sont les affaires de la marmaille (37–38).

6. Tu détestes le Français-France qu'elle veut te contraindre à parler et, du même coup, tu prends en grippe le français plus gouleyant en usage dans ta famille. Tu ne veux plus t'exprimer qu'en créole et elle te déclare la guerre. Elle dispose d'un piège imparable: le premier qu'elle surprend à parler créole dans l'enceinte de l'école, elle lui passe au cou un collier fruste, au bout duquel pendouille une espèce de molaire (de "manicou," affirment les élèves, désignant ainsi, dans notre langue, l'opposum des tropiques) (79).

7. Ce soir-là, l'institutrice a fêté sa promotion en se faisant coquer toute debout derrière une porte par Parrain Salvie. Très curieusement, elle a semblé avoir oublié l'idiome sacré puisqu'elle a hurlé: "*Ba mwen dòt! Dòt! Dòt!*" (Donne-m'en encore, mon chéri! Encore! Encore!) (83).

8. Notre maîtresse est une dame de France, bien qu'elle soit noire comme un péché mortel, car elle se poudre les joues de rose et porte des talons hauts. Nous n'avions jamais soupçonné qu'elle puisse comprendre notre créole jusqu'au jour où elle calotte un élève qui a injurié son voisin d'un rétentissant "*Bonda manman'w!*" (le cul de ta mère) (81–82).

9. Jugeant que désormais nous nous trouvons en honorable compagnie,

tante Emérante t'interdit l'usage de l'idiome des coupeurs de canne à sucre et te fait la lecture *d'Intimités* chaque soir, afin que tu améliores ton vocabulaire français. . . . Elle ne peut réprimer un petit cri de chat-pouchine quand elle se rend compte de la masse effrayante qui se meut dans la noireté, comme prête à bondir sur le bourg pour l'engloutir. Ce dernier est silencieux. Le monde dort raide-et-dur, et même les chiens ne jappent point. *"Yo pa pou konnèt, fout!"* (Ils n'en ont cure!) soliloque-t-elle, incrédule et admirative à la fois, retrouvant, sans même s'en étonner, la langue honnie (165).

10. À Terres-Sainvilles, on n'entend que le créole le plus rude, fait de mots imprononçables pour les mulâtres du centre-ville et de jurons interminables qui ont le don de te ravir. Car, en Ville aussi, tes proches n'ont pas réussi à te dépersuader de t'accointer avec les rebuts de l'humanité (197).

11. L'enfance pour toi, s'est achevée au bout de tes neuf ans. Finie la douce errance créole entre les grand-mères, la marraine, les tantes et leurs amis, toutes personnes de grand maintien et d'ardente amour. Fini le fol enliannement dans la parlure des nègres qui, par bonheur, ne s'écrit point et dont on n'a donc point à s'échiner pour respecter un quelconque Ordre Orthographique (243).

12. Raphaël Confiant est martiniquais. Il vit dans une case antillaise. Les objets de la modernité occidentale se résument à un fax, un téléphone et un poste de télévision. Entre femme et enfants, sa machine à écrire, ses livres et ses cabris, c'est là que naissent ses romans. Pour créer, pour inventer, pour se souvenir, il a besoin de son île, de ses paysages, de ses habitants et de sa mémoire. Chez lui, le succès n'a rien d'ostentatoire, au point d'en être presque agaçant! Son regard n'est pas tourné vers l'Europe ou l'Amérique, il scrute la Martinique, sa Martinique. Son cadre de vie est volontairement modeste. Une façon, peut-être de montrer que sa richesse est ailleurs, un ailleurs bâti sur une langue, le créole (Sabbah, "Raphaël Confiant," 99).

13. Nous sommes tout à la fois, l'Europe, l'Afrique, nourris d'apports asiatiques, levantins, indiens, et nous relevons aussi des survivances de l'Amérique précolombienne. La Créolité, c'est *"le monde diffracté mais recomposé,"* un maelström de signifiés dans un seul signifiant:une Totalité. Et nous disons qu'il n'est pas dommageable pour l'instant, de ne pas en avoir une définition (*Eloge de la Créolité*, 27; emphasis in the original).

14. Le fils, né et vivant à Pékin, d'un Allemand ayant épousé une Haïtienne, sera écartelé entre plusieurs langues, plusieurs histoires, pris dans l'ambiguïté torrentielle d'une identité mosaïque. Il devra, sous peine de mort créative, la penser dans toute sa complexité. *Il sera en état de créole* (*Eloge de la Créolité*, 52; emphasis in the original).

15. Au contraire! Je découvre une plus grande liberté. Le créole est une langue rurale, habituée à désigner des réalités immédiates. Son niveau conceptuel est très limité. Lorsqu'on s'exerce à écrire un roman dans une langue orale et rurale, on a beaucoup de difficultés, parce qu'un concept doit être exprimé à

travers des périphrases. La liberté, pour les écrivains créoles, paradoxalement, c'est le français, parce que le français est déjà une langue constituée avec laquelle on peut jouer. Quand j'écris en créole, je ne peux pas jouer parce que je suis obligé de construire un outil. . . . Je maintiens que l'écriture en français est un plaisir et qu'en créole, c'est un travail. Je suis beaucoup plus à l'aise dans la description en français. Un paysan ne décrit pas un arbre, par exemple. Il vit en intimité complète avec la nature. Le créole n'a pas de niveau descriptif: il manque d'adjectifs permettant de décrire un paysage (4).

16. C'est cette troisième langue, le français-banane—ou plus exactement une version francisée, occidentalisée par l'acte littéraire lui-même—qu'emploie le plus fréquemment Raphaël Confiant dans ses souvenirs d'enfance (Lepape, "Le Feuilleton," 3).

17. Le français, dit "français banane" qui est au français standard ce que le latin macaronique est au latin classique, constitue, à n'en pas douter, ce que l'interlangue récèle de plus stéréotypé, et par quoi, irrésistiblement, elle donne dans le comique. . . . Quant à nous, notre éloge de la Créolité ne sera jamais celui de l'accroupissement désoeuvré et infécond à faire autre chose que parasiter le monde. Or, toute une série de productions verbales peuvent aisément, si on n'y prend garde, faire fortune à se comporter en plantes épiphytes, enclines de surcroît, à détourner le fleuve langage de son embouchure créole (*Eloge de la Créolité*, 49).

18. In her excellent article "La Créolité à l'oeuvre dans *Ravines du devant-jour* de Raphaël Confiant," Valérie Loichot agrees with my statement by asserting that Confiant "creolizes" French by different creative strategies in his autobiography: "Les mots français, intrusion d'abord, sont pourtant adoptés par l'auteur—son récit d'enfance, récit intime, est d'ailleurs écrit en français—mais pas avant d'avoir été reforgés, minés, infiltrés de l'intérieur dans un processus de créolisation. Nous ne citerons ici que quelques exemples de ces entrelacs de mots dans le texte, comme l'écrit si bellement Confiant 'ce fol enlianement de la parlure des nègres' (Ravines, 201). Les mots français peuvent être enliannés au Créole par des procédés de calques ou l'on reprend la structure d'une expression pour la modifier de l'intérieur comme dans l'expression 'au beau mitan' (Ravines, 13), conservant la structure d' 'au beau milieu' et remplaçant le mot 'milieu' par son équivalent créole, le 'mitan.' Le mot ainsi enchâssé dans une structure importée permet l'adoption par hybridation d'une structure de la langue française. Même si le mot mitan est un vieux mot français, il est perçu comme créole par le lecteur de la métropole. Cette relique oubliée est rajeunie et remotivée dans le français créole et perçue comme une création alors qu'elle est un emprunt de la langue originelle. D'autres mots sont créolisés par l'adjonction d'affixes eux aussi français. Dans ce cas, c'est le processus même de juxtaposition qui fait la créolisation, même si et le mot et l'affixe sont tous deux français. Je cite quelques exemples: 'fénéantiseur' pour fainéant, 'doucine' pour douceur, 'tendreté' pour tendresse, 'belleté' pour beauté. Selon ce procédé, un habitant, un autochtone devient un zabitant, une écrevisse autochtone devient naturellement

une 'écrevisse-zabitant.' Le mot français est ainsi créolisé (zabitant). La prothèse héritée de la prononciation du nom pluriel accompagné d'un article (les habitants) devient à son tour un suffixe acclimatisant le mot dans le contexte créole. L'hybridation des mots alors qu'elle serait considérée comme une erreur infantile dans la langue française (un zabitan, un zoiseau) se fait procédé de grammatisation, de normalisation dans le français créolisé" (629–30).

19. Du coup, nous voilà nous-mêmes transformés en voyeurs, en amateurs de pittoresque, en ramasseurs d'exotique, en picoreurs d'expressions singulières, de saveurs patoisantes et de parler délicieusement incongrus. Nous voilà des touristes d'un livre dont nous sentons pourtant à chaque instant qu'il délivre bien autre chose que des volées de cartes postales. Nous admirons et nous sommes en même temps honteux de notre plaisir; invités à la table, gavés de mets succulents, mais gentiment exclus de la famille des hôtes, de leurs allusions, de leurs plaisanteries, de toute cette vie qui se poursuit sous les ornements de la fête (Lepape, "Le Feuilleton," 3).

20. Notre valetaille a coutume de proférer d'un air énigmatique: "Papa Loulou est chimérique." Dans *notre parlure*, ce mot renvoie à de brusques éclairs qui ennuagent soudain le regard de celui qui est en train de vous entretenir de propos dénués d'importance (19; emphasis mine).

21. "Les déclarations d'intention de l'autobiographe sont tout à fait repérables; elles seront l'une des aunes auxquelles le lecteur ne pourra s'empêcher de mesurer ses attentes" (Jaccomard, *Lecteur et lecture*, 35).

22. All these genres are generally defined according to their finality: tragedy leads to death, while comedy's purpose is to make the spectator or reader laugh, and drama is a mixture of both playing with the serious and grave. I am using this simplistic definition, as these are not plays, but rather narratives that are dominated by a certain tone.

CHAPTER 6: MARYSE CONDÉ

1. Jonathan Ngaté, an African critic, reads Maryse Condé in her controversial relationship with Africa as it is reflected in her novels, especially *Heremakhonon*. To him, Condé is "recalcitrant" because she refuses to endorse Africa as "mother Africa," but rather as a stepmother: "Recalcitrant daughter of 'Afrique-mère' as Condé very soon will be shown to be, the analysis of the African situation in *Mort d'Oluwémi d'Ajumako* nonetheless parallels others, say, Nigerian writings, both pre-and post-Civil War" (8). Ngaté is critical of Condé's paradox with Africa: her harsh representation and critique of Africa and Africans, yet her inclusion of Africa as a central theme in her novels: "That counts for something, and surprisingly enough the whole interview confirms one in the belief that while it would be foolish to deny that Maryse Condé is indeed a Caribbean woman, she is also one for whom Africa has been and remains an essential point of reference. . . . Her strength is in the way in which

she both reveals and conceals her awareness of the ambiguity of her position as an Afro-Caribbean woman thinking and writing primarily about, and as, a woman caught up in the male/female, African/Afro-Caribbean dichotomy" (18). Ngaté ironically adopts Condé as "that cousin from Guadeloupe."

2. Condé, *Tales from the Heart*, 54. In this chapter, I quote from the English version of Condé's work, as translated by her husband, Richard Philcox. I am providing the corresponding quotes from the original French in the notes. (Maryse Condé strongly believes that any of her translated work is no longer hers and has instead become another product.) The quote in the original French follows: "À cause de cette paranoïa de mes parents, j'ai vécu mon enfance dans l'angoisse. J'aurais tout donné pour être la fille de gens ordinaires, anonymes. J'avais l'impression que les membres de ma famille étaient menacés, exposés au cratère d'un volcan dont la lave en feu risquait en tout instant de les consumer. Je masquais ce sentiment tant bien que mal par des affabulations et une agitation constantes, mais il me rongeait" (Condé, *Le Coeur à rire et à pleurer*, 40–41).

3. In *Conversations with Maryse Condé*, answering a question posed by Françoise Pfaff, Condé herself attributes the unfavorable reception of *Heremakhonon* to the political and cultural environments both in Africa and in the Caribbean:

FP: How were your first two novels received in France?

MC: They went almost unnoticed. There were very few reviews, though rather favorable ones, especially *A Season in Rihata*. I recall that Jerome Garcin defended it on the radio program *Le masque et la plume*. But that's all. Magazines such as *Jeune Afrique* and *Afrique-Asie* royally ignored them. A friend told me that *Afrique-Asie* had even refused to publish his article on *Hermakhonon*. Neither of those two novels was "politically correct."

FP: What happened in Africa and in Guadeloupe?

MC: In Africa, apart from a moralizing article by a friend, Bernard Zadi, in *Ivoire Dimanche*, there was the same conspiracy of silence. However, the word-of-mouth system worked, and I was labeled as a person who detests and says bad things about Africa. I was tagged a reactionary. But in the West Indies, critics broke loose. An article in *Le Naïf*, signed by someone whose name I will not mention, called me a "voyeur and a whore," added that "an odor of sperm could be smelled" in the book and ended up comparing me to Mayotte Capécia. Instead of laughing about it, I cried (46).

In the context of postcolonial Africa of the 1970s where communism and socialism were seen as positive avenues for the liberation and development of the newly independent nations, the critical representation of a tyrannical regime (easily identified as that of Sékou Touré) in *Heremakhonon* did not sit well with *Jeune Afrique* and *Afrique-Asie,* both leftist newspapers. In a way, the negative representation of Africa in *Hermakhonon* was then perceived as contributing to the "Afro-pessimism" undermining the development and positive representation of Africa.

In "Mediations of Identity Through the Atlantic Slave Trade," a chapter in her book *Autobiographical Tightropes*, Leah Hewitt reveals the shifts in Condé's trial to disassociate herself with Véronica and autobiography: "Condé's interview with Ina Césaire a few years after the publication of *Heremakhonon* affords intriguing insights into Condé's particular resistance to, and affinities for autobiography. In the first part of the interview, Condé takes her distance from formal autobiography in a categorical way: 'Everything one writes has autobiographical roots. But Véronica's story is not mine and I have no desire to recount my life'" (186). For Hewitt, Condé posits Véronica as an "Anti-me," to erase any connection between the writer and the main character.

4. Condé, *Tales from the Heart*, 95. The quote in the original French reads: "Ma mère n'entretenait de relations suivies qu'avec l'un de ses cousins de Marie-Galante. De vingt ans son cadet, il répondait au prénom céleste de Séraphin. C'était un gros garçon taciturne et embarrassé qui respirait de loin son bitako. Dans sa bouche, le français prenait des allures de créole et il s'emmêlait aussi bien dans les articles que dans les adjectifs possessifs. . . . Ce garçon respectueux était la risée de mes frères et soeurs parce que lors des repas dominicaux, quand ma mère lui proposait de se resservir, il répondait à chaque fois en secouant poliment la tête: —Merci cousine Jeanne, j'ai mangé mon content!" (Condé, *Le Coeur à rire et à pleurer*, 89).

5. Condé, *Heremakhonon*, 13. In the original French, this passage reads: "Nous avions un cousin quand même, cousin Séraphin. Parfois il venait déjeuner le dimanche avec sa femme cousine Charlotte. A la fin du repas, il disait: —Merci cousine Marthe, j'ai mangé mon content" (Condé, *En Attendant le Bonheur [Heremakhonon]*, 34).

6. Condé, *Heremakhonon*, 34. In the original French, this passage reads: "Notre maison était une des plus jolies de la ville. Il y avait un balcon, de hautes fenêtres et des bougainvillées sur le balcon. Ma da s'appelait Mabo Julie; elle portait un jupon empesé sous sa robe. Elle, m'aimait. Elle prenait toujours ma défense et me faisait avaler de grosses tranches de gâteau marbré dans la cuisine. Et des tasses de chodo. Malheureusement, elle est morte quand j'avais seize ans. J'ai été initiée, la même année, à l'amour et à la mort" (Condé, *En Attendant le Bonheur [Heremakhonon]*, 64).

7. Condé, *Tales from the Heart*, 46. In the original French, this passage reads: "Mabo Julie était la bonne qui m'avait charroyée dans ses bras et promenée sur la Place de la Victoire pour faire admirer à tous ceux qui avaient des yeux pour admirer mes casaques en soie, en tulle ou en dentelle. Elle m'avait aidée quand j'apprenais à marcher, relevée, consolée à chaque fois que je tombais. . . . Moi, je l'adorais à l'égal de ma propre mère qui en était jalouse, je le sais" (Condé, *Le Coeur à rire et à pleurer*, 46–47).

8. Condé, *Heremakhonon*, 122. In the original French, this passage reads: "Ils cherchaient un prétexte pour se pavaner à Saint-Claude, dans ce fief de la mulâtraille où les Noirs marchaient sur la pointe des pieds, les békés s'étant

refugiés encore plus haut dans les hauteurs. On les a donc eues ces vacances à Saint-Claude. On a loué la villa de mulâtres désargentés qui possédaient une boulangerie-pâtisserie à Trois-Rivières où ils habitaient désormais. Et là, croyez-moi, ce fut l'anonymat le plus complet. A quatre-vings kilomètres de la Pointe, où son nom faisait tant de bruit, le marabout mandingue était un inconnu. . . . A Saint-Claude nous n'étions pas des intrus. Simplement, nous n'existions pas" (Condé, *En Attendant le Bonheur [Heremakhonon]*, 182–83).

9. Condé, *Tales from the Heart*, 117. In the original French, this passage reads: "Selon la rigide géographie sociale de ce temps-là, les régions de Trois-Rivières, Gourbeyre, Basse Terre appartenaient aux mulâtres. Mes parents, quant à eux, avaient leur place à Grande-Terre. Saint-Claude et Matouba étaient les fiefs des blancs-pays qui les disputaient aux Indiens. Mes parents, quant à eux avaient leur place en Grande-Terre. . . . Ce que je sais, c'est que nous fumes ignorés. Mes parents avaient beau rouler en Citroën C4; ma mère avait beau garrotter son cou de son collier chou et mon père plastronner son ruban de la Légion d'honneur qui faisait tellement d'effet à La Pointe, personne ne nous prêtait attention" (Condé, *Le Coeur à rire et à pleurer*, 107).

10. "Maryse Condé: La révolte et la pitié."

11. Source http://www.fluctuat.net/scenes/paris99/sorties/ athevain.htm.

12. Richard est aussi mon traducteur: il se désole de mon indifférence. Mes livres en anglais ne m'intéressent plus. Lors de leur parution, il est seul à guetter le New York Times et le Village Voice. Je ne doute pas de ses talents et ne lui applique pas l'adage "Traduttore, traditore." Simplement, je ne ME retrouve pas. Les mots, c'est bien connu, ne servent pas seulement à créer du sens. Ils jouent, ils font l'amour. Ils composent une musique. Je ne suis pas sensible à la musique d'un texte traduit, créé avec des sons étrangers, donc différents, indépendants de mon choix (6; Condé's emphasis).

13. Pfaff, *Conversations with Maryse Condé*, 41.

CONCLUSION

1. L'anormal, c'est ce que j'ai fait: publier cinq livres en créole et m'en tenir pendant douze longues années à ce refus. Ce n'était qu'un refus public, bien entendu, parce que, tout en publiant mes livres créoles et en défendant mes positions, très "nationalitaires," j'écrivais chez moi en français! En Martinique, mes romans créoles peuvent se vendre à trois cents exemplaires, alors que mes romans français atteignent quatre mille ventes. Je ne pouvais pas y être indifférent (De Ceccaty, "Carrefour des littératures européennes").

2. See Gusdorf, "Conditions and Limits of Autobiography," 28–48; and Gusdorf, *Lignes de vie*.

WORKS CITED

Aggarwal, Kusum. *Amadou Hampâté Bâ et l'africanisme: De la recherche anthropologique à l'exercice de la fonction auctoriale.* Collection sociétés africaines et diaspora. Paris: L'Harmattan, 1999.

Aide sociale, Web site with information for helping youth (listed Amadou Hampâté Bâ's *Amkoullel* in their catalog). July 25, 2007. http://www.ac-1limoges.fr/CAFA/ressources/aide-sociale.htm (accessed July 23, 2009).

"Un Air d'Afrique va souffler sur Vitré." *Ouest France*, June 29, 2007 (accessed on the Web, August 2, 2009).

Aperçus culturels, Web site of an online magazine for the Franch-Conte region of France. February 2004. http://www.cr-franche-comte.fr/apercusculturel/mensuel42/affiche.php ?idsite=18&idpage=375&idpage=375&idrub=1&idmenupage=490 (accessed July 25, 2009).

Arnold, James. "The Novelist as Critic." *World Literature Today* 67, no. 4 (1993): 711–16.

Ashcroft, Bill, Gareth Griffiths, and Helen Tiffin. *The Empire Writes Back: Theory and Practice in Post-Colonial Literatures.* London: Routledge, 1989.

Bâ, Amadou Hampâté. *Aspects de la civilisation africaine: Personne, culture, religion.* Paris: Présence Africaine, 1995.

———. *L 'Éclat de la grande étoile. Suivi du Bain rituel. Récits initiatiques peuls de Amadou-Hampâté Bâ.* Paris: Armand Colin, 1974.

———. *L'Empire peul du Macina.* Collection "Le monde d'outre-mer passé et présent, Etudes XV." Paris: Mouton, 1962.

———. *L'Étrange destin de Wangrin ou Les roueries d'un interprète africain.* Paris: Union Générale d'Éditions, 1982.

———. *Histoire du Sahel occidental malien: Des origines a nos jours.* Bamako, Mali: Editions Jamana, 1989.

———. *Jésus vu par un musulman.* Dakar, Senegal, and Abidjan, Ivory Coast: Nouvelles Editions Africaines, 1976.

———. "The Living Tradition." In *General History of Africa*, vol. 2. Berkeley: UNESCO/University of California Press, 1981.

———. *Mémoires 1: Amkoullel, l'enfant peul.* Arles, France: Actes Sud, 1991.

———. *Mémoires 2: Oui, mon Commandant!* Arles, France: Actes Sud, 1994.

———. *La Notion de personne en Afrique noire.* Groupe de recherche 11: Etude des phénomènes religieux en Afrique occidentale et équatoriale. Paris: n.p., 1971.

———. *Petit Bodiel: Une Poignée de poussières; contes peuls.* Paris: Stock, 1994.

———. *Le Petit frère d'Amkoullel.* With illustrations by Christian Kingué Épanya. Paris: Syros, 1994.

———. *La Poignée de poussière: Contes et récits du Mali.* Abidjan, Ivory Coast: Nouvelles Editions Africaines, 1987.

———. *Sur les traces d'Amkoullel, l'enfant peul.* Edited by Bernard Magnier, with photography by Philippe Dupuich. Arles, France: Actes Sud, 1998.

———. *Vie et enseignement de Tierno Bokar, le sage de Bandiagara.* Paris: Editions du Seuil, 1980.

Bâ, Amadou Hampâté, and Marcel Cardaire. *Tierno Bokar: Le sage de Bandiagara.* Paris: Présence Africaine, 1957.

Bâ, Amadou Hampâté, and Germaine Dierterlen. *Koumen texte iniatique des pasteurs peuls.* Paris and La Haye: Mouton, 1966.

Bâ, Amadou Hampâté, and Lilyan Kesteloot. *Kaïdara.* Paris: Julliard, 1969.

Barry, Kesso. *Kesso, Princesse peuhle.* Paris: Seghers, 1988.

Bernabé, Jean, Raphaël Confiant, and Patrick Chamoiseau. *Eloge de la Créolité.* Bilingual edition. Translated by M. B. Taleb-Khyar. Paris: Gallimard, 1989.

———. "La Riposte (circonstanciée)/Cabort a soif d'une reconnaissance toujours refusée." *Karibèl,* no. 17 (May 1992): 23.

Bianciotti, Hector. "L'Enfant Chamoiseau." *Le Monde* (France), November 2, 1990.

"Bibliographie nationale française Livres - Cumulatif 2001." Bibliographie nationale française. September 2007. http://bibliographienationale.bnf.fr/livres/cum_01.h/ cadre92–4.html (accessed July 23, 2009).

Boahen, A. Adu. "Africa and the Colonial Challenge." In *General History of African VII: Africa Under Colonial Domination, 1880–1935,* edited by Adu A. Boahen. London: Heinemann, 1985.

Borgomano, Madeleine. "A l'écoute de Ahmadou Kourouma." *Mots Pluriels,* September 2002. http://motspluriels.arts.uwa .edu.au/MP2202mb.html (accessed August 20, 2009).

Bourdieu, Pierre. *La Domination masculine.* Paris: Seuil, 1998.

Bugul, Ken. *The Abandoned Baobab: The Autobiography of a Senegalese Woman.* Chicago: Lawrence Hill Books, 1991.

———. *Le Baobab fou.* Vies Africaines. Dakar, Senegal: Nouvelles Editions Africaines, 1997.

Cabort-Masson, Guy. "La Dérive culturelle/Les puissances d'argent à la Martinique." *Karibèl*, no. 17 (May 1992): 22–23.

———. *La Mangrove mulâtre: roman historique martiniquais.* Saint-Joseph, Martinique: La Voix du Peuple, 1986.

———. *Martinique comportements et mentalités: Créolisation assimilation nationalisme.* Saint-Joseph, Martinique: La Voix du Peuple, 1998.

———. *La Passion de Raziéla.* Saint-Joseph, Martinique: La Voix du Peuple, 1989.

———. *Pourrir, ou Martyr un peu.* Saint-Joseph, Martinique: La Voix du Peuple, 1987.

———. *Les Puissances d'argent en Martinique: l'État français, la caste békée et les autres.* Saint-Joseph, Martinique: Laboratoire de recherches de l'AMEP, 1987.

———. *Qui a tué le béké de Trinité?* Saint-Joseph, Martinique: La Voix du Peuple, 1991.

Camara, Laye. *L'Enfant noir.* Paris: Plon, 1953.

Certeau, Michel de, Luce Giard, and Pierre Mayol. *L'Invention du quotidien.* Paris: Gallimard, 1990.

Césaire, Aimé. *Le Cahier d'un retour au pays natal.* Paris: Présence africaine, 1960.

Chamoiseau, Patrick. *Antan d'enfance.* Paris: Hatier, 1990. Reprint, Paris: Gallimard, 1993. Reprinted as *Une Enfance créole I, Antan d'enfance* with a new preface, Paris: Gallimard, 1996. Translated by Carol Volk as *Childhood,* Lincoln: University of Nebraska Press, 1999.

———. À Bout d'enfance. Paris: Gallimard, 2005. Reprinted as *Une Enfance créole III, À bout d'enfance.* Paris: Gallimard, 2006.

———. *Biblique des derniers gestes: Roman.* Paris: Gallimard, 2002.

———. *Chemin d'école.* Paris: Gallimard, 1994. Reprinted as *Une Enfance créole II, Chemin d'école,* Paris: Gallimard, 1996.

———. *Chronique des sept misères.* Paris: Gallimard, 1988.

———. *Un dimanche au cachot: Roman.* Paris: Gallimard, 2007.

———. *Ecrire en pays dominé.* Paris: Gallimard, 1997.

———. *L'Esclave vieil homme et le molosse.* Paris: Gallimard, 2006.

———. *Manman Dlo contre la fée Carabosse: Théâtre conté.* Paris: Editions Caribéennes, 1982.

———. *Les Neuf Consciences du malfini: Roman.* Paris: Gallimard, 2009.

———. *Solibo magnifique: Roman.* Paris: Gallimard, 1991.

———. *Texaco.* Paris: Gallimard, 1994.

Chamoiseau, Patrick, and Raphaël Confiant. *Lettres créoles: Tracées antillaises et continentales de la littérature, Haïti, Guadeloupe, Martinique, Guyane; 1635–1975.* Paris: Hatier, 1991.

Chaulet-Achour, Christiane. Ministère de l'Education nationale. October 2000. http://eduscol.education.fr/D0033/actfran _francophonie.pdf (accessed August 20, 2009).

Chehat, Fayçal. Review of *Sur les traces d'Amkoullel, l'enfant peul.* Africultures. January 17, 2002. http://www .africultures.com/index.asp?menu=affiche_article&no=558 (accessed July 25, 2009).

"En Classe de Seconde." Éducnet, August 3, 2007. http://www2 .educnet. education.fr/educnet/sections/lettres/pratiques5675/lycee/se-conde/11128675218247 (accessed August 20, 2009).

"Le Coeur à rire et à pleurer de Maryse Condé au musée Dapper." *Gens de La Caraïbe.* March 31, 2004. http://www .gensdelacaraibe.org/index2. php?option=com_content&do_pdf =1&id=1152 (accessed July 28, 2009).

Commager, H. Steele, Raymond Henry Muessig, and Vincent Robert Rogers. *The Nature and the Study of History.* Ohio: Charles E. Merrill Books, 1965.

Condé, Maryse. "Chercher nos vérités." In *Penser la créolité,* edited by Maryse Condé and Madeleine Cottenet-Hage, 305–10. Paris: Karthala, 1995.

———. *Le Coeur à rire et à pleurer.* Paris: Robert Laffont, 1999. Translated by Richard Philcox as *Tales from the Heart,* New York: Soho Press, Inc., 2004.

———. *Conversations with Maryse Condé.* Interview by Françoise Pfaff. Lincoln: University of Nebraska Press, 1996.

———. *En Attendant le bonheur (Heremakhonon).* Paris: Robert Laffont, 1997. Translated by Richard Philcox as *Heremakhonon,* Boulder, CO, and London: Lynne Rienner Publishers, 2000.

———. "Interview de Maryse Condé." In *La Parole des femmes: Essai sur des romancieres des Antilles de langue francaise,* 124–29. Paris: L'Harmattan, 1993.

———. "J'essaie en vain de joindre Abidjan; mon journal de la semaine." *Libération* (France), November 4, 2000, 6. LexisNexis (accessed May 5, 2009).

———. *Maryse Condé Speaks from the Heart.* Interview directed by Susan Wilcox. Produced by Ann Armstrong Scarboro. Videodisc. Boulder, CO: Mosaic Media, 2003.

———. "Parce que tu es une négresse. . ." *L'Humanité* (France), May 10, 2006, 9. LexisNexis (accessed June 3, 2007).

———. *Ségou: les murailles de terre: Roman.* Paris: Robert Laffont, 1984.

———. *La Vie scélérate: Roman.* Paris: Seghers, 1989.

Confiant, Raphaël. *Adèle et la pacotilleuse: Roman.* Paris: Mercure de France, 2005.

———. *Aimé Césaire, une traversée paradoxale du siècle.* Paris: Stock, 1993. Reprint, Paris: Écriture, 2006.

———. *L'Allée des soupirs: Roman*. Paris: Grasset, 1994. Reprint, Montréal: Mémoire d'encrier, 2008.

———. *L'Archet du Colonel: Roman*. Paris: Mercure de France, 1998.

———. *La Baignoire de Joséphine*. Paris: Mille et une nuits, 1997.

———. *Le Barbare enchanté: Roman*. Paris: Écriture, 2003.

———. *Bassin des ouragans*. Paris: Mille et une nuits, 1994.

———. *Barrancos del alba: Literatura francocaribeña novela*. Havana, Cuba: Casa de las Américas, 1993.

———. *Bitako-a: Roman*. Schoelcher: GEREC; Paris: l'Harmattan, 1985.

———. *Brin d'amour: Roman*. Paris: Mercure de France, 2001.

———. *Le Cahier de romances*. Collection Haute Enfance. Paris: Gallimard, 2000.

———. *Case à Chine: Roman*. Paris: Mercure, 2007.

———. *Commandeur du sucre: Récit*. Paris: Écriture, 1994.

———. *Dictionnaire des néologismes créoles*. Petit-Bourg, Guadeloupe: Ibis Rouge, 2000.

———. *Dictionnaire créole martiniquais-français*. Matoury, Guyane: Ibis Rouge, 2007.

———. *Dictionnaire des Titim et sirandanes: Devinettes et jeux de mots du monde creole*. Kourou: Ibis Rouge, 1998.

———. *Eau de café: Roman*. Paris: Grasset, 1991.

———. *L'Hôtel du bon plaisir*. Paris: Mercure, 2009.

———. *Jik dèyè do Bondyé: Nouvelles*. Martinique: Grif An Tè, 1979.

———. *Jou Baré: Poèmes*. Martinique: Grif An Tè, 1981.

———. *Kôd Yanm: Roman*. K.D.P., 1986.

———. *La Lessive du diable*. Paris: Serpent à Plumes, 2003.

———. *Mamzelle Libellule: Roman*. Paris: Serpent à Plumes, 1994.

———. *Marisosé: Roman*. Schoelcher: Presses Universitaires Créoles, 1987.

———. *Le Meurtre du Samedi-Gloria*. Paris: Mercure, 1997.

———. *Morne-Pichevin*. Paris: Bibliophane-Daniel Radford, 2002.

———. *Le Nègre et l'Amiral: Roman*. Paris: Grasset, 1988.

———. *Nègre marron: Récit*. Paris: Écriture, 1998.

———. *Nuée ardente*. Paris: Mercure, 2002.

———. *La Panse du chacal*. Paris: Mercure, 2004.

———. "Patrick Chamoiseau ou la réconciliation avec notre entour." *Antilla*, no. 408, November 9–15, 1990, 38–40.

———. *Ravines du devant jour*. Collection Folio. Paris: Gallimard, 1993.

———. *Régisseur de rhum: Récit*. Paris: Écriture, 1999.

———. *La Savane des Pétrifications*. Paris: Mille et une nuits, 1995.

———. *Les Ténèbres extérieures: Récit*. Paris: Écriture, 2008.

———. *La Vierge du grand retour*. Folio 4602. Paris: Gallimard, 2007.

Confiant, Raphaël, and Jean Bernabé. *Lettres créoles: Tracées antillaises et continentales de la littérature; 1635–1975*. Paris: Hatier, 1991.

Confiant, Raphaël, Jean Bernabé, and Patrick Chamoiseau. *Eloge de la créolité*. Paris: Gallimard, 1989.

Confiant, Raphaël, and Gerry L'Etang. *Le Gouverneur des dés*. Nouveau cabinet cosmopolite. Paris: Stock, 1995.

"Conseils de lecture." Collège Jean Moulin Le Pecq. August 20, 2007. http://www.ac-versailles.fr/etabliss/clg-moulin-lepecq/FRANCAIS/conseils%20de%20lecture.htm (accessed July 23, 2009).

Crosta, Suzanne. "Marronner le récit d'enfance: *Antan d'enfance* de Patrick Chamoiseau et *Ravines du devant-jour* de Raphaël Confiant." *Récits d'enfance antillaise*. Sainte-Foy, Québec: Université Laval, GRELCA, 1998. Available on the Web site Ile en île, July 16, 1999. http://www.lehman.cuny .edu/ile.en.ile/docs/crosta/chamoiseau_confiant.html (accessed August 24, 2009).

"Cultures." *L'Humanité* (France), May 22, 2004. http:// www.humanite.fr/po-pup_imprimer.html?id_article=394172 (accessed July 25, 2009).

Dadié, Bernard Binlin. *Un Nègre à Paris*. Paris: Présence Africaine, 1959.

D'Almeida, Irène Assiba. "Kesso Barry's *Kesso*, or Autobiography as a Subverted Tale." *Research in African Literatures* 28 (summer 1997): 66–82.

"Dans la Presse: Chronique des trois bonheurs." *Antilla* (Martinique), no. 411, November 30–December 6, 1990, 40–41.

De Ceccatty, René. "Carrefour de littératures européennes: La bicyclette créole ou la voiture française? Un entretien avec l'écrivain antillais Raphaël Confiant qui définit son paradoxe de romancier: vouloir faire vivre une langue et en écrire une autre." *Le Monde* (France), November 6, 1992, 1–2. LexisNexis (accessed July 2, 2009).

"Décédé mercredi: Hampâté Bâ inhumé hier." *Fraternité Matin* (Ivory Coast), no. 7984, May 17, 1991.

Deffontaines, Thérèse Marie. "La mémoire et l'écrit; Amadou Hampâté Bâ." *Le Monde* (France), December 13, 1999. LexisNexis (accessed February 12, 2009).

Delcroix, Olivier. Interview with Fabrice Luchini and Erik Orsenna. *Le Figaro* (France), June 21, 2007. LexisNexis (accessed February 2, 2009).

Desportes, Georges. "Une conscience d'adulte dans un regard d'enfant." Review of *Antan d'enfance* by Patrick Chamoiseau. *Antilla*, no. 412, December 7–13, 1990, 39–40.

———. Review of *Ravines du devant-jour* by Raphaël Confiant. *Antilla*, no. 550, September 10, 1993.

Diallo, A. B. "Kesso-Princesse peuhle." *Amina*, no. 220, August 1988, 66.

Dietrich, Claire. "Nouveaux programmes de Terminale. Atelier Colonisation, décolonisation, Tiers-Monde, les Sud." Académie de Grenoble. August 20, 2007. http://www.ac-grenoble.fr/histoire/programmes/lycee/classique/terminale/ hist/colo.pdf (accessed July 25, 2009).

Du Bellay, Joachim, and Henri Chamard. *La deffence et illustration de la langue francoyse (1549)*. Paris: A. Fontemoing, 1904.

Edie, James M. *Merleau-Ponty's Philosophy of Language: Structuralism and Dialectics*. Pittsburgh, PA, and Washington, DC: The Center for Advanced Research in Phenomenology / University Press of America, 1987.

"L'Enfance de Chamoiseau: Après Bernard Pivot, l'écrivain martiniquais sera l'invité de Bernard Rapp dans l'émission 'caractère.'" *Antilla* (Martinique), no. 402, September 28–October 4, 1990, 38.

L'Essor (Mali), May 19, 1991. Newspaper notice on the death of Amadou Hampâté Bâ.

Fanon, Frantz. *Peau noire, masques blancs*. Paris: Éditions du Seuil, 1952.

Ficatier, Julia. "Figures spirituelles du XXè siècle: Islam." *La Croix*, November 21, 1995. LexisNexis (accessed May 7, 2008).

Flaherty, Dolores, and Roger Flaherty. "A Child's Garden of Alienation." *Chicago Sun-Times*, February 1, 2004, 13. LexisNexis (accessed May 7, 2009).

Gallimore, Rangira Béatrice. "Écriture féministe? Écriture féminine? Les écrivaines francophones de l'Afrique subsaharienne face au regard du lecteur/critique." Études Françaises 37, no. 2 (2001): 79–98. http://www.erudit. org/ revue/etudfr/2001/v37/n2/009009ar.pdf.

Geesey, Patricia. "Why African Autobiography?" *Research in African Literatures* 28, no. 2 (summer 1997): 1–4.

Glissant, Edouard. *Le Discours antillais*. Paris: Gallimard, 1997.

Gottin, Marius. Interview with Raphaël Confiant. *France-Antilles Magazine*, June 11, 1993, 37.

Gusdorf, Georges. "Conditions and Limits of Autobiography." In *Autobiography: Essays Theoretical and Critical*, edited by James Olney, 28–48. Princeton, NJ: Princeton University Press, 1980.

———. *Lignes de vie*. 2 vols. Paris: Odile Jacob, 1991.

Heckmann, Hélène. "Genèse et authenticité des ouvrages l'Etrange destin de Wangrin et la série des Mémoires." Postface in *Oui mon Commandant! (Mémoires II)* by Amadou Hampâté Bâ, 389–94. Paris: Actes Sud, 1994.

Herzberger-Fofana, Pierrette. "Interview de Kesso Barry (Guinée)." In *Littérature féminine francophone d'Afrique noire*, 393–96. Paris: L'Harmattan, 2000.

Hewitt, Leah. *Autobiographical Tightropes: Simone de Beauvoir, Nathalie Sarraute, Marguerite Duras, Monique Wittig, and Maryse Condé*. Lincoln: University of Nebraska Press, 1990.

Holub, Robert C. *Crossing Borders: Reception Theory, Poststructuralism, Deconstruction*. Madison: University of Wisconsin Press, 1993.

Horoya: Organe National d'Information: Comité Militaire de Redressement National (Guinea), "Rencontre avec. . . Ahmed Tidiane Cissé: poète, écrivain, dramaturge guinéen," no. 436, August 1988, 6.

Horoya: Organe National d'Information; Comité Militaire de Redressement National (Guinea), "Union Nationale des Ecrivains de Guinée: Remise de prix aux lauréates du concours de poésie, de nouvelle et de conte," no. 426, May 7, 1988, 8.

Huggan, Graham. *The Postcolonial Exotic: Marketing the Margins.* London and New York: Routledge, 2001.

Hugo, Victor. *Les Misérables.* Paris: J. Hetzer, 1862.

Jaccomard, Hélène. *Lecteur et lecture dans l'autobiographie française contemporaine.* Geneva: Librairie Droz, 1993.

Jauss, Hans Robert. "The Identity of the Poetic Text in the Changing Horizon of Understanding." In *Reception Study: From Literary Theory to Cultural Studies,* edited by James L. Machor and Philip Goldstein, 7–28. New York: Routledge, 2001.

———. *Toward an Aesthetic of Reception.* Minneapolis: University of Minnesota Press, 1982.

JPA. "Le Passé murmuré de Raphaël Confiant." *Le Point,* no. 1083, June 19, 1993.

Kane, Hamidou Cheikh. *L'Aventure ambiguë.* Paris: Julliard, 1962.

Kane, Mohamadou. "L''écrivain africain et son public." *Présence Africaine* 58 (1966): 8–31.

Kundera, Milan. "Les Cent dix-sept sortilèges de Patrick Chamoiseau." *Le Nouvel Observateur,* November 1990. Print. Reprinted in *Antilla,* no. 411, November 30–December 6, 1990, 41.

Kwateh, Adams. "L'Odorat et l'enfance." *France-Antilles Magazine,* June 5–11, 1993, 37.

"La lecture au lycée dans les documents d'accompagnement." Académie d'Amiens. August 20, 2007. http://www.ac-amiens .fr/pedagogie/lettres/lycee/lect2–1.htm (accessed July 25, 2009).

"Lectures en classes de seconde et première." Académie de Nancy-Metz. Inspection Pédagogique Régionale des Lettres. September 2001. http://www.ac-nancy-metz.fr/enseign/   lettres/Inspection/FrSeconde/acc_2nde_1ere/ Lectures _lycee.pdf (accessed July 25, 2009).

Le Fol, Sébastien. "Les livres vedettes de 1999." *Le Figaro,* December 30, 1998. LexisNexis (accessed February 14, 2007).

Lepape, Pierre. "Le Feuilleton: Le malaise du français-banane." *Le Monde,* June 18, 1993, 3. LexisNexis (accessed March 8, 2008).

Lejeune, Philippe. *Je est un autre.* Paris: Seuil, 1980.

———. *Moi aussi*. Paris: Seuil, 1986.

———. *Le Pacte autobiographique*. Paris: Editions du Seuil, 1975.

———. "Récits de naissance." In *Récits de vie: Modèles et écarts*. Paris: Cahiers de Sémiotique textuelle, 1985.

———. *Récits de vie et institutions*. Nanterre: Centre de sémiotique textuelle, Université (de) Paris X, 1986.

Léotin, Georges-Henri. "Pour fêter une enfance." *Karibèl*, no. 26, July 1993.

Levin, David. *In Defense of Historical Literature: Essays on American History, Autobiography, Drama and Fiction*. New York: Hill and Wang, 1967.

Lioust, Mariane. "L'Enfance toujours recommencée." *Le Monde*, February 22, 2005.

Loichot, Valérie. *Orphan Narratives: The Postplantation Literature of Faulkner, Glissant, Morrison, and Saint-John Perse*. Charlottesville and London: University of Virginia Press, 2007.

———. "La Créolité à l'oeuvre dans *Ravines du devant-jour* de Raphaël Confiant." *The French Review* 71, no. 4 (March 1998): 621–31.

Lokoho, Tumba Shango. "Autobiographies, Autoscopies." Université de la Sorbonne Nouvelle, Paris III. September 2005. http://www.univ-paris3.fr/ ue_libres_sl4_detaillee.htm (accessed August 20, 2009).

Lüsebrink, Hans-Jürgen. "Du Journal de voyage au témoignage: Autobiographies fragmentaires d'auteurs africains dans la presse ouest-africaine à l'époque coloniale (1916–50)." In *Genres autobiographiques en Afrique: Actes du 6e. Symposium International Janheinz Jahn (Mainz-Baireuth, 1992)*, edited by János Reisz and Ulla Schild, 83–100. Berlin: Dietrich Reimer Verlag, 1996.

Lyotard, Jean-François. *Phenomenology*. Translated by Brian Beakley. Albany: State University of New York Press, 1991.

Machor, James L., and Philip Goldstein, eds. *Reception Study: From Literary Theory to Cultural Studies*. New York and London: Routledge, 2001.

"Maryse Condé: La révolte et la pitié; Autobiographie: Pour comprendre l'adulte qu'elle est devenue, la romancière antillaise sauve des éclats de mémoire; Un passionant éclairage sur la naissance d'une conscience." *Le Temps* (France), January 30, 1999. Listed under the rubric "Samedi culturel." LexisNexis (accessed June 3, 2007).

Médeuf, Serge. Review of *Antan d'enfance* by Patrick Chamoiseau. *Antilla*, no. 405, October 19–26, 1990, 40–41.

Merleau-Ponty, Maurice. *Phénoménologie de la perception*. Paris: Gallimard, 1976.

Meudal, Gérard. "Un Enfant Confiant: Ni Nègre ni Blanc, ni métis ni mulâtre: 'Ravines du devant-jour' ou l'enfance de Raphaël Confiant, gamin à la fois haï et redouté." *Antilla*, no. 547, July 30, 1993. Originally published in *Libération* (French newspaper), 1993.

"Monde des livres." *Le Monde* (France), August 31, 1990. LexisNexis (accessed July 15, 2009).

Montesquieu, Charles Louis de. *Lettres persannes*. Amsterdam: Chez les Libraires associés, 1764.

Mounier, Bernard. "Amadou Hampâté Bâ, maître de la parole." *Sud Ouest*, "La Rochelle; Culture I," November 28, 2002. LexisNexis (accessed February 8, 2009).

Moore-Gilbert, B. J. *Postcolonial Life-Writing: Culture, Politics and Self-Representation*. London and New York: Routledge, 2009.

Mudimbé, Valentin Y. *Les Corps glorieux des mots et des êtres*. Montréal and Paris: Humanitas & Présence Africaine, 1994.

———. "I as an Other, Sartre and Levi Strauss or an (Im)-Possible Dialog on the Cogito." *American Journal of Semiotics* 6, no. 1 (1988): 57–68.

———. *Parables and Fables*. Madison: University of Wisconsin Press, 1991.

———. *Shaba Deux: Les Carnets de Mère Marie-Gertrude*. Paris: Présence Africaine, 1989.

N'Diaye, Christiane. "Les mémoires d'Amadou Hampâté Bâ: Récit d'un parcours identitaire exemplaire." In *Récits de vie de l'Afrique et des Antilles*, edited by Suzanne Crosta, 13–36. Québec: GRELCA, 1998.

Ngara, Emmanuel. *Stylistic Criticism and the African Novel*. London: Heinemann, 1982.

Ngaté, Jonathan. "Maryse Condé and Africa: The Making of a Recalcitrant Daughter?" *A Current Bibliography of African Affairs* 19, no. 1 (1986–87): 5–20.

Nkashama, Pius Ngandu. *Livre littéraire: Bibliographie de la littérature du Congo (Kinshasa)*. Paris: L'Harmattan, 1995.

"The Nonfiction List." *Washington Post*, September 9, 2001, T05. LexisNexis (accessed May 4, 2009).

"Nouveau Programme de français en classe de 2° A." Académie d'Amiens. January 2000. http://www.ac-amiens.fr/ pedagogie/lettres/lycee/experim1. htm (accessed July 25, 2009).

"Nouvelles et romans d'Afrique francophone." Les dossiers de Weblettres. April 26, 2005. http://www.weblettres.net/ spip/article.php3?id_article=370 (accessed August 20, 2009).

Olney, James. "The Value of Autobiography for Comparative Studies: African Vs. Western Autobiography." In *African-American Autobiography: A Collection of Critical Essays*, edited by William L. Andrews, 212–23. Englewood Cliffs, NJ: Prentice Hall, 1993.

Ormerod, Beverley, and Jean-Marie Volet. *Romancières africaines d'expression française: Le sud de Sahara*. Paris: L'Harmattan, 1994.

Ouologuem, Yambo. *Le Devoir de violence*. Paris: Seuil, 1968.

"Patrick Chamoiseau Lauréat du Prix Carbet." *Antilla* (Martinique), no. 413, December 14–20, 1990, 37.

Péroncel-Hugoz, Jean-Pierre. "Romans: Les métamorphoses d'une nonne africaine. Monde des Livres." *Le Monde*, April 20, 1990. LexisNexis (accessed August 12, 2008).

Pfaff, Françoise. *Entretiens avec Maryse Condé*. Paris: Karthala, 1993.

Prince, Gerald. "Introduction to the Study of the Narratee." In *Reader-Response Criticism*, edited by Jane P. Tompkins, 7–25. Baltimore, MD: Johns Hopkins University Press, 1980.

"Prix littéraires." *Le Monde* (France), November 5, 1999. LexisNexis (accessed March 25, 2007).

Riesz, János. "Genres autobiographiques en Afrique et en Europe: Déterminismes historiques de l'histoire d'une vie et rêve d'une autre vie." In *Genres autobiographiques en Afrique: Actes du 6e. Symposium International Janheinz Jahn (Mainz-Baireuth, 1992)*, edited by János Reisz and Ulla Schild, 9–32. Berlin: Dietrich Reimer Verlag, 1996.

"Les romans et récits pour la classe de sixième." Savoirs CDI. April 1, 2004. http://savoirscdi.cndp.fr/fonds/ AideAuChoix/Bibrecom/BibRecom15.htm (accessed July 25, 2009).

Sabbah, Laurent. "Raphaël Confiant: Portrait d'un combattant." Postface in *Bassin des Ouragans*, by Raphaël Confiant, 93–95. Paris: Mille et une nuits, 1994.

"La Saga du commando fada." *L'Humanité* (France), May 22, 2004, 42. LexisNexis (accessed June 3, 2007).

Saint-John Perse. *Éloges: La gloire des rois; anabase; exil*. Paris: Gallimard, 1967.

Salvaing, François. "Une enfance martiniquaise." *Antilla*, no. 545, July 16, 1993. Originally published in *L'Humanité Dimanche*, 1993.

Sartre, Jean-Paul. *Les Jeux sont faits*. Paris: Nagel, 1947.

———. *Les Mots*. Paris: Gallimard, 1964.

Semujanga, Josias. "De l'autobiographie intellectuelle chez V-Y Mudimbé." In *Récit de vie de l'Afrique et des Antilles*, edited by Suzanne Crosta, 53–99. Québec: GRELCA, 1998.

Smith, Sidonie, and Julia Watson. *Reading Autobiography*. Minneapolis: University of Minnesota Press, 2001.

Sow, Salamatou A. "Le bâton de berger et la calebasse. Patrimoine et matrimoine chez les Peuhls pasteurs." April 25, 2006, 1–8. http://www.lemangeur-ocha.com/fileadmin/ images/sciences_humaines/SALAMATOU_SOW_caf_s_g_o.pdf (accessed August 26, 2009).

Steedman, Carolyn. *Past Tenses: Essays on Writing, Autobiography and History*. London: Rivers Oram Press, 1992.

Stephan, Mark. "Ricoeur and Merleau-Ponty on Narrative Identity." Netcolony.com. August 15, 2001. http:// www.netcolony.com/arts/markstefan/merlric.html.

Taylor, Robert. "Bookmaking: Robert Taylor Is the Retired Chief Book Critic of the Globe." *The Boston Globe*, November 28, 1999, H2. LexisNexis (accessed May 4, 2009).

Théâtre Artistic Athevains. Fluctuat.net. November 5, 2000. http://www.fluctuat.net/scenes/paris99/sorties/athevain.htm (accessed August 26, 2009).

"Théâtre Sans Frontières." Théâtre Sans Frontières. July 25, 2007. http://www.tsfront.co.uk/peul.html (accessed July 20, 2009).

Thébaud, Marion. "Artistic Athévains; Femmes Artistes Caraïbes." June 2, 1999.

"Thierno Bokar." Theatreonline. October 12, 2004. http:// www.theatreonline.com/guide/detail_piece.asp?i_Region=0&i_Programmation=10430&i_Genre=&i_Origine=&i_Type= (accessed July 25, 2009).

Tiffin, Helen. "Rites of Resistance: Counter-Discourse and West Indian Biography." *Journal of West Indian Literature* 3, no. 1 (1989): 28–46.

Upchurch, Michael. "Between Two Worlds." *Washington Post*, October 24, 2001, C04. LexisNexis (accessed May 5, 2009).

Velter, André. "Une enfance africaine." *Le Monde*, September 28, 1991. LexisNexis (accessed March 6, 2009).

Wardlaw, Ruth Pierson. "Recasting the Self: The Interaction of Metaphor and Personal History in American Immigrant Autobiography." PhD diss., Emory University, 1976 (UMI, Ann Arbor, Michigan 46106).

Watts, Richard. *Packaging Postcoloniality: The Manufacture of Literary Identity in the Francophone World*. Lanham, MD: Lexington Books, 2005.

Wimsatt, William K. Jr., and Monroe C. Beardsley. "The Intentional Fallacy." In *The Verbal Icon: Studies in the Meaning of Poetry*, 748–56. Lexington: University of Kentucky Press, 1954. Reprinted in *The Critical Tradition: Classic Texts and Contemporary Trends*, edited by David H. Richter, Boston: Bedford, 1998.

Wise, Christopher. *Yambo Ouologuem: Postcolonial Writer, Islamic Militant*. Boulder, CO: Lynne Rienner Publishers, 1999.

Wylie, Hal. "Child Abuse or Conflict of Interest?: Maryse Condé's Autobiographical Writings." In *Africanizing Knowledge: African Studies Across the Disciplines*, edited by Toyin Falola and Christian Jennings, 289–96. New Brunswick, NJ, and London: Transaction Publishers, 2002.

INDEX